JEWISH HISTORY IN MODERN TIMES

Jewish History in Modern Times

Joseph Goldstein

sussex
ACADEMIC
PRESS

First published 1995 by

SUSSEX ACADEMIC PRESS
18 Chichester Place
Brighton BN2 1FF, United Kingdom

Distributed in the United States by
International Specialized Book Services, Inc.
5804 N.E. Hassalo St.
Portland, Oregon 97213-3644
USA

British Library Cataloguing in Publication Data
A CIP catalogue record for this book is available from the British Library.

ISBN 1–898723 06 0 (hardcover)

Copy-edited and typeset in 10 on 12 Palatino
by Grahame & Grahame Editorial, Brighton, East Sussex
Printed and bound in Great Britain by Biddles Ltd, King's Lynn and Guildford

To my family

Contents

Glossary	viii
Acknowledgments	xi
Introduction	1
1 Migration	6
2 Emancipation	28
3 Cultural Revolution	47
4 Anti-Semitism	76
5 Zionism and the State of Israel	104
Conclusion	146
Appendix	150
Notes	158
Index	199

Glossary

Admor – The title by which a hasidic rabbi is known.

Agudat Israel – World organization of Orthodox Jews seeking to preserve Orthodoxy by adherence to *halakhah* as the principle governing Jewish life and society. Founded in 1912.

Aliyah – Heb.: Settling in Israel.

Achdut Ha'avoda – Zionist-Socialist party in Palestine. Founded in 1919. Merged in 1930 with *Ha-po'el Ha-tza'ir* Labor Party of Erez-Israel, Mapai.

Balfour Declaration – A statement by British Foreign Secretary Arthur James Balfour promising a National Home for the Jews in Palestine. Issued on 2 November 1917.

Benei Moshe – (Lit.: "Sons of Moses") Secret order of Hovevei Zion. Founded in 1889 to implement Ahad Ha'am's ideas.

Bund – (abbr. of Algemeyner Yidisher Bund in Lita, Poyln un Rusland; General Jewish Workers' Union in Lithuania, Poland and Russia), Jewish socialist party founded in Russia in 1897.

Conservative Movement – One of the religious responses to the situation in which Jews found themselves in the era of emancipation. Founded in the middle of the nineteenth century both in Europe and in the United States.

First Aliyah – *Aliyah* movement to Palestine between 1881 and 1903.

Ghetto – Urban area serving as compulsory residence for Jews.

Haganah – (Lit.: Defense). The underground military organization of the yishuv in Erez Israel from 1920 to 1948.

Halukah – (Lit.: distribution) Financial allowance for the support of the inhabitants of Erez Israel provided by their co-religionists in the Diaspora.

Hasidism – A popular religious movement giving rise to a pattern of communal life and leadership as well as a particular social outlook which emerged in Judaism and Jewry in the second half of the eighteenth century.

Haskalah – (Lit.: Enlightenment) Movement and ideology that had its roots in the general Enlightenment movement in Europe which began within Jewish society in the second half of the eighteenth century.

Heder – (pl.: Hadarim) Jewish school for Orthodox children age 4–14.

Hibbat Zion – (Lit.: Love of Zion) The first national Jewish movement founded in Russia in 1881.

Histadrut – General Federation of Labor for Jewish Workers in Erez Israel. Founded in Haifa in 1920.

Hovevei Zion – (Lit.: Lovers of Zion) The adherents of Hibbat Zion.

Jewish Agency – International body which is the executive and representive of the World Zionist Organization, whose aims are to assist and encourage Jews throughout the world and to help in the development and settlement of Erez Israel.

Kabbalah – Term for the esoteric teachings of Judaism and for Jewish mysticism.

Kahal – Jewish institutions which ruled and served the Jewish people in eastern Europe from the Middle Ages until 1844.

Knesset – (Lit.: Assembly) The parliament of Israel.

Kristallnacht – (Ger: Night of Broken Glass). On 9–10 November 1938, gangs of Nazis in Germany murdered 36 Jews; 30,000 were arrested; more than 7,500 businesses were torched and plundered; 191 synagogues were destroyed.

Kvutza, Kibbutz – (Lit.: group) In 1909 a new form of agricultural settlement, based on full cooperation among the members in work and equal profit-sharing, was set up near Lake Kinneret.

Ma'barah – (pl.: Ma'barot) Transitional immigrants' camp or quarter in the early 1950s in Israel.

Mapai – (Hebrew initials of Mifleget Po'alei Erez Israel – The Palestine Labor Party. A Zionist-Socialist party founded in 1930.

Maskil – An adherent of Haskalah.

Mitnaggedim – (Lit.: Opponents) A designation for the opponents of the Hasidim.

Mizrachi – The religious faction of the World Zionist Organization. Founded in 1902.

Moshav – (pl.: Moshavot) A smallholding settlement, the first type of Jewish village in Erez Israel.

Numerus clausus – The quota system imposed on the entry of Jews into Russian high schools and universities (1887).

Poalei Zion – (Lit.: The workers of Zion) A general term for labor Zionist groups.

Reform Judaism; Reform movement – A modern interpretation of Judaism in response to the changed political and cultural conditions brought about by emancipation.

Second Aliyah – *Aliyah* movement to Palestine between 1903 and 1914.

Servi Camerae Regis – (Lat.: Servant of the Royal Chamber) Definition of the status of the Jews in Christian Europe in the Middle Ages. First used in the thirteenth century.

Talmud Torah – A school for basic study for Orthodox children, usually comunally supported and larger than heder.

Third Aliyah – *Aliyah* movement to Palestine between 1919 and 1923.

Wannsee Conference – The Nazi conference which decided to coordinate the activity of the government to carry out the extermination of the Jewish people (the "final solution").

Yeshiva – (pl.: Yeshivot) A school for advanced Talmudic study.

Yishuv – The term denoting the organization of the Jewish community in Erez Israel before the establishment of the State of Israel.

Zhid – Jew.

Acknowledgments

In writing this book I had help from many quarters. Above all, I am deeply indebted to my teacher and mentor, Professor Shmuel Ettinger, of blessed memory. It was in a conversation with him, some twenty years ago, when I was just embarking on my doctoral thesis (for which he and Professor Jonathan Frankel were my advisors), that I raised the ideas which form the book's intellectual core. Professor Ettinger responded by saying that if I intended to put forward a thesis along these lines – one with which he disagreed absolutely – I must first acquire years of scholarly experience. Above all, he said, I would need the courage of my convictions in order to withstand the rebuttals of my colleagues, whose approach was deeply at odds with mine. Fortunately, I had the good sense to heed the advice of that wise man. It took me fifteen years to think those ideas through and to be certain that I stand behind them, however controversial they may be.

I also have the pleasant duty to thank many others without whom this book would not have been published. I am grateful to my wonderful family; to my colleagues, particularly at Haifa University; to my friend and teacher Professor Jonathan Frankel; to my ever-patient publisher; to my translators, Ralph Mandel and Moshe Shalvi; and to David Rechter, who read the manuscript and corrected my mistakes. I owe a special debt of gratitude to my students at Haifa University: they have often been my teachers and I have benefited from their stimulating feedback to the thesis I adduce here. It is to my students that I dedicate this book.

Introduction

This book is an inquiry into the central processes and events that changed the course of Jewish history in the modern era. It attempts to answer a major question in Jewish historiography: What were the principal developments that propelled Jewish history into "modern times"? What, indeed, was the true watershed that heralded a dramatic shift in Jewish history?

In order to find out, five central historical processes in Jewish history that began in the final third of the nineteenth century and concluded in our era are identified and discussed in depth. The time frame chosen for the genesis of those processes derives from the revolutionary upheavals experienced by the Jewish people in the 1870s and 1880s. The roots of the issues of emigration, emancipation, secularization, anti-Semitism and Zionism date from before, but it was at this time that they entered a *dynamic* stage. Marginal historical movements, ripples of which some scholars discern as early as the seventeenth century, became surging, irreversible currents from the 1880s to our own day.

Emigration: Two crucial demographic developments radically altered Jewish population distribution: the huge emigration of Jews from Russia to the United States which began in the 1880s, continued unabated for more than forty years, and ultimately encompassed two and a half million Jews who crossed the Atlantic Ocean in search of a brighter future; and the emigration, again beginning in the 1880s, of more than two million Jews to Palestine/Israel from Europe and Islamic lands. These waves of migration set in motion a process that dramatically reduced the size of the Jewish community in eastern Europe (Russia and Poland), still the world's largest at the end of the nineteenth century. This is contrasted with the building, in the same years, of the Jewish communities in the United States and Israel, the new centers of the Jewish people in the modern era.

Emancipation: French Jewry were already accorded equality of rights at the end of the eighteenth century, and the rest of European Jewry received it a generation later. But 90 percent of world Jewry still had a long wait for emancipation. Not until the end of the 1860s were a million and a half Jews in Austria-Hungary and Germany granted emancipation, while more than five million Jews in Russia had to wait fifty years after that. Moreover, even that equality was short-lived. The Nuremberg laws of 1935 again undermined the basic principles of Jewish equality with the surrounding society. Then, in the Second World War, the Germans deprived the majority of the world's Jews not only of emancipation but of the right to life. Paradoxically, the Nürnberg laws and the Germans' attempt to apply them constituted the true turning point in the emancipation of the Jews.

Social-cultural revolution: Two major events preceded the secularization process undergone by the Jewish people in the past hundred years: the growth of Hasidism into the largest religious-social movement the Jews had known, and the cultural-social activity of the *maskilim* in the first part of the nineteenth century. In the 1870s and 1880s new processes began that radically affected Jewish society. Within a few generations secularization processes generated a cultural-social revolution that expressed itself in every facet of Jewish life, including a dramatic change in the basic approach of most Jews toward their religion. Attachment to Judaism was based more on sentiment and nationalism than on religious faith as such. From the end of the nineteenth century two new streams in Judaism – Reform and Conservatism – assumed a growing influence within Jewish society.

Anti-Semitism: Anti-Jewish ideology in the last third of the nineteenth century took its argument from modern doctrines of nationalism, economic and social developments, and scientific advances. Hitler and the Nazis adopted race theory in particular, and translated it into the murder of six million Jews. The development of anti-Semitism after World War II, particularly in the Soviet Union and the Arab states, is contrasted with the historical roots of such attitudes.

Zionism: The developments that led to the proclamation of Israel's independence – the Balfour Declaration in 1917 and the 1948–49 war – are linked to the emergence, in the 1880s, of a national movement that aimed to create a Jewish entity in the Land of Israel, encompassing, in 1897, the founding of the Zionist Organization by Theodor Herzl.

During the autumn of 1868 the historian Heinrich Graetz completed the last volume of his monumental work, *Geschichte der Juden von den aeltesten Zeiten bis auf die Gegenwart* (The History of the Jews from the Earliest Times to the Present Day). In it he reached the second half of the eighteenth century, the "start of the Mendelssohn epoch." Two years later he completed his magnum opus, carrying the description of Jewish history until 1848. In these two volumes Graetz became the first to give material form to the conception of "modern times" in Jewish history, an idea he first raised in 1846.[1] Graetz aimed to show that since the era of Mendelssohn, German Jews had undergone dramatic developments as a result of which their problems, interests, goals and way of life were similar to or identical with those of his own era. Thus they launched a new age in the history of the Jewish people. One of Graetz's premises was that problems that perturbed him, issues he found interesting, goals he strove for, and his way of life were relevant to the Mendelssohn epoch. This may have been so, but it is most improbable that they were identical or even similar to our period or to other periods since Graetz's time. Here lies the source of the debate among historians about Graetz's view of the beginning of "modern times." Another distinguished historian, Ben Zion Dinur, wondered whether "the problems that perturbed people in those generations, the matters they dealt with, the goals they set themselves and the manner in which they endeavored to achieve them are really comprehensible to us or very close to us; whether they resemble our approach, our aspirations or our ways of doing things. Therefore, is the history of those generations modern history? Do past and present intermingle unknowingly, according to the matter at hand?"[2]

Some historians disputed Graetz's dating for the genesis of modern Jewish history, or argued that he was mistaken about the reasons for the changes among the Jews. Two major historical schools were represented. One group agreed with Graetz that "modern times" began in the second half of the eighteenth century. However, Simon Dubnow, Raphael Mahler and, indirectly, Yitzhak Baer, differed with Graetz about why this particular period should be considered the start of the modern age. According to Graetz (and, implicitly, Baer, though for different reasons), the activity of Mendelssohn and his disciples transformed the Jews "from a constrained force to an active force" in order "to elevate that people from its abject condition." Thus began a new stage in their history.[3] In contrast, Dubnow and Mahler singled out the events surrounding the French

Revolution as the spark for the dramatic changes undergone by the Jews. Specifically, Dubnow pointed to the granting of emancipation to the Jews by the French National Assembly as the date when they entered the modern era;[4] Mahler, drawing on the method of dialectical materialism, argued that the French Revolution had launched a new era in the history of the European nations, the Jews among them.[5]

Despite their different reasoning, all four of these renowned historians agreed that the time frame for the start of "modern times" in Jewish history was the second half (more precisely, the last third) of the eighteenth century. However, historians of the "Jerusalem School," such as Gershom Scholem, Ben Zion Dinur and Shmuel Ettinger, as well as their great adversary, Salo Baron, focused on the early eighteenth century, or even the latter part of the seventeenth. Scholem considered the Sabbatian movement crucial in the emergence of a new era in modern Jewish history.[6] Ettinger and Baron sought to prove, each by his own method, that the rise of the absolutist state in Europe was a central factor in bringing about changes which set apart Jewish history in the modern era from earlier periods.[7] Dinur looked to changes that occurred somewhat later, in the early eighteenth century – a time when both individuals and groups within the Jewish community were revising their attitude toward the Land of Israel – as the starting point of the modern era in Jewish history. More specifically, the immigration to Erez Israel of Rabbi Judah He-hasid and his followers signaled the renewal of the Jewish people's ties with their Holy Land and thus portended a new epoch in their history.[8] So this group of scholars, who exercised a decisive influence on modern Jewish historiography, linked the emergence of a new trajectory in Jewish history with various events that occurred in the second half of the seventeenth century and the early part of the eighteenth.

A closer perusal reveals that these historians, like others,[9] interpreted the new course taken by Jewish history in the light of their own historical period. For example, the struggle for emancipation in western Europe and the dramatic changes wrought by the *Haskalah* (Enlightenment) movement induced Graetz to search out the roots of those phenomena. His findings led him to the conclusion that Mendelssohn and his disciples had caused the vast transformation undergone by the Jewish people in the modern era. The same syndrome is apparent in Dinur. Seeking the origins of what he identified as the two most dramatic developments in modern Jewish history[10] – the success of Zionism and the creation of the State of Israel – he arrived at the year 1700, when Rabbi Judah He-hasid was active. We may surmise that the others followed the same path. Consciously or unconsciously, their understanding of the roots of the transformations that marked modern Jewish history was based on the conditions of their own time.

Can these theories, published in the course of a century, between 1868 and 1965, account for all the changes that occurred in the twentieth century? Most notably: the shift of the former east European Jewish centers to the United States and Israel, the cultural revolution and the secularization experienced by the Jewish people, the Holocaust of European Jewry and the establishment of Israel. Dinur's question (raised within the context of his refutation of Graetz and Dubnow) is still apposite. Did there not remain, he reflected, "beyond the pale, or at least . . . by the roadside, whole areas of the utmost importance in the life of the Jewish people during those generations, indeed precisely those areas in which the actual 'historical enterprise' of those ages was enacted?"[11] Is it not possible that those neglected areas are the very ones that could enable us to determine exactly when the Jewish people's "modern times" began?

This book, then, endeavors to answer these questions by describing the critical events and principal developments that changed the course of Jewish history in the modern era.

1

Migration

Jewish migration and the establishment of Jewish communities all over the world have existed since the emergence of the Jewish people as a religious and ethnic entity. The dispersion of the Jews throughout many countries was a major factor in ensuring their continued existence.[1] The Jews conquered Erez Israel as nomadic tribesmen, making it their historic center. After migrating to Egypt in the south and Assyria in the east, they transferred their centers to the Greek and Roman provinces and to Babylonia; and in the late Middle Ages and the sixteenth and seventeenth centuries to Spain and the Kingdom of Poland–Lithuania. In modern times, migration increased, and from the 1880s until 1994 there were revolutionary changes in trends, directions, goals and numbers. What were the major factors that brought about such changes? Were they a continuation of previous trends? What impact did the migrations have on Jewish development?

In the course of the nineteenth century the number of Jews increased from 2.5 million to more than 10 million.[2] During the first half of the twentieth century the growth rate declined by half, with the slaughter of six million Jews by the Nazis serving to exacerbate this process. During the subsequent thirty years (1950–80) the number of Jews increased steadily, though in relatively smaller proportions than in the past;[3] since the 1980s growth has again slowed down, finally ceasing altogether.

Between the beginning and end of the nineteenth century, growth rates of Jews reached about 400 percent; by the year 2000 world Jewish population is projected to be[4] 12.43 million (see Appendix, Table 1, for the increase in world Jewish population from 1880 to 1990[5]). If we compare this figure with the general population, we see that the growth rate amongst Jews was more than 200 percent that of the general population.[6] Though this phenomenon was unique in its time it soon occurred in developing countries all over the world. The fact that in the recent past demographers and sociologists termed the Jewish demographic growth a "miracle," ascribing it to the special nature of Jewish religion and customs,[7] can be explained by the fact that they were unaware of the relevant data indicating similar developments amongst nations all over the world in the twentieth century, as well as of data on the demographic growth of Jews in Islamic countries.[8] The urbanization process, the rise in standard of living, improved sanitary conditions and the level of services, all brought about an acceleration in world demographic growth.[9] Advances in medicine, particularly preventive medicine, brought about a dramatic decrease in the death rate and a significant increase in the life expectancy of world population, further accelerating the process of growth.[10]

While urbanization and the relative improvement in standard of living were factors contributing to Jewish population growth in the nineteenth century, they were precisely the factors that caused a decline in the natural birth rate in the twentieth. As with all western societies, the improved standard of living also produced a slow down in demographic growth among Jews, primarily as a result of a decline in the birth rate. For example, while in 1890 about 3.5 percent of the Jewish population in Russia were children, twenty years later the figure was 1.1 percent. In Romania, children constituted about 4 percent of the Jewish population in 1900 and 1.7 percent thirty years later. This was the trend in most of the Jewish centers.[11] In other words, a dramatic decrease in the number of births caused a decline in the size of the population. After the Holocaust, a new development occurred: accelerated economic development, combined with the social revolution undergone by Jews in the Islamic countries and incentives given by the Israeli government to encourage an increased birth rate, produced a relatively moderate increase in the number of Jews 35 years after World War II. But in the 1980s changes occurred which reversed this trend. An increased standard of living and life expectancy as well as mixed marriages precipitated – and, according to demographic forecasts, will continue to cause – a decrease in the world Jewish population.[12]

The accelerated demographic growth induced many Jews to seek new sources of livelihood. In the first stage, which began in the 1820s, thousands of Russian Jews migrated from the traditional regions in which they had made a living, such as Lithuania,

Belorussia, Ukraine and the outlying regions of Poland, to the Polish cities and the southern regions of the Ukraine (Kherson, Yekaterinoslav [Dnepropetrovsk], and Yelizavetgrad [Kirovgrad]).

At the same time there was an internal migration of Jews from the Austro-Hungarian Empire (both parts of Galicia), from Germany (Poznan), and from France (Alsace) to major cities of central and western Europe – Vienna, Berlin, Budapest, Paris, London and other large cities. A much smaller number of Jews migrated to the United States. Thousands of Jews left the villages and towns of Lithuania, Belorussia, Ukraine and Poland for the rapidly developing cities. Łódź and especially Warsaw were the major attractions for Jewish migrants. In Łódź the Jewish population increased from 2,775 in 1856 to 98,677 in 1897. In Warsaw the population increased from 40,922 in 1856 to 219,198 in 1897[13] and to 337,074 in 1914. The attraction of these Polish cities was their accelerated economic and industrial development, in which Jews played a central role.[14] For example, in 1907 more than 64 percent of the means of production were in the hands of Jewish capital (although Jews constituted only 34.6 percent of the total population). The number of Jewish factory workers was even higher, reaching about 75 percent of the work force.[15]

The cities of New Russia also attracted Jews. The lower tax rates and other incentives extended by the Russian government and the hope that it would be possible to improve living conditions induced thousands of Jews to migrate to cities like Yekaterinoslav, Yelizavetgrad and even Simferopol in the Crimea. The Jewish community of Odessa grew remarkably, this port city on the shores of the Black Sea proving a special attraction for Jews, who were drawn by the city's dynamic economic development and its unique pluralistic cultural character. Its Jewish population was 138,915 in 1897, while in 1857 it had numbered about 17,000.[16]

The internal migrations of Jews within Russia and the migrations from troubled areas in central and eastern Europe like Romania, Galicia (a region in Poland formerly in Austria-Hungary) and Germany to the large cities, provided a slight improvement in the standard of living for thousands of Jews. However, others who sought a decent income failed to find it. Some researchers estimate the number of unemployed Jews in Russia at the end of the nineteenth century at more than 25 percent of the work force, and slightly less in other eastern and central European communities. While others give a lower figure, all agree that economic distress was considerable.[17] Add to this the Russian regime's discrimination against Jews and one has the reasons why about 2.5 million Jews from Russia and tens of thousands from central European countries emigrated between 1880 and 1914. The minority – about half a million – went to western Europe, the rest to the United States of America.[18]

From the 1820s there was an acceleration of large-scale migration of Jews to the large cities of central and western Europe. It soon transpired, however, that the absorptive capacity of these cities was restricted. The relatively limited means of production did not supply employment for the thousands of migrants. Furthermore, incidents of anti-Semitism, which grew ever more severe, reaching their peak in the last third of the nineteenth century (surprisingly, in those countries where the Jews had been granted equal rights, like the Hapsburg Empire and Germany and even France,[19] where Jews had been granted these rights at the end of the eighteenth century), ultimately made the large cities less attractive. From the early 1880s many Jews sought a different solution for their problems. Thus began the process of millions of Jews emigrating to the United States. Even earlier the new "promised land" had attracted Jews. About 150,000 Jews arrived in the United States after 1820, increasing the Jewish community (initially founded by Portugese Jews who arrived in the seventeenth century), from 8,000 (1820) to 280,000 (1880). Most of the immigrants came from Germany. For two generations they integrated relatively successfully into American society, becoming an efficient and wealthy component of that society.[20]

The migration of Jews from Europe to the United States was part of an overall migratory process of millions of people. From 1846 until 1932 some 57 million people migrated from Europe, more than half of them at the end of the nineteenth century and the beginning of the twentieth: 18 million from Great Britain, 10 million from Italy, 5 million from Germany, 5 million from Austria-Hungary, 4.6 million from Spain, 2.2 million from Russia, 1.8 million from Portugal. The vast majority (about 32 million) emigrated to the United States, while the rest headed for Argentina (6.4 million), Canada (5.2 million), Brazil (4.6 million), Australia (2.5 million) and other countries (chiefly in Latin America). Millions of emigrants, about one-tenth of the world's population, hoped to find in their new countries a standard of living higher than that of their homelands.[21] So it was with the Jews, particularly those from eastern Europe, who hoped to change the penury of their current life for a better one in the countries to which they migrated.

The first eastern European Jews to arrive in the United States in the 1880s found a Jewish community whose members differed from themselves in cultural inclinations and even in religious beliefs. Most of the German Jews had joined the reform movement.[22] But it was this German-Jewish community which served as a model for the newly-arrived eastern European immigrants; they provided a model of successful integration into American society. Furthermore, Jewish motivation for migrating to the United States was heightened by the fact that during the nineteenth century millions of people had migrated there. The overwhelming majority had been absorbed and thousands more were waiting to come in order to satisfy the growing demand for labor in the work force. As a result, more than 2 million Jews came between 1881 and 1920.[23]

At first (1880–90), an average of twenty thousand arrived each year. In the 1890s, forty thousand arrived annually and in the next decade (1900–10) their numbers increased to an annual average of about one hundred thousand, later declining to about forty thousand per year between 1910 and 1920. The peak years were between 1903 and 1908, during which 710,000 Jews immigrated. Most of them came from Russia (68%), the rest from Austria-Hungary (14.6%), Romania (5.6%) and other countries.

Life in the United States was not easy for first- and second-generation Jewish immigrants. Most of them suffered economic and social hardships; but the inherent possibilities of the "promised land" finally led to their secure establishment. The prime factor in absorption was the possibility of finding work.[24] A large proportion of the Jews who arrived in New York (which received more than 70 percent of the Jewish immigrants) found immediate employment. The rest were soon absorbed in the work force. The expertise they had gained in the clothing trade in eastern Europe helped in their speedy absorption. Allowed to enter New York, many of them joined one of the thousands of "sweatshops" that operated in private homes in the city, while others found work in stores. News of the immigrants' success in finding work reached Russia, encouraging thousands of others to leave for the United States. The equal rights they were granted, the rarity of anti-Semitic incidents, the social and economic success of German-Jewish immigrants and, in particular, the increased number of eastern European Jews who were financially established, provided additional reasons for the attraction exerted by the United States. Furthermore, in the United States it was possible to retain the unique character of eastern European Jewish life, with its religious, educational and cultural institutions, and to develop a cultural and social life in Yiddish. This was particularly noticeable with the publication of several Yiddish newspapers which were in great demand in many Jewish households. All these factors spurred many more Jews to set out for the "new world." Over the years Jewish voluntary aid organizations for immigrants were established, to instruct immigrants from the moment of their arrival in the United States as to how to take advantage of all the available opportunities. The establishment of HIAS (United Hebrew Sheltering and Immigrant Aid Society), which coordinated a large number of these aid organizations, represented the peak of the aid process. Potential Jewish immigrants in eastern Europe knew that someone – either family or representatives of the mutual aid societies – would meet them upon their arrival in the United States. This knowledge encouraging them to leave their homeland for the land of unlimited opportunities.

Migration to the United States altered the distribution of Jewish communities in the world. At the end of the nineteenth century and the beginning of the twentieth, Russia was still considered the largest Jewish center, but emigration to the United States now made the latter the second largest community and soon afterward it achieved first place. New York was preferred to Warsaw and Odessa and became the largest Jewish community.

The hundreds of thousands of Jews who migrated to the United States between 1881 and 1914 sought to solve their economic and social problems simply and rapidly. The major problem for the emigrant lay in reaching the United States. This entailed leaving Russia (a feat which usually involved an illegal border crossing), making one's way to a gathering point in one of the transit cities in central Europe, such as Brody, Vienna or Berlin, and proceeding from there to the ports of embarkation for the United States: Hamburg and Bremen in Germany, Amsterdam and Rotterdam in the Netherlands, and other ports in France and Great Britain. They would then cross the Atlantic in a ship packed with emigrants to experience the immigration inspection at Castle Garden or Ellis Island in New York City, in the knowledge that there was a slight chance of being denied permission to enter. The feeling among those who wished to leave Russia was that when they reached the United States they would manage somehow, and reports of absorption difficulties failed to alter this feeling. On the other hand, there was a relatively negative impression regarding other emigration destinations such as Latin America (Argentina and Brazil), English-speaking countries (Canada, Australia and South Africa) and, above all, Erez Israel, the general opinion being that economic and social conditions in Erez Israel were much worse than in the United States. (See Appendix, Table 2, for the distribution of Jews according to continents, 1800–1914.[25])

Furthermore, even intellectuals who did not believe that emigration alone would solve the Jewish problem, and those who sought to attribute a nationalist connotation to emigration, preferred the United States. The writer Judah Leib Levin (1844–1925, known by the acronym Yehalel), for example, believed in the possibility of establishing a Jewish state in the United States, which would solve the Jewish problem.[26] This was also the opinion of the members of the *Am Olam* Society (founded in 1881 in Odessa with the aim of establishing agricultural colonies in the United States), who preferred the United States to Erez Israel as a national solution for the Jews.[27] Even Judah Leib Pinsker (1821–91), in his pamphlet *Autoemancipation,* published in 1883 (before he was chosen to head the *Hovevei Zion* movement ["Lovers of Zion"]),[28] maintained that the United States could serve as a solution for the Jewish problem and that they would be able to establish their own state there.[29] In contrast, a small group of intellectuals, public leaders and rabbis in eastern Europe insisted that the United States could never solve the Jewish problem. Personalities such as Moses Leib Lilienblum (1843–1910) and Rabbi Samuel Mohilever (1824–98) preferred Jews to emigrate to Erez Israel, even if it required far greater resources than those needed for emigration to the United States.

Thus, in 1881 Jews began to emigrate to Erez Israel in order to "pave the way for settling [our] brethren in the Holy land so that they may work the land and fulfill the *mitzvot ha-teluyot ba-aretz* ('precepts peculiar to the Land of Israel'), thus exalting the people of Israel with honor and so that they will no longer be a mockery among the nations."[30] The several thousand emigrants who arrived in Erez Israel,[31] most of them in two waves which were later respectively designated the First *Aliyah* (1881–1903) and the Second *Aliyah* (1904–14), wished to impart a different meaning to emigration. The terminological change from "emigration" to "*aliyah*" was just one of the characteristics of this new meaning of emigration to Erez Israel.[32] No longer was it merely a move from country to country in the context of changing one's place of abode or attaining reasonable economic conditions for absorption, but rather Jewish emigration for nationalist reasons. (See Appendix, Table 3, for the waves of Jewish immigration to, and emigration from, Erez Israel.)

The immigrants (Hebrew: *olim*) who arrived in Erez Israel in 1881 did not find an unpopulated country. About 450,000 Arabs lived there,[33] more than 70 percent of them in villages and the rest in twelve towns.[34] Jerusalem had a population of 14,000 Arabs – both Muslims and Christians – and 17,000 Jews. Despite a relatively dense population, the Ottoman Turks who ruled the country did not develop a significant economic base. Only a small number of Jewish *olim* took root in Erez Israel between 1881 and World War I. The waves of immigration were relatively short, lasting on average a year or two. Most of the *olim* failed to establish themselves for lack of a suitable infrastructure. The belief held by many before their *aliyah* that in Erez Israel they would find a solution to their economic, social and cultural problems soon proved unfounded, breeding frustration which in turn led many to defect.

During the First and Second *Aliyot* the net number of *olim* was about 20,500 (out of a total of some 60,000). In other words, about 66 percent left the country, a small number returning to their countries of origin while the majority went to the United States.

Even the large sums of money invested by Baron Edmond de Rothschild (1845–1934), the French Jewish philanthropist and patron of Jewish settlement in Erez Israel, which totalled about 40 million French francs between 1882 and 1899, failed to succor more than a dozen *moshavot* (Heb. "colony," the earliest type of Jewish village in modern Erez Israel) with a population of several thousand Jews.[35]

Since the Jewish masses preferred to migrate to the United States, the significance of the *aliyah* to Erez Israel between 1881 to 1914 cannot be compared to the emigration to the United States. In 1914 a majority of the Jewish settlers in Israel lived off the "allocations" funds[36] and only a few earned their living by working. However, for some of these Jews living in Erez Israel was a way of expressing their national aspirations. The belief that in Erez Israel one would, in due course, be able to solve the Jewish problem was deeply rooted amongst many Jews, although it was clear to most of them that without the creation of an economic and social infrastructure the country would be unable to absorb additional waves of immigration in the future.

Jewish emigration to Argentina was relatively more successful than the *aliyah* to Erez Israel. There was much in common between the two countries and it is therefore not surprising that when

Theodor Herzl planned his Jewish State he chose Argentina as an alternative to Erez Israel.[37] In 1891 the Jewish financier and philanthropist Baron Maurice de Hirsch (1831–96) founded the ICA (Jewish Colonization Association) for the purpose of settling 3.5 million Jews in Argentina and thus solving the problems of eastern European Jewry. Hirsch believed that the economic and social conditions in Argentina, with its promising economic potential, could serve as an alternative to the harsh conditions in Russia, Romania and even Galicia. He attempted to implement his plan and over a five-year period (1891–96) succeeded in attracting 6,575 Jews who settled on 910 farms.[38] But even this emigration (like that to Erez Israel) was not a sufficiently attractive solution for the distressed Jews, despite the fact that in Argentina, the "destined land" according to Hirsch, there was a much firmer economic infrastructure than in Erez Israel. Argentina was not a sufficiently appealing destination for the Jewish masses of eastern Europe. Ultimately, more than 70,000 Jews emigrated to Argentina by 1910. In the final instance, though, the United States of America – "the land of unlimited opportunity" – proved more attractive to the potential eastern European Jewish emigrant than either Erez Israel (the "Promised Land") or Argentina (the "Destined Land").

During World War I the Jews underwent further migrations – both voluntary and involuntary. At the very beginning of the war some 100,000 Jews from the Polish districts of Radom, Łomza and Lublin were expelled on the orders of the Russian military authorities, apparently for fear that they might collaborate with the German and Austro-Hungarian enemy. This expulsion reached its peak on 30 May 1915 when thousands of Jews from Kovno and Kurland (today a province of Latvia on the east Baltic shore) were ordered to leave their homes within 48 hours. From the districts of Poland, western and eastern Ukraine and Galicia, a total of more than 600,000 Jews were expelled or fled from their homes during the war. Many of them were directed towards the eastern districts of the Pale of Settlement (the territory in tsarist Russia where Jews were permitted to live) while others were removed to territories in which they had hitherto been forbidden to settle. With the de facto abolition of the Pale of Settlement in August 1915 by the Russian authorities, many Jews settled in the internal areas of the empire, chiefly in the two capital cities of Moscow and Petrograd.[39]

The expulsion of the Jews and their removal from frontier areas during World War I was a continuation of the Russian regime's policies toward the Jews which had their beginnings after the three Polish partitions (1772, 1793, 1795). Thereafter, Jews were compelled to leave their homes from time to time by force of decrees issued by the authorities, whose pretexts for these expulsions were security and socioeconomic factors. In 1804 Tsar Alexander I had already issued a series of decrees ("Jewish Statutes") which forced the Jews to leave the villages in the northeastern part of the Pale of Settlement for villages in the south. To justify these decrees, Alexander argued that it was necessary to make the Jews more "productive." Persuaded by his advisors that the major Jewish activities in the villages – leasing property and selling alcoholic beverages – were not sufficiently productive, he set about effecting a dramatic change. From 1807 government inspectors began enforcing these decrees. Many Jews were expelled from their villages, while others left of their own accord. According to one estimate, more than 200,000 Jews were expelled, but some place the number even higher.[40] Seventy years later, Tsar Alexander III followed in the footsteps of Alexander I, ordering about 25,000 Jews resident in Moscow to leave the city on the grounds that laws promulgated in the distant past forbade their living there.[41] The expulsion decree was issued on 29 March 1891 and within a year most of Moscow's Jews were forced to find new homes in the Pale, leaving only about 5,000 who were allowed to continue residing in the capital.

The other reason given for the expulsions was security. In 1825 Alexander I issued a decree which forbade Jews to live within 53 kilometers of the Austro-Hungarian and Prussian borders (excluding those Jews who lived in towns and villages where they had large communities). Although the decree was not fully implemented because of Alexander's death on 1 December 1825, the authorities did expel several thousand Jews, who were forced to migrate to areas in the Pale in the north and the west. Ninety years later, at the start of World War I, Jews were again forced to migrate into Russia, away from the German and Austro-Hungarian borders.

The shock felt by the Jews at the beginning of World War I continued into the days of the Bolshevik revolution. Jews were forced to take their possessions and migrate from areas of danger, chiefly the towns and villages in Ukraine where they were molested by the mobs, to the large cities – Kiev and Kharkov – or to safer cities in the heart of Russia. Jewish migration from the Pale of Settlement – an area which they were forbidden to leave for a period of more than

120 years – to central Russia brought about a further revolution in the dispersion of the Jewish population in eastern Europe. During the second half of the nineteenth century Jews wandered in the direction of Novorussia (specifically to Odessa, Yekaterinoslav and Yelizavetgrad) and the towns of Poland. But from the beginning of World War I the direction changed. Moscow and St. Petersburg became attractive cities for Jewish emigrants. This process gathered strength by the end of World War I when about 2.6 million Jews from Russia (which became the Soviet Union after the Bolshevik revolution) found themselves cut off from the Jews of Poland and the newly-independent Baltic states, and from the areas annexed by Romania. The Jewish communities of Moscow and Leningrad grew dramatically, totalling 600,000 (350,000 in Moscow) by 1939. (See Appendix, Table 4, for the dispersion of Jews in Russia and the Soviet Union from 1897 to 1939, in areas which were retained by the Soviet Union from 1918 to 1939.[42])

A further phenomenon associated with Jewish migration in the twentieth century is the establishment of the Jewish autonomous region of Birobidzhan in eastern Siberia. In March 1928 the presidium of the central executive committee of the Soviet Union approved the establishment of a Jewish autonomous region in Birobidzhan. Although the Soviet authorities intended to transfer hundreds of thousands of Jews to the area, undertaking to subsidize their mode of livelihood and provide jobs for the settlers, only 29,544 Jews moved there between 1927 and 1937, and some of them later returned to their former places of residence.[43]

In contrast to the successful settlement of hundreds of thousands of Jews in central Russia, despite the fact that the authorities, at least initially, were (to put it mildly) dissatisfied with this phenomenon, the failure of the Birobidzhan plan proved above all that the demographic dispersion of Jews generally stemmed from economic needs. Although the Soviets attempted to provide a socioeconomic solution for the Jewish problem, all the additional components essential to their absorption were non-existent. In Moscow, Leningrad, Kiev, or Kharkov the conditions for absorption were better and as a result thousands of Jews streamed to these cities rather than to Birobidzhan.

The establishment of independent states in central and eastern Europe – the Baltics (Lithuania, Latvia and Estonia), Poland, Hungary, Czechoslovakia, Yugoslavia, Romania and Bulgaria – brought about a dramatic change in the situation of the Jews.

Suddenly, more than one-third of the world's Jewish population found themselves living under regimes which had not previously existed. (See Appendix, Table 5, for the number of Jews in eastern Europe (excluding the Soviet Union) from 1918 to 1939[44]).

The political changes in the countries of central and eastern Europe somewhat alleviated the economic and social situation of the Jews living in these areas. Many Jews experienced equal rights for the first time, and for others there was the hope that the promises of national autonomy made by the Allies in the Versailles Treaty would be fulfilled. Nevertheless, one can discern that some Jews were dissatisfied with the changes and wished to migrate (see chapter 2). Several thousand left Poland every year, most of them for the United States and the rest for Erez Israel and Latin America. Others wanted to leave Romania and Bulgaria. From 1924 the improvements seemingly heralded at Versailles proved illusory. The gates of the United States were almost completely closed by restrictive laws passed by Congress and as a result only 200,000 Jews emigrated to the United States between 1924 and 1939 as compared with more than 150,000 who emigrated between 1919 and 1924.[45]

The options for Jewish emigration in the late 1920s were Erez Israel, Latin America and Canada. In fact, between the two World Wars many emigrated to Argentina (107,000), Brazil (45,951), Uruguay, Chile[46] and Canada (51,063). However, even there they failed to find solutions to their problems. Latin America and Erez Israel were economically still relatively backward. The accelerated economic development which was started by the British in Erez Israel, and the private and public investments of the Jewish sector there, failed to create sufficient jobs. Consequently many Jews in Poland and Romania felt that their aspirations, like those of their forebears, would not be readily fulfilled in migration.[47]

The situation of the Jews in Erez Israel at the outbreak of World War I was difficult. The Turks perceived them as a hostile community, some of whom sympathized with the Allies.[48] Those most at risk were the 25,000 non-Ottoman subjects amongst the Jews. At the beginning of the war a decree issued by the authorities ordered Jews with foreign nationality to adopt Turkish nationality. Many among the ten thousand Jews who did not adopt Turkish nationality were expelled, while others left of their own volition. During the war there were additional expulsions and thousands of others fled. The Jewish population in Erez Israel, which numbered about 85,000 at the beginning of the war, was reduced to 55,000 by the end.

With the end of the war, however, Erez Israel became an attractive destination for Jews. There were several reasons for this: the liberal image of the British administration and the Balfour Declaration in November 1917; recognition by the British authorities that Palestine was a strategic asset and their consequent readiness to invest in the country and develop an economic infrastructure;[49] the fact that from 1924, emigration to the United States was mostly closed to Jews; an increased investment by the Zionist Organization, which regarded the establishment of Erez Israel as an independent and developed Jewish economy with a large absorptive capacity as a major objective.[50] All these factors induced thousands of Jews to emigrate each year. The first wave brought back some of the expellees from World War I. These were joined by thousands of immigrants who later became known as the Third *Aliyah*. Between 1919 and 1923 Jewish immigration totalled 35,183 persons, increasing the Jewish population to 84,000.

In the 1920s and 1930s *aliyah* escalated as a result of the expansion of the economic infrastructure through British capital investments and capital imported by the Zionist Organization (and from 1929 by the Jewish Agency) as well as by the *olim* themselves. The nationalist pioneering fervor which the new immigrants brought with them was augmented by economic vigor. The growing distress of eastern European Jewry and persecution of Jews in Germany in the 1930s accelerated the flow of emigrants and made Erez Israel a haven for endangered Jews comparable to the United States at the beginning of the twentieth century. (See Appendix, Table 6, for *aliyah* to Erez Israel from 1919 to 1939.[51])

Three waves of immigration reached Erez Israel during the 1920s and 1930s. The *olim* from Russia and Poland were conspicuous in the first wave (Third *Aliyah*, 1919–23). Many of them were imbued with an idealistic fervor, wishing to create in Erez Israel a society based upon socialist and nationalist values in order to "organize, expand, transfer and arrange productive elements for Erez Israel and in particular to create the cultured agricultural laborer."[52]

From 1924 to 1926 an additional wave of immigration began, with *olim* coming mainly from Poland. What characterized the Fourth *Aliyah* was that many of the immigrants settled in the urban areas, in contrast to their predecessors who had wished to consolidate the agricultural settlements. The city of Tel Aviv absorbed more than 50 percent of the *olim*, its population growing from 21,000 in 1924 to 40,000 in 1926. The immigrants of the Fourth *Aliyah* urged a recognition of the centrality of urban settlement in the Zionist enterprise and in Erez Israel.[53]

The years 1932 to 1938 brought another wave of *aliyah*, the Fifth. Many *olim* arrived from Germany and settled in the large cities. Hitler's anti-Semitic policies, which constituted a serious threat to Jewish lives, drove thousands of them to seek a safer haven.[54] As time passed and the British administration established itself, Jews found absorption relatively easier. In the first years after the waves of immigration of the Third and Fourth *Aliyot* the inability of the economy to absorb such large numbers[55] had created a serious crisis, leading thousands to work at jobs initiated by the British. From 1920 to 1921, in 1923, and again from 1926 to 1928, there had even been a negative balance of immigration. But in the 1930s, despite the doubling and trebling of the Jewish population in a period of several years, the Jewish sector in Erez Israel flourished economically.

The number of settlements grew from 160 in 1927 to 233 in 1938,[56] businesses doubled in numbers from 3,388 to 6,200 (1933–39) and the annual industrial output during the same period increased from 5 million Palestine pounds to 13.3 million. The accelerated economic development of the Jewish sector in Erez Israel prevented the Arab population and even the British rulers of the country from stopping the immigration. Both bureaucratic and politically-motivated ordinances aimed at limiting *aliyah*, and Arab riots and insurgency against the *yishuv* (1920–21, 1929, 1936–39), failed to stop *aliyah*. Only just before the end of World War II, with the British decision to limit Jewish immigration by an Administrative Order (White Paper), did immigration in fact totally cease for a few years.

The tragic events of World War II – the brutal murder of six million Jews and the displacement and flight of millions more – accelerated the changes in the Jewish diaspora. Essentially, this process was the transfer of the center from eastern Europe, westward to the United States and later to Erez Israel. (See Appendix, Table 7, for the Jewish world population from 1939 to 1948.[57])

The magnificent 700-year-old Jewish community of Poland was almost totally annihilated in the gas chambers, by Nazi bullets or by deliberate starvation. The remnants fled eastward to the Soviet Union,[58] some of them, after a long and arduous migration, eventually reached western Europe, the United States and Erez

Israel. Such was also the fate of the rest of the Jewish communities in eastern Europe. Of the half of world Jewry living in eastern Europe before the war, more than two-thirds of those in the Soviet Union and Poland, and about 40 percent of those in Romania, Hungary and Czechoslovakia, were annihilated. However, the three largest communities outside Europe – the United States, Erez Israel and the Islamic countries – were unaffected. The community in the United States now became the largest in the world, as the process of its growth intensified and reached its peak at the beginning of the twentieth century.

In the late 1930s the United States was still home to the largest Jewish community, with New York City as its center. As such, it replaced the Jewish community of eastern Europe, which had lived, before World War I, under the Russian regime, and between the wars, in the Soviet Union, Poland, Hungary, Romania and the Baltic states. After World War II the Jewish community of eastern Europe was the second largest, but within two generations most of its members had emigrated to Israel, while a minority moved to the United States.

Jews in the Islamic countries fared better than their European co-religionists. Their communities expanded even before World War II.[59] From the beginning of the twentieth century until 1939 the demographic increase of the Jews in Egypt and Algeria was more than 100 percent, in Morocco 60 percent, with a slight decline in Tunisia. The events of the war and the demographic increase amongst North African Jews caused a doubling of the percentage of their relative position amongst world Jewry from 2.4 to 5.1 percent.

The annihilation of the Jews by the Nazis was carried out in a systematic and measured fashion. Only the Allied conquest of Europe prevented them from murdering the remaining Jews as they had planned at the Wannsee Conference in January 1942.[60] At the end of the war about 200,000 Jews survived in the various Nazi camps (*She'erit ha-Pelitah* [lit. "the surviving remnant"]). Some of the Jewish displaced persons turned westward to France, the Netherlands and Belgium, while a small number (chiefly Hungarian Jews) returned to their countries of origin. However, the majority, originally from Poland, the Soviet Union and Lithuania, refrained from returning to their countries despite the cajoling of the Allied authorities. Many of them moved westward (*Berihah*, "flight", is the name of an organized clandestine operation from 1944 to 1948 to move Jews out of Europe and transport them "illegally" to Erez Israel), crowding the displaced persons camps in Germany, Austria and Italy.[61] From these camps the majority wanted to reach Erez Israel. They were joined by thousands of Jews, formerly from the Soviet Union, Poland and Germany, who had been saved from Nazi extermination. Between 1946 and 1948 many of them managed to reach Erez Israel despite strong British and Arab opposition. Others were forcibly removed by the British from the ships which brought them to Erez Israel and interned in camps on the island of Cyprus. About one-third dispersed over Europe and even reached the United States. The establishment of the state of Israel accelerated the arrival of the others. About half a million Jews emigrated from Europe to Erez Israel between 1946 and 1951.

The establishment of the state of Israel and the promulgation of the Law of Return (July 1950), which declared that every Jew has the right to settle in Israel as an *oleh* and that every *oleh* shall be an Israeli national, made Israel the main destination for Jewish emigrants. Concurrently, and chiefly after the DPs from Europe and the camps in Cyprus arrived in the country, the Jews from the Islamic countries began their emigration. The first to arrive were the Yemenites ("Operation Magic Carpet," August 1950) followed by waves of immigration from Iraq, Egypt and Libya, culminating with the immigration from the Maghreb countries – Algeria, Tunisia and Morocco. The Jewish population of Israel grew dramatically: when the state was established on 15 May 1948, there were 649,000 Jews in the country. Three and a half years later, 676,749 Jews had emigrated to Israel and during the subsequent thirteen years (1952–64) a further 522,534 came. Of the total of 1,199,283 immigrants about 640,000 were Jews from Islamic countries.[62] The reasons for the *aliyah* of these Jews and the dissolution of most of their communities are complex and in many instances related to local factors such as their economic situation, or the severe friction between Jews and their Muslim neighbors generated by the Israeli-Arab conflict. There are, however, a number of additional reasons for the mass *aliyah* from the Islamic countries which have their roots in the second half of the nineteenth century. From the time of the European conquest of North Africa, many of the Jews living in these countries, in particular the social strata living in the large cities, adopted modern European values and ways of life. Adopting these values was usually an element in the process of Jewish identification with the colonial conquerors, which militated against their integrating into local society. World War II and the de-stabilization of the colonial regimes, with the consequent loss of influence by the British and French in the Mediterranean basin, exacerbated the alienation of the Jews from the Muslim population. The events of the War of Independence to a large extent destroyed the psychological barriers which protected the Jews against Arab hostility. The intensification of the Arab-Israel conflict, events of the War of Independence, the fervent enthusiastic response of the Jewish communities in the Islamic countries to the establishment of the state of Israel and the opening of its gates to Jewish immigration, which coincided with the anti-Jewish riots and economic restrictions – were all factors which paved the way for the almost total dissolution of the Jewish communities in the Islamic countries and their mass emigration to Israel.[63]

The absorption of the immigration from the Islamic countries was essentially different from that of their predecessors. For the first time, absorption was organized by a central governmental authority which cared for the immigrant from the moment of arrival. Although the Jewish Agency continued to finance a considerable part of the cost of *aliyah* and absorption, the government of Israel invested money and other resources, assuming responsibility for dealing with the immigrants from their arrival until their absorption. This method gave the new immigrants an advantage over their predecessors, since the authorities were able to concentrate their efforts in order to provide the immigrants with housing and employment.[64] However, absorption was far from easy since the *yishuv*, which had been forced to mobilize almost all of its resources for war,[65] immediately afterwards (within three months) found itself with more than 600,000 immigrants, who almost doubled the Jewish population. Each successive year between 1952 and 1961 brought an additional 30,000 immigrants. Furthermore, the good intentions displayed by the leaders of the state in their desire to integrate the immigrants from the Islamic countries with the indigenous society (*kibbutz galuyyot*, "ingathering of the exiles," as it was then designated) ultimately had the opposite effect of widening the cultural and social gap.[66] The veteran pre-state society tried to impose its "Ashkenazi" cultural values upon the "Oriental" culture brought by the new immigrants.[67] It took many years for them to realize and accept that these cultural differences were positive and desirable, and an even greater period of time to overcome the trauma caused by the entire experience.[68]

For about four years, beginning in 1965, mass immigration ceased. But even so, every year there were some twenty thousand immigrants (a total of 72,836), which was partly offset by the emigration of Jews from Israel, particularly to the United States and western Europe. The absorption of mass immigration between 1948 and 1961 can be divided into five periods, the differences between which are attributable to the different character of the *olim* in each period and to the varied nature of their absorption. The first period, extending from the declaration of the state until 1951, during which the Jewish population of the country doubled within a relatively short period, was characterized more than anything else by the overwhelming number of *olim* that flooded the newly-established state. Despite the fact that it appeared as if the service infrastructure built during the Mandate would not sustain the volume of immigrants, no real housing shortage was felt during this stage. Many of the immigrants settled in Jaffa, Ramle, Lod, and in Arab neighborhoods of other cities, particularly Jerusalem, Haifa and Acre, which had been abandoned by the Arabs during the War of Independence. Some of the immigrants were housed for a certain period in temporary camps, which were, however, vacated after a relatively short time. By contrast, the next wave of immigration, which ended in 1952, suffered from a housing shortage and severe unemployment. These immigrants were billeted in tent camps and *ma'barot* (immigrant transit camps) and it seemed as if the absorption structure would collapse. The services supplied in these camps were minimal and the traumatized immigrants bore the resulting scars for many years. During the second half of 1952 government institutions began a better planned absorption program. Jerry-built housing estates partially solved the problem of accommodation. But the most effective factor was the cessation of the mass immigration. During the years 1952 to 1954 the average number of immigrants per year dropped to 18,022 in contrast to 189,000 for the previous three years. This enabled government institutions to tighten organization, with the result that during the next period, from August 1954 until mid-1956, there was a marked improvement in absorption services, which included the beginning of a massive dispersion of newly-arrived immigrants (joined by some of the veteran immigrants) to border areas and to the newly-established towns and villages.[69] From 1957 until 1968, 482,127 immigrants came to Israel (an average of about 40,000 per year). This decline in relation to the previous period was accentuated by the emigration from Israel of about 100,000 Jews who sought their fortune elsewhere. In 1969 a new stage of *aliyah* began: from that year until 1974 the rate of *aliyah* doubled. The relaxation of Cold War tensions between the East and West as a result of the détente, together with Israel's new image after the Six Day War, resulted in the opening of the gates of the Soviet Union and a large Jewish *aliyah*. In these five years 227,258 immigrants came to Israel, about half from the Soviet Union.[70] In addition to the Soviet Jews, the period also saw a significant increase in immigration from western European communities, Latin America and the United States, which was stimulated by Israel's victory in the Six Day War. This wave ended in the middle of the 1970s, with an average annual rate of 14,000 for the years 1975 to 1988. In this period (1975 to 1988), however, immigration was offset by emigration and a point was reached when the latter exceeded the former.

Mikhail Gorbachev's rise to power in 1986 and the implementation of the *glasnost* and *perestroika* policies, accompanied by a severe economic crisis, again caused a dramatic turn in Soviet immigration to Israel. In line with Gorbachev's policy, from 1989 any Jew could leave the Soviet Union. Parallel to this policy came a limitation by the United States on the number of entry visas issued to Jews. Until then all Jews who could prove they had first-degree relatives in the United States had been allowed entry. As a result of pressure from the Israeli government, from 1989 the number of visas for Jews was limited to 40,000 per year and in 1990 to 30,000. The serious economic crisis in the Soviet Union, which grew steadily worse from 1988 on, combined with an improved standard of living in Israel, intensified the motivation of Jews to immigrate.[71] During 1990–93 the number of immigrants reached about 420,000,[72] a hitherto unprecedented number even in the days of the mass immigration immediately after the founding of the state.

Increased immigration once again altered the proportion of Jews to Arabs in Israel, which has changed significantly since 1948. In 1947, prior to the establishment of the state, the non-Jewish population, which was composed primarily of Muslim Arabs, numbered 1,340,345 as against a *yishuv* of 630,000. The War of Independence caused the flight and expulsion of hundreds of thousands of Arabs from their settlements in Erez Israel. Jordan annexed the West Bank, and Egypt took over the Gaza Strip. As a result, the proportion of Arabs to Jews in Israel declined dramatically: 80 percent of the population of Israel were Jews. The balance in favor of the Jews increased after the mass immigration, and reached 91 percent in 1961. However, after the Six Day War in 1967 the trend was reversed, since the Arab population in the areas conquered by Israel – the West Bank and the Gaza Strip – was 954,848. As a result the proportions between Jews and Arabs again changed, the non-Jewish population, consisting mainly of Muslims (94%), reaching about 38 percent of the total population – a factor with far-reaching political and social implications for the development of the Jewish community in Israel. (See Appendix, Table 8, for the ratio of Jews to Arabs in Palestine and Israel between 1947 to 1988.[73])

Jewish emigrants during the period 1948 to 1994 did not come only to Israel. Although the resources made available by the government and the national institutions for their absorption encouraged most of them to emigrate to Israel, some preferred the United States and western European countries. Thus, during those years about 200,000 Jews emigrated from the Magreb countries, particularly Algeria, to France, whose culture they had absorbed from the time of the colonial conquest.[74] Between 1945 and 1994, more than 550,000 Jews emigrated to the United States,[75] from both the Soviet Union and Israel. The "land of unlimited opportunities" still retains pre-eminent drawing power and only the severe immigration laws prevented many more from settling there. Nevertheless, the *aliyah* to Israel from its beginnings until 1991 reached more than 2 million Jews, equalling Jewish emigration to the United States at the beginning of the twentieth century and resulting in a dramatic turn in the history of the Jews in modern times. Furthermore, since the 1950s there has been a decline in the Jewish birth rate in the diaspora.[76] In the 1970s and 1980s this decline reached a point of negative growth and the number of Jews waned. This was, however, not the case in Israel, where the birth rate remained positive and relatively high in comparison with other western countries. (See Appendix, Table 9, for emigration of Jews to Israel, 1991 to 1993.[77])

Jewish emigration to Erez Israel began at the end of the nineteenth century, accelerating from 1948 to 1989 and reaching its peak in 1994. As a result of emigration to Israel, there have been major shifts in the distribution of the world's Jewish population. (See Appendix, Table 10, for the Jewish world population, 1948 to 1988.[78])

Looking back, we can see that emigration has been a central process in the history of the Jews in modern times. Its various directions – migration within Russia and then to the major cities of central and western Europe, emigration from eastern Europe to the United States, and *aliyah* to Israel from Europe and the Islamic countries – have given the concept of the "wandering Jew" a new relevance. The modern period is notable for the migrations of millions of people, the majority going of their own volition and out of a desire to seek a better life, the minority forcibly and against their will. The migration of Jews was part of a general process in which about one-tenth of the world's population participated, chiefly from Europe to the United States, in search of a new life. Yet in this great sea of migrants the Jews were a phenomenon unto themselves – different from other migrations not only in size but in nature and in mode of development.

Two examples will suffice to make this clear. First, while of every hundred emigrants to the United States at the beginning of the twentieth century 70 were men, and more than 80 percent were young, aged between 14 and 44; amongst Jews the proportion of males to females was two women to three men and only 60 percent were young (between 14 and 44), while the number of children under the age of 14 was very high, reaching 25 percent. In other words, the Jewish emigration was family oriented.[79] Secondly, amongst the Jews the number who returned to their countries of origin was very small. Of the non-Jewish Poles who emigrated from the beginning of the twentieth century, about 40 percent returned to Poland, of the Italians 56 percent, and of the Romanians 67 percent, but amongst the Jews the number was only about 7 percent.

There is no single explanation for Jewish migratory phenomena during the last one hundred and thirteen years (1880–1994). The causes are clearly related to the political and social distress in which Jews often found themselves, and also to the hatred of Jews and the anti-Semitism which in many cases were endemic to the societies in which Jews lived. However, it would seem that above and beyond all these reasons, the migrations stemmed from a socioeconomic oppression which cannot always be understood or measured by objective means, and from the psychological impact of contrasting a dark and dismal future in one place with a set of positive expectations and great hopes held out by another country.

From the last third of the twentieth century, migration created a revolution in the distribution of the Jewish population, as their traditional center in eastern Europe was transferred to the United States and Israel. The migration processes and the transfer of the Jewish centers caused extraordinary cultural, social and economic changes. The central point of reference in the history of the Jewish people in modern times is the 1880s – the period which saw the onset of the mass emigration to the United States and the nationalist *aliyah* to Erez Israel.

2

Emancipation

In March 1917 the Kerensky government granted the Jews of Russia
full civil rights, thus, as it were, completing a process begun 130
years earlier when the American Congress and the French National
Assembly granted them full emancipation. Other countries had
followed suit, first in western Europe and later – at the end of the
1860s – the two central European powers, Austria-Hungary (1867)
and Germany (1869–70), and finally Russia (1917). However, only
one generation after the Russian emancipation the Nazis not only
abrogated the civil rights of most of European Jewry but seriously
threatened their lives, finally fulfilling this threat and causing the
greatest tragedy in the history of the Jewish people.

Had the circle been closed in March 1917, it might well have
been appropriate to embrace the widely-accepted contention of
the historian Heinrich Graetz (1817–91) that Moses Mendelssohn's
(1729–86) activities and philosophy inaugurated a new era in Jewish
history by paving the way for the idea of integrating the Jews in their
environment; or the equally widely-endorsed argument of historian
Simon Dubnow (1860–1941), that the French Revolution was the
dawn of a new era in Jewish history.

However, the laws and activities of the Nazi regime rendered
both these theories inaccurate and left us with the question as to
how one should view the emancipation process and its relation to
modern times.

In the middle of the seventeenth century there was a change in
the way Jews were perceived in Europe. Up to this point, they
were recognized as a religious community and a self-contained
corporation.[1] Their status was that of *servi camerae regis* ("servants
of the royal chamber"), their right of residence was dependent upon
special permission from the ruler, and their Christian neighbors saw
them as "conditional residents."[2] The changes in European society

at the end of the Middle Ages gradually revised the attitude toward the Jews, which found a prominent expression in the European emancipation philosophy. In Britain at the end of the seventeenth century and at the beginning of the eighteenth, deists such as Roger Williams, John Toland and John Locke argued that one should not disenfranchise the Jews because of their religion.[3] Similarly, the German author and dramatist Ephraim Lessing in 1729 maintained that one must recognize the Jews as human beings entitled to human rights.[4] In the 1780s French philosophers and politicians like Honoré-Gabriel Riqueti Mirabeau and Jean-Jacques Rousseau stated that the vision and personality of Jews such as Moses Mendelssohn ("the good Jew") demonstrated the need to relate positively toward them. The changed attitude toward the Jews in central and western Europe in modern times is related to transformations in religious and philosophical outlooks as well as economic and social developments. Rationalism, which was a dominant social and philosophical trend in post-Renaissance Europe, bestowed upon the individual a much greater value in society and rejected any discrimination on grounds of social affiliations. The rulers of Europe adopted these basic principles and saw themselves as "benevolent despots" working for the general welfare.[5]

Society at large changed its attitude toward religion and belief, causing a devaluation of religious institutions which also brought about a change in relations with the Jews. The deep-seated antagonism toward Jews displayed by Christian institutions became less relevant over the years, as the egalitarian attitude which was an inseparable part of rationalistic philosophy played a positive role in the gradual elimination of discrimination in society. From the sixteenth and seventeenth centuries onward, European society underwent a process of economic change as a result of the agricultural and industrial revolutions. These changes accelerated the shift of large segments of the rural population to the towns and cities, which then became prime economic centers. The Jews, urban dwellers, assumed an important position in the modern economy, chiefly due to their involvement in the financial sector. In short, the call by various circles in Europe for a changed relationship toward Jews and an equalization of their status with that of other citizens was partially implemented in the mid-eighteenth century in central and western Europe and to a lesser degree in eastern Europe.

Toward the second half of the eighteenth century the change in the

Jewish situation found its expression in various legislative activities in central and western Europe, which aimed at ameliorating their status by gradually narrowing the gap between them and other citizens. Thus in 1740 a law was passed in Great Britain which enabled Protestants and foreigners (including Jews) to become naturalized in the British colonies. In 1753 Parliament passed the Jewish Naturalization Bill, granting similar privileges to Jews in Great Britain. Despite the fact that the law was repealed the following year due to popular agitation and opposition, the act exemplified the new image of the Jews and perhaps even more so the radical changes which had taken place in western European society regarding the place and status of the individual in society.[6]

Thirty years later, in 1782, the Holy Roman Emperor Joseph II issued a *Toleranzpatent* for the Jews of Austria which decreed that they should be allowed to share the "common welfare" with the rest of the citizenry, so that "their general industriousness should increase in every respectable manner."[7]

The new image of Jews in central and western Europe in the seventeenth and eighteenth centuries found its expression in their socioeconomic status. Some Jews – such as Samson Wertheimer (1658–1724), Joseph Suess Oppenheimer (*c.* 1698–1738), or the Gomperz family (widely dispersed throughout central Europe, active in banking in the seventeenth, eighteenth, and nineteenth centuries) – were able to attain high positions at the royal courts of Europe as "court Jews," suppliers and purveyors to the army and the court, and tax collectors, clearly proving that the image of the Jew had undergone a radical change.[8] But most Jews lived in the shadow of the old, negative image and even enlightened people like Voltaire or Diderot called them "pimps" and "rags" whose beliefs as well as behavior could only be seen by every cultured nation as an enigma in its alienness.[9]

The French Revolution accelerated the dramatic changes that overtook the Jews in Europe. Members of the French National Assembly equalized the national rights of the Jews with those of other citizens, thus inaugurating a new era which influenced the other peoples of Europe.[10] But the initiators of the revolutionary legislation in the United States preceded such champions of the Jews in the French National Assembly as Abbé Grégoire (1750–1831) and Comte de Clermont-Tonnerre (1759–92) and their colleagues. The American Declaration of Independence (1776) emphasized that "all men are created equal"[11] and article six of the Constitution of the

United States of America states that "No religious test shall ever be required as a qualification to any office or public trust under the United States." However, while the granting of equal rights to the Jews of the United States did not affect other Jewish communities in Europe, the decision of the French National Assembly was a signal for other European nations to follow suit.

In contrast with the Americans, the French had difficulties regarding the status of the Jews – equal rights did not seem so obvious to them as to the Americans. Several years before the French Revolution (1785–87) an essay competition was held in Metz by the Société Royale des Arts et Sciences on the subject "Is it possible to make the Jews more useful and happier in France?" The essays received indicated an ambivalent attitude toward the Jews on the part of French society. Abbé Henri Grégoire, one of the three prize winners, wrote a work entitled *Essay on the Physical, Moral and Political Reformation of the Jews*, in which he claimed that the shortcomings of the Jews were due to their persecution by others and that granting them equal rights would bring them relief and giving them freedom would be a "great step forward towards reforming their character."[12] By contrast, others argued that while Jews should be granted equal rights, their base character, despicable religion, money-grabbing profession and a culture which incites to isolation and segregation required that one first bring about a dramatic change in their customs and religion and only afterwards try to draw them into French society. Thus on the eve of the French Revolution equal rights for Jews were not a foregone conclusion. It took another year and a half of heated debate in the National Assembly before Jews achieved full emancipation through the National Assembly's decree of 27 September 1791.[13] Furthermore, even after the decree, sectors of the French population, such as farmers, clergy and nobility, disapproved of the decision, appealing to Napoleon Bonaparte to dispossess them of equal rights. In 1806 Napoleon convened an Assembly of Jewish Notables who faced twelve questions to test whether there was any conflict between Jewish religious law and French civil law. Despite being assured that there was no contradiction between the two, Napoleon issued an edict in 1808, commonly referred to by the Jews as the *décret infâme* ("the infamous edict"), which in fact abrogated Jewish equality, limiting their rights and their choice of profession. After Napoleon's banishment, the decree was cancelled and civil equality for the Jews reinstated. However, it took several generations before Jews were generally accepted in French society and became clear to the majority of French citizens that the Jews were in fact equal in the eyes of the law.[14]

While France was the first European state to grant equal rights to the Jews, Jewish communities in other countries had to wait many years before achieving the same status. Opposition to the emancipation of the Jews generally stemmed from their long-standing negative image in the eyes of society and from the social and economic tensions which fanned hatred against them, chiefly after the Napoleonic wars.[15] Furthermore, even many Jews were far from anxious to demand equal rights, fearing they would be obliged to relinquish certain privileges obtained in the past, like the right to separate communal organizations in which they could observe Jewish religious laws relating to personal status and the right to maintain separate rabbinical courts.

In the second half of the eighteenth century, Moses Mendelssohn tried to reconcile the apparent contradictions between the civil and religious obligations of the Jews.[16] Mendelssohn distinguished between personal belief in God and the rabbinical and religious institutions which serve this belief. The latter, he felt, were necessary for the welfare of the individual. He suggested abolishing the institutions of *niddui* (a preliminary and lighter form of excommunication) and *kherem* (total and severe excommunication), which the leaders of the community used to impose their will, arguing that affiliation to the community must be voluntary and unimpeded by any form of religious coercion. Nevertheless, he was in favor of the continued existence of a separate Jewish community and understood that ritual laws were the main force which protected this community.[17] At the same time he wanted to impose upon the Jews the laws of the countries in which they resided, religion being a matter of individual conscience.[18] In other words, belief and religion exist exclusively to serve the needs of the individual, while social affiliation and loyalty belong to one's immediate environment and not to the Jewish community.[19]

The struggle between those in favor and those opposing legal emancipation for the Jews in the German states continued for eighty years or even, as some claim, a century.[20] It was only at the end of the 1860s that the Jews of the Hapsburg Empire and the German principalities achieved complete equal rights. While the arguments used by the respective parties varied over an extended period, according to time and place, they did have much in common. The dissenters argued that one should not relate to the Jews as to other citizens because of their peculiar religion, nationality and economic character.[21] Others argued that the Jewish demand for civil rights should be rejected because of their social alienation and the fact that they continued to practice a despicable tradition.[22] Thus there are no essential differences between the anti-Semitic arguments of Friedrich Jakov Fries of Heidelberg (1773–1843) in his pamphlet *Über die Gefahrdung des Wohlstandes und Charakters der Deutschen durch die Juden*, 1816 ("On the Jewish Threat Against German Welfare and Character") and those of Heinrich Treitschke (1834–96), the German historian and philosopher, who in his short work on Judeo-Christian relations, *Unsere Aussichten* ("Our Prospects–Outlook"), coined the phrase *Die Juden sind unser Ungluck* ("The Jews are our misfortune"). Conversely there were those like Saul Ascher (1767–1822) or Alois Zuker (1783–1851) who were in favor of granting equal rights to all, regardless of religion, race or sex.

One of the major factors accelerating emancipation was the extent of Jewish involvement in the central European economy. Jews became prominent in economic sectors which were vital to urban development, a fact that was responsible for enhancing their socio-economic status. Until the mid-eighteenth century the Jews constituted a sort of corporation which chiefly specialized in money lending and retail trade. From the eighteenth century, there was a gradual change and Jews began to enter various professions. The fact that most of them lived in towns, particularly large ones which became the economic and social centers of the modern world, spurred their speedy integration and accounted for their relatively disproportionate involvement in economic activity, compared with other ethnic and religious groups. While many Jews still engaged in small trade or in the crafts – occupations lacking status and prestige – there was an appreciable increase in the number of Jewish wage earners who specialized in professions that were essential for developing modern society, such as stock investment, venture initiation, international financial activities and the liberal professions. As a result the Jews projected an image of a group with economic power. In particular, the Rothschild family, with its world-wide financial activities operating in Frankfurt on the Main, Paris, London, Berlin and Vienna, personified the modern Jew in the eyes of non-Jewish society,[23] despite the fact that only two to three percent of Jews benefitted directly or indirectly from similar occupations.[24] This economic development affected the situation of Jews in society, and, inter alia, the granting of equal rights. There is no doubt that the general attitude toward Jews, as well as the desire to grant them equal rights, were affected first and foremost by the social, economic and political changes occurring in Europe. In a period of ferment and revolution – during the Napoleonic wars, during the 1830s, and particularly at the beginning of the revolutions of 1848 – emphatic demands were heard by those who favored granting emancipation for the Jews, as the strengthened liberal forces supported this idea as part of their demands for a social revolution. On the other hand, the post-Napoleonic period, which was dominated by the powerful Austrian statesman and state chancellor (from 1821–48) Prince Klemens von Metternich, saw the rise of reactionary forces which, after the revolutions of 1848, joined with the reigning monarchs to oppose any liberal factions which might foment revolutionary ideas and activities, including granting equal rights to the Jews.

Between 1772 and 1795 the Kingdom of Poland–Lithuania ceased to exist, undergoing three partitions among the neighboring powers. Prussia annexed Polish Pomerania and Ermland in the north-west, Austria annexed Galicia in the south-west, and Russia annexed the major part of the kingdom which included Lithuania, Belorussia, Ukraine, Volhynia and Podolia. These partitions had a decisive influence on modern Jewish history. Approximately 900,000 Jews who resided in pre-partition Poland – about half the world's Jewish population – were granted Russian citizenship whereas prior to the partition Jews (as well as subjects of other religions and non-eastern Orthodox Christians) were not allowed to reside in the tsarist kingdom.[25]

The annexation of the Polish territories forced the Russian regime to face the Jewish problem for the first time, the major issue being the status of these new subjects. The Jewish policy of Catherine II, Empress of Russia (1762–96), was a mixture of conflicting attitudes: on the one hand she held the traditional eastern Orthodox Christian stance, which was basically anti-Jewish, but on the other hand her admiration for the European enlightenment movement, which also had advocates in Russia, tended to emphasize the talents and capabilities of Jews. Until her death in 1796 Jews were granted certain rights, such as permission to participate in elections for local government institutions; however, they were restricted in various other matters and were forbidden to settle outside those areas of

Poland where they had resided until the partition. These areas became part of what was designated as the Pale of Settlement under Tsar Nicholas I (1825–55). Toward the end of her reign (1791–96) Catherine regressed from her previous liberal policies.

Catherine's heir, Emperor Paul (1796–1801), attempted to deal with the Jewish problem in a more systematic fashion. In 1799, governor Ivan Friesal (1740–1802) and senator Gabriel Derzhavin (1746–1816) were appointed to investigate the Jewish problem and submit proposals. Paul died in 1801, but his successor Alexander I (1801–25) continued Paul's policy and the work of Derzhavin and Friesal. On 9 November 1802 he established a Public Committee for the Betterment of the Jews, whose function was to deal with the Jewish problem and relate to the report submitted by Friesal and Derzhavin.

The report's proposals were incorporated in a series of laws issued in 1804, known as the "Jewish Statute" (The Statute Concerning the Organization of the Jews). Under this statute Jews continued to have a special status – different from that of the general population. They were to be confined to settling in certain areas and were not allowed to live outside the borders of historic Poland, except for areas in which the government was interested in encouraging settlement, such as southern Ukraine and eastern Lithuania; the government would do everything possible to direct Jews toward employment in productive occupations such as agriculture and industry (their current occupations being leasing of fixed assets and distilling of alcoholic beverages); and to integrate and assimilate them within the general society by providing free education and granting incentives for those who availed themselves of such education. In other words, the Jews would not acquire the equal rights of their French brethren nor would they gain the rights granted in Austria-Hungary and Germany unless they drastically changed their occupations, education and way of life. The call by Alexander I and his ministers for reforming the Jewish population, and the greater severity of his successor Nicholas I, generated despair amongst the Jews, who accused the authorities of attempting to disrupt the fabric of their traditional life-style, something they wished to prevent at all costs.[26]

The expulsion order issued by Alexander I for Jews living in villages (the purpose of which was to force them to change their employment from leasing of fixed assets and distilling alcoholic beverages to more productive occupations) and the particularly oppressive measures of Nicholas I, such as compulsory military service for Jewish children; the attempt to dramatically change the Jewish educational system by developing a network of Jewish government schools; the restriction of publication of Jewish books to only two authorized presses; and the abolition of the autonomous Jewish community board (*kahal*), were all seen by many Jews as a hostile attempt by the regime to impose a way of life which would endanger their religious belief.[27] The threat felt by the Jews during the reign of Nicholas I abated somewhat during the early part of the reign of his successor, Alexander II (1856–81), whose ascension raised great expectations because he declared that he would abolish the oppressive Jewish statutes, and in 1856 he rescinded the special system of recruiting Jews for the army.[28] Alexander's emancipation of the serfs in 1861 strengthened the hope that the liberal policies of his regime would also alleviate the distress of his Jewish subjects. There were even Jewish intellectuals who hoped that in the final instance Alexander II would grant the Jews full emancipation. However, he too disappointed them and in the second half of his reign (1868–81) he resumed the oppressive anti-Jewish policy of his predecessors. Indeed, he issued statutes which still further restricted Jewish rights of residence and occupations. Furthermore, from the beginning of the 1870s the Jews' feeling of insecurity increased as they experienced disappointment in his regime.

To sum up, Russia, which had half the world's Jewish population as its subjects, not only failed to grant the Jews emancipation but even worsened their conditions. The trends established in the United States and France, and manifested eighty years later in Germany and Austria-Hungary, did not penetrate Russia. In the 1870s and 1880s many Jewish intellectuals felt they must radically alter their goals, since the hoped-for salvation which emancipation was to have brought was as far from fulfillment as it had been one hundred years earlier.

The Jewish policy of Alexander II remained unchanged under his successors Alexander III (1881–94) and Nicholas II (1894–1917). Barring the period of the first revolution (1905–6), when Nicholas was temporarily forced to abandon his reactionary policies for more liberal ones, the reign of the last Russian tsar was a difficult one for the Jews. Far from granting emancipation to its five million Jewish subjects, the government imposed further restrictions regarding residence, occupation, and children's education. From 1881 there was a growing feeling of insecurity amongst the Jewish population

due to the pogroms which erupted in southern Russia in 1881
and 1882 ("Storms in the South" known in Hebrew as – "*Sufot
Ba-Negev*")[29] and in other parts of the kingdom between 1903 and
1906.[30] In the 1880s scores of discriminatory laws and statutes were
issued restricting leasing activities, entrance into the professions,
attendance at high schools and institutions of higher learning (1887,
numerus clausus).[31] As a result of the pogrom of 1881–82, Alexander
III, upon the advice of his Minister of Interior, Count Nikolai
Ignatyev (1832–1908), appointed a "Jewish Committee" composed
of several cabinet ministers whose task was to decide upon steps to
be taken to prevent a further occurrence of the anti-Jewish riots.[32]
The results of these deliberations were the promulgation of the
"temporary laws" in May 1882 (also known as the "May laws")
which imposed further harsh restrictions upon the Jews, who were
blamed for causing the riots by their economic exploitation of the
general public.

However, many of the anti-Jewish measures enacted during the
nineteenth century were either altered or not complied with. For
example, when Alexander I ordered the Jews to educate their
children in a spirit which was alien to their way of life, or Nicholas
I ordered them to change their mode of dress, the Jews disobeyed
these statutes, most of which were abandoned with time. Four times
statutes were issued ordering the Jews to leave their villages, but
each time they were disobeyed. Often laws were changed due to
pressure of liberal circles who sought to ameliorate or cancel the
anti-Jewish laws. Such was the case during the reign of Alexander
I when the liberal governor Ivan Friesal wished to moderate the
anti-Jewish proposals of Senator Gabriel Derzhavin, or during the
reign of Alexander III when individuals like Alexei Lopukhin
(1864–1928), head of the gendarmerie, and Count Sergey Witte
(1849–1915), minister of finance, tried to restrain the demands
of the reactionary circles led by the head of the Holy Synod,
Konstantin Pobedonostev (1827–1907), to be more stringent with
the Jews. There was a heated debate about the Jewish problem at
all levels of the Russian government and the decisions reached were
variously influenced by the strength of the conservative circles and
the ability of the liberal circles to mitigate these decisions.[33]

At the end of the nineteenth century factors in Russia's economic
development influenced the decision-making process of the Tsar's
regime regarding the Jewish problem. From the last third of the
nineteenth century Russia needed huge loans in order to accomplish

the development program initiated by the government. This forced the government decision makers to recognize the sensitivity of international public opinion to the plight of Russian Jewry. Consequently, officials in the ministry of finance, headed by Sergey Witte, pressured the ministers of the interior to moderate their actions against the Jews. Similar pressure was exerted by wealthy and influential Jews. From the 1850s and 1860s, Jewish occupations underwent a change, as the traditional trades in which Jews had engaged for hundreds of years – leasing of fixed assets and distilling of alcoholic beverages – were, in a relatively short period, exchanged for others.

At the beginning of the nineteenth century 60 percent of the wage earners were engaged in leasing and the distilling industry, 12 percent in crafts and the rest in commerce and agriculture,[34] while in 1897, 39 percent of Jewish wage earners engaged in commerce, 40 percent in crafts and industry and a smaller number in agriculture and services. Another significant factor was the high percentage of Jews in liberal professions – 5 percent in relation to 2 percent for the general population. Furthermore, 3 percent of Jewish wage earners belonged to the upper bourgeoisie, the entrepreneurs among the merchants and capitalists.[35] Throughout the entire nineteenth century, these Jewish entrepreneurs participated in the development of the railway system, transportation on Russia's rivers and seas, particularly the Dnieper and its tributaries, the establishment of banks, and the expansion of trade and commerce with western European countries by promoting agricultural exports and related industries such as milling and sugar, and developing the wood industry, coal mining and petroleum.[36] Jewish entrepreneurs were conspicuous in the development of all levels of industry in Polish cities. In 1900, 75 percent of all factories in Łódź and Warsaw were owned by Jews, while their proportion in the general population in Warsaw did not exceed 33 percent.[37] Although in cities outside Poland, in the Pale of Settlement, the number of factory owners failed to reach such high proportions, it was nevertheless above the percentage of Jews in the general population.

Inevitably, the large number of Jewish entrepreneurs obliged the authorities to accord them special treatment, which no doubt contributed to the negative image of the Jews, in particular the demonic stereotype from the 1880s depicting them as striving to control the Russian economy.[38] Thus Sergey Podolinski, one of the leaders of the Nationalist and Socialist party in the Ukraine and an anti-Semite, maintained "We would not be mistaken if we assumed that the source of livelihood of more than a million Jews among the *zhidim* who live in our country is the sucking of our blood."[39] However, others, like Sergey Witte, saw things differently. Witte, whose priority was the development of Russia as a European power, realized the importance of the Jews in this process. He therefore insisted upon improving their status, and when serving as Prime Minister in 1905, he even proposed granting them emancipation.[40] Although he later withdrew his proposal he continued to oppose the oppressive measures demanded by reactionary circles. One can also assume that wealthy Jews like the Guenzburgs (Baron Joseph [1812–78] and his son Horace [1833–1909]); the Poznanski brothers; the Polyakov brothers – Jacob (1832–1909), Samuel (1837–88) and Eliezer (1842–1914); Leon Rosenthal (1817–87) and others often succeeded in their intercession with government officials regarding the plight of the Jewish community.

The life-style and culture of some of these wealthy Jews became Russified. As members of the first guild they were free to reside anywhere in Russia, send their children to any educational institution and enjoy many additional privileges. Their status further accentuated the dismal plight of their brethren, who were not only denied the emancipation granted to Jewish communities in central and western Europe, but were more harshly oppressed by the Russian regime between 1881 and 1914.

World War I brought about a change in the status of Jews because hundreds of thousands were forced to flee as refugees from their homes to the hinterland beyond the Pale of Settlement.[41] Having no option, from 1915 the authorities allowed the Jews to enter these areas, thus unwittingly abolishing the Pale of Settlement. Jews began settling in places which hitherto had been out of bounds for all but the very few privileged, like St. Petersburg and Moscow. The events of the February 1917 revolution (which led to the Bolshevik takeover of 7 November 1917) caused an additional dramatic change in the situation of Jews, who were granted full equal rights by the Kerensky government on 22 March 1917. As an integral part of Bolshevik policy, Kerensky's successors, headed by Lenin, further strengthened Jewish emancipation by forbidding all discrimination. Furthermore, for the first time a law was promulgated which declared anti-Semitism a crime.[42] The fact that there was such a high proportion of Jews among the revolutionaries no doubt played an important role in determining the Bolshevik Jewish policy.

During the first ten years of the Soviet regime Jews were especially conspicuous in all government ranks. In 1922 they constituted more than 10 percent of all Communist party members, although they were only 1.8 percent of the total population in the Soviet Union. They constituted a quarter of the members of the Central Committee and the Politburo, which formed the country's leadership, and held 6.5 percent of the senior positions in the Soviet hierarchy (27 out of 414).[43] Thus the Jews not only won complete emancipation but within a few years had attained key positions in the new regime. Despite these achievements there remained a Jewish problem in the Soviet Union. In the early 1920s the question arose of granting the Jews national rights. From the time they received emancipation some Jewish circles laid claim to national autonomy like that granted to other nationalities, hoping that under Soviet patronage it would be possible to develop Jewish culture and schools, and that the legitimacy of their religious institutions would be recognized. The Soviet leadership did partially acknowledge this claim, establishing a Commissariat on Jewish Affairs and "Jewish Sections" (Yevsektsiya) in branches of the Communist party to deal with matters specifically related to the Jews and to facilitate the setting up of a wide range of Jewish institutions.[44] In 1928 the Soviet authorities decided to recognize the Jews as a nation entitled to their own territory and allocated Birobidzhan in the Soviet Far East for this purpose.[45] Here they believed the Jews would be able to develop their own nationality and solve the Jewish problem. Special incentives were granted to encourage Jewish settlement in Birobidzhan, but only a few thousand Jews moved to this remote eastern region and the scheme eventually failed. Most of the Jews felt that they could express their Jewish nationality far from Birobidzhan and that the establishment of this Jewish Autonomous Region was a transparent ruse on the part of the authorities, whose real intent was to distance the Jews from the major cities of the Soviet Union.

In the mid-1930s and, to a greater extent, after World War II a new chapter in the history of Soviet Jewry began. Renewed persecution, this time by the Soviets led by Joseph Stalin, reached its peak between 1948 and 1953. These persecutions began in the 1930s when Stalin attempted to eradicate all religious institutions and education in the Soviet Union as part of his overall policy toward religion. The educational, religious and cultural institutions of the eastern Orthodox and Catholic churches as well as Muslim and Jewish institutions were affected by this policy. The secret police closed

most of the Jewish religious and cultural institutions, harassed rabbis, teachers, cultural activists and dispensers of religious services.
Some were arrested and sent to work-camps, others were executed.
The second half of the 1930s saw the persecution of many Jews who
had previously held important positions in the Bolshevik regime,
as part of Stalin's persecution of opposition elements who might
endanger his regime. Scores of Jews were tried, exiled, executed or
murdered.[46]

Unlike what had happened in Nazi Germany the Soviet Jews did
not view the Stalinist purges of the 1930s as a retreat from their
emancipation, despite their taking place against the background
of Nazi persecutions. However, it was clear to all that legally
prohibiting anti-Semitism did not suppress the negative attitude
of Russian society toward the Jews; their persecution was not
seen as something unique on the part of the regime toward the
Jews but rather as part of the regime's overall policy. However,
the Nazi atrocities against the Jews in the conquered areas of the
Soviet Union between 1941 and 1945 and the collaboration of sectors
of the conquered population with the Nazis against the Jewish
population intensified the mistrust that many Jews felt toward the
Soviet authorities. Stalin's persecution of the Jewish intellectuals
between 1948 and 1951 marked the high point of these sentiments.
Although no laws regarding equal rights for the Jews were changed
de jure, many Jews felt that the equal rights granted by the Kerensky
government and his Bolshevik successors in 1917 had not taken root
in the Russian consciousness even thirty or forty years later.

The Balfour Declaration of 2 November 1917 aroused great hopes
amongst the Jews. The fact that Great Britain, the greatest power in
the world, not only recognized the Jewish right to self-determination
but was willing to support the establishment of a "national home"
in which Jews could fulfill their national aspirations was of great
significance to world Jewry.[47] A few generations earlier, just a small
number of intellectuals had supported the idea that Jews should be
granted emancipation. It took more than eighty years for legislators
in central Europe to emulate the United States Congress and the
French National Assembly and grant the Jews equal rights.

Russian Jews – 50 percent of the world's Jewish population –
received equal rights only half a year before the Balfour Declaration when His Majesty's Government suddenly recognized the
legitimacy of Zionism's demands for the establishment of a "national
home" for the Jews in Palestine.

Shortly after the German capitulation in November 1918, Woodrow Wilson, the President of the United States, announced the opening of the Paris Peace Conference on 18 January 1919, which then led to the signing of the peace treaty at Versailles on 28 June 1919. The Conference carved out a number of new states from the pre-war European empires and signed minorities treaties with them and with the defeated states, intending thus to protect the autonomous civil, political and religious rights of minorities (including the Jews). A large contingent of Jews came from all parts of the world and formed a delegation which participated in the negotiations regarding the minorities treaties and Jewish autonomy.[48] Newly-formed independent states like Ukraine and Lithuania granted the Jews national autonomy even before the opening of the peace conference.[49] The expanded Romania and reconstituted Poland signed treaties which provided for the granting of national autonomy for the Jews at a future date and a promise that Jews – like other ethnic groups – would be given national rights.[50]

The post-World War I developments were especially important for Polish Jewry. For a country in which Jews constituted 10 percent of the population (and one quarter of the world Jewish population), the success of national autonomy could have served as an example for other countries which had large Jewish populations. Unfortunately, the greater the expectations, the greater the disillusionment. Only a few years after the signing of the Versailles Treaty it became clear to Polish Jews that they would not receive national autonomy and that even the equal rights granted them were unstable and insecure. There was a delicate balance between the pressures of the right wing, who had an anti-Semitic tradition, and those of the liberal left-wing parties who wished to protect equal rights for the Jews. So long as the liberals had an influence on the regime, this balance was maintained. For sixteen years, chiefly the ten years of Marshal Jozef Pilsudski's government (1926–35), the Jews on the one hand did not receive autonomy as was promised, but on the other hand were not deprived of civil rights.[51] They suffered discrimination in civil service posts, the army and educational institutions but were able to develop their own economic, cultural and religious life and combat discrimination.[52] Jewish politicians were elected to the Polish Sejm as representatives of Jewish political parties and Yitzhak Gruenbaum (1879–1970) was one of the outstanding Jews who, in the early 1920s, led the national minorities bloc in the Sejm. Jewish emancipation in Poland and the improved standard of living found its expression in the greater variety of occupations in which they were engaged, particularly crafts and industry. (See Appendix, Table 11, for Jewish occupations in Poland – 1897 to 1931.[53])

The most significant occupational change was in the liberal professions, where a marked increase occurred – particularly in the percentage of Jews in law and medicine. In 1931 Jews constituted 49 percent of the 6,538 lawyers and legal advisors in Poland and 40.5 percent of the medical practitioners.[54] The enormous increase in these two professions demonstrated the effects of Jewish emancipation in Poland, particularly in everything relating to the acceleration of the modernization processes and the spread of education. However, the fact that Jews were under-represented in a number of other liberal professions, such as agronomy or veterinary medicine, accentuated the fact that emancipation was not always dependent upon laws but rather upon the goodwill of the dominant society. Medicine and law were professions less dependent upon non-Jewish employers and thus attracted more Jews.[55]

The non-acceptance of the Jews as an integral part of Polish society was particularly conspicuous in 1935 and 1936. At the end of the 1920s there was an economic crisis which continued for a number of years and escalated in the mid-1930s. The economic crisis, the death of Jozef Pilsudski, the influence of Nazi rise to power in Germany and their amazing success, all intensified discrimination against the Jews, which found its expression in the occupationary structure of Polish Jewry. At the end of the 1930s more than one-third of Jewish wage earners in Poland were unemployed and more than 40 percent required welfare assistance. The unemployment and welfare figures for other class sectors of the Polish population were much lower. Equal rights for the Jews were not formally revoked, but Polish society discriminated against them. Thus the great hopes harbored by Polish Jewry at the end of World War I dissolved by the end of the 1930s, just like those of the Jews of Romania, Hungary and the Baltic states. If at first, encouraged by the victorious allied powers, they demanded national autonomy, in the end they could only hope that the formal equality granted them would not be revoked.

The equal rights achieved by the Jews in Austria-Hungary and Germany (1867–70) marked the end of a period of struggle between the pro- and anti-emancipation forces. From that point until the beginning of the 1930s many Jews succeeded in integrating into German society.[56] The German and Austrian Jewish intellectual élite that developed included such outstanding personalities as

Albert Einstein, Sigmund Freud, Franz Rosenzweig, Franz Werfel
and Stefan Zweig. Among other examples of integration were the
100,000 Jews who fought in the German army in World War I –
the armed forces being a sector which had in the past been closed
to any non-German ethnic group; and outstanding German-Jewish
politicians of the 1920s, like Hugo Preuss, Walter Rathenau and Rosa
Luxemburg. But the opponents of Jewish equality in Germany and
Austria were stronger than in any other part of Europe, becoming
even more powerful in the last third of the nineteenth century.
Political parties adopted platforms which demanded the abolition of
Jewish emancipation,[57] and anti-Semites were elected to parliaments
and government positions. Outstanding among the latter was Karl
Lueger (1844–1910), the anti-Semitic mayor of Vienna (1897–1910).
Until the 1930s, however, all of these phenomena were relatively
marginal and ineffectual because the forces in favor of Jewish
integration were more powerful. The failure of Adolf Hitler's
putsch in 1923 was perhaps an indication that German society
was not yet ripe for the ghastly ideas outlined in *Mein Kampf*.

However, the extended economic crisis of the 1920s and the early
1930s, political instability and the strengthening of those forces
which embodied a megalomaniac, nationalistic and anti-Semitic
world view, brought about a dramatic change in the attitude
toward Jews. At the beginning of the 1930s there was an upsurge of
political forces demanding the abolition of Jewish emancipation. In
January 1933 Adolf Hitler came to power. Four months later, having
promised to eliminate not only Jewish emancipation but the Jews as
well, he set about doing so.

In the first stage (1933–35) Hitler abolished equal rights for Jews,
first by a boycott of Jewish businesses and services ("Don't buy
from Jews") which climaxed in the official boycott of 1 April 1933.
Thereafter laws were enacted which stated that the "non-Aryan
officials should be pensioned while those who hold honorary
positions should immediately be dismissed." In September 1935
the Nazis enacted the "Nuremberg Laws", the first of which, the
Reich Citizenship Law, rescinded the political rights of the Jews
by designating them "state subjects" whereas "Aryan" Germans
were "citizens of the Reich." The second law – "the Law for the
Protection of German Blood and Honor" – prohibited marriages
and extramarital relations between Germans and Jews. Although
the Jews were systematically ousted from various branches of the
economy they were still able to engage in commerce and industry

up to 1937. In 1939 the forced deportations began, at first of Jews who had Polish citizenship. A further high-point of anti-Jewish activity was reached on 9 and 10 November 1938, *Kristallnacht*, when Nazi stormtroopers and street mobs burned synagogues, demolished Jewish-owned stores and physically assaulted Jews throughout Germany and Austria. Following the pogrom some thirty thousand Jews were arrested and sent to concentration camps. The Jewish community was fined one billion Reichmarks, which amounted to one-third of its assets.[58]

In a speech before the German parliament (Reichstag) on 30 January 1939 Hitler declared, "If international-finance Jewry inside and outside of Europe should succeed once more in plunging nations into another world war, the consequence will not be the Bolshevization of the earth and thereby the victory of Jewry but the annihilation of the Jewish race in Europe."

Hitler meant what he said and throughout World War II the Germans carried out the "Final Solution" (the Nazi program for the extermination of the Jews). In all the territories conquered by the German army the first stage of the anti-Jewish measures was cutting them off from the general population, forbidding their employment in most crafts, expropriating their property (homes, shops and factories) and prohibiting the possession of cash and merchandise. The next stage was concentrating the Jews in special districts or quarters (ghettos), which were formally administered by Jewish Councils (Judenräte). The ghettos served as temporary collection points whence Jews were either sent to work-camps or concentration camps. From the inception of the ghettos until their final destruction about one-quarter of the population died of starvation and disease. The last stage was mass murder. From September 1939 until early 1942 the Jews were murdered by various means – enforced starvation, mass shootings by mobile execution units (*Einsatzgruppen*) and gas vans. On 20 January 1942 a top-level meeting of Nazi officials was held at a villa in Wannsee, Berlin (later known as the Wannsee Conference), to discuss the implementation of "an overall plan" for the "final solution to the Jewish question." In order to accelerate and streamline the mass murder of Jews the Germans erected a series of extermination camps using gas as the killing method. The first camp, Chełmno (in the Łódź district) was put into operation on 8 December 1941. Other camps included Auschwitz-Birkenau, Belzec, Sobibor and Treblinka. By the end of the war the Germans had murdered some six million Jews, 3.5 million of them in the gas chambers of the extermination camps. The Nazi racist ideology not only denied the Jewish right to emancipation but viewed the Jews as parasites and political conspirators who threatened the world and must therefore be exterminated.[59]

Paradoxically, the defeat of Nazi Germany terminated the emancipation process. The nations of the world recognized not only that Jews were entitled to equal rights wherever they resided but that they were entitled to self-determination and their own state. Formally this recognition found expression in the United Nations General Assembly's decision of 29 November 1947. Moreover, even countries which had not accepted the rule of democracy and where not all citizens were equal in the eyes of the law, accepted the principle that one must not discriminate against the Jews because of their religion, unless they were identified as enemies of the regime. Thus, for example, the Jews were denied their freedom in a number of Arab countries like Iraq, Egypt, Morocco and Tunisia in the 1950s and 1960s, or in Syria till 1994,[60] on the grounds that they identified with Zionism and the State of Israel and were therefore enemies of the regime. But in a post-Nazi world, countries and governments, even those with totalitarian regimes who declared they were in a state of war with Israel, were careful not to discriminate against Jews because of their religious or ethnic affiliations. Thus we see that the process which began at the end of the eighteenth century culminated after the greatest Jewish catastrophe, in which the Jews were not only deprived of equal rights but were deprived of the right to life.

The process of granting equal rights to Jews was sporadic rather than ongoing and uniform. In the United States, the equality of Jews was taken for granted within the framework of the principle expressed in the American Constitution – that all people were created equal and therefore one must not discriminate against any person on grounds of religion, sex or race (excluding blacks, who later had to struggle for emancipation). But this formula was not self-evident with regard to European Jews. Even in countries where Jews were granted full emancipation, this was later rescinded: in Great Britain in 1753; fifty years later by Napoleon Bonaparte in France; and in Germany and Austria in the 1930s. Nevertheless, one may categorically state that as the twentieth century draws to its close, the process of Jewish emancipation has been completed.

3

Cultural Revolution

During the 1870s and 1880s, Jews experienced a cultural-social revolution – mass secularization. What was the significance of this phenomenon from an historical perspective? Was it a continuation of trends initiated in the last third of the eighteenth century as a result of the activities of Israel ben Eliezer Ba'al Shem Tov (*Besht*, 1700–60) the founder of Hasidism, which came to dominate large segments of eastern European Jewry;[1] or was it caused by the coincidental establishment of the *Haskalah* movement in Germany, which adopted the ideas of its leader, Moses Mendelssohn (1729–86)?[2] Or was the secularization a unique cultural-social phenomenon, sui generis in essence and dimension, signifying a turning point in the history of the Jews in modern times?

The historical background for the emergence of Hasidism is related to the socioeconomic and spiritual crisis which beset the Jews of Poland–Lithuania in the second half of the seventeenth century. Due to the gradual disintegration of the Polish–Lithuanian commonwealth which began with the Chmielnicki revolt in 1648 and ended with the final partition of Poland between her neighbors (1772–1795), the economy was gradually undermined. The Jews, caught between the Polish nobles and the peasants, were an integral part of that economic system and when it collapsed they too were affected[3] although to a less dramatic extent than their neighbors.[4] At the same time the Jews experienced a religious crisis which expressed itself in the rise of the Sabbateanism. This ecstatic messianic outburst, which climaxed with the fall of Shabbetai Zevi in 1666, caused a spiritual crisis[5] that in turn resulted in the widespread activities of Kabbalists and the establishment of Hasidic circles.[6]

The founder of Hasidism, the *Besht*, was active in Medzibezh, a town in the Podolia province in the Ukraine, from about 1740 until his death in 1760. Performing miraculous acts of healing, he earned the name *ba'al shem* ("the noteworthy") and became a spiritual leader. The Hasidic circles in Medzibezh and the surrounding towns recognized his rare spiritual qualities and original thinking and in due course he became the outstanding personality of the group.[7] After his death, his disciple Dov Baer, the *Maggid* of Mezhirech (a village in the Rovno province of the Ukraine), was recognized as his successor and together with other contenders for succession, led by Rabbi Jacob Joseph of Polonnoye, spread the teachings of Hasidism as attributed to the *Besht*.[8]

The essence of the *Besht*'s teaching was emotional experience, which emphasized the salvation of the individual's soul through *devekut* ("the clinging of the soul to God") and *hitlahavut* ("burning enthusiasm for God") in fulfilling the *mitzvot* (commandments). Hasidism contained mystic elements based upon Kabbalistic traditions which were combined with popular traditions of ecstasy and mass enthusiasm. The movement created a new type of religious leader, the charismatic *zaddik* (the righteous, the leader of Hasidism), whose followers, members of his court, recognizing his spiritual superiority, sought his spiritual protection.

During the first half of the nineteenth century Hasidism spread throughout Russia. The *Maggid* and his disciples disseminated the teachings of the *Besht* among the Jewish communities in the Ukraine, Lithuania, Reisen and central Poland, and their successors extended their activities to the remaining parts of the Pale of Settlement, even spreading to many communities in Galicia, Hungary and Romania. During the reign of the *Maggid*, who was still considered the undisputed leader of Hasidism, a number of other Hasidic centers were established – in Belorussia by Rabbi Menahem Mendel of Vitebsk; in Lithuania by Rabbi Aaron (the Great) of Karlin. *Zaddikim* (the righteous) recognized the *Maggid*'s leadership but in their courts they became leaders in their own right. After the death of the *Maggid* in 1772 the movement split into numerous groups, each led by a *zaddik* who gloried in being the *Besht*'s heir.

In the long run the proliferation of Hasidic courts caused an irreparable split in the movement. This split was further exacerbated by a number of factors: the plurality of leadership, which became a tradition even during the lifetime of the *Besht* and the *Maggid*;[9] the enormous distances between the eastern European communities; the political instability in the Pale of Settlement during the period of the Polish partitions; the opposition stirred up by Hasidism. Perhaps most critical of all was the lack of a single leader acceptable to all the Hasidim.

Already in the 1820s there were scores of Hasidic courts and by the 1850s their number grew to hundreds, each with thousands of followers. Relations between the courts were minimal and conflicts between them increased in direct proportion to the movement's expansion. The nature of these conflicts varied, ranging from a desire to expand spheres of influence to disagreement over type of dress and mode of customs. However, despite this dissension the expansion of Hasidism spurred the reorganization of Jewish communities. The *kehillah* ("community"), with all its traditional functions, lost much of its significance and was replaced by an umbrella organization whose spokes were the Hasidic courts.

From the beginning of the nineteenth century, the more than 50 percent of world Jewry who lived in eastern Europe underwent a cultural and sociological revolution whose sources were Kabbalah, Sabbateanism and the laws of the Torah and *halakhah*.[10] Hasidism represented a new stage in the religious development of the Jews. Having spread and established its centrality amongst the populace, the movement which at first seemed opposed to orthodox Judaism became the focal element of orthodox Jewish society.

The struggle against Hasidism, which had begun during the lifetime of its founder, the *Besht*,[11] gained momentum after his death, by which time Hasidism had established itself as a major factor among the Jews of eastern Europe. The outstanding personality among the opponents of Hasidism was Rabbi Elijah ben Solomon Zalman (The "Vilna Gaon," 1720–97), who led a fierce and unwavering battle against the new movement, pronouncing a ban on it and disseminating letters of condemnation.[12] Hasidism, according to Elijah, conflicted with traditional Judaism which placed its major emphasis upon the centrality of Torah study and the ideal of total commitment to the study of holy texts. From 1772 Vilna became the center of the *Mitnaggedim* (opponents) movement against Hasidism, spreading throughout Lithuania, Belorussia and Galicia.

Opposition to Hasidism grew even as the movement expanded throughout the Pale of Settlement. It reached a peak in 1794 when the "Vilna Gaon" ordered the public burning of the *Testament of the Besht*.[13] However, during the nineteenth century the intensity of the conflict gradually diminished despite the differences between the two camps, which also found expression in a large body of polemical literature. The feud abated under the influence of internal and external factors such as the pro-Hasidic stand taken by the Russian authorities in Vilna, who in April 1798 issued an edict permitting Hasidim to pray in their own congregations, and the Statute of 1804 issued by Tsar Alexander I, granting each Jewish sect the right to organize its own synagogue and choose its own rabbi. However, the conflict subsided primarily because Hasidism had rooted itself firmly in the majority of the communities in Russia, Galicia, Romania and Hungary,[14] while the *Mitnaggedim* became a minority based mainly in Lithuania and a number of communities in Belorussia and Galicia. In addition, the steady rise of the *Haskalah* movement in the 1840s and 1850s equally affected both Hasidim and *Mitnaggedim*, serving to tone down their quarreling and even uniting them against its threat.

The *Haskalah* movement, which originated in Berlin, reached the Pale of Settlement two generations after it had spread through central and western Europe.[15] From the middle of the eighteenth century, individuals and, later, groups adopted the life-style of their German environment. First they sought to acquire a general education[16] for themselves and their children. Later they adopted Christian customs, abandoning most of the uniquely Jewish outer signs of identification.[17]

The philosophical basis for the Enlightenment movement was shaped by Moses Mendelssohn (1729–86), who was born in Dessau, Germany. From the 1760s he became the chief spokesman of the German *maskilim* (adherents of the Enlightenment movement). In his treatise *Jerusalem or On Religious Power and Judaism* (1783), Mendelssohn explained why it was necessary to establish a new system of relations between the Jews and their environment – one which would enable them to preserve their religion and customs, based on a deep recognition of the truth of Judaism, yet at the same time to be accepted with equal rights into society. He recognized that the tenets of Judaism were essentially in harmony with reason and the principles of Enlightenment and therefore advocated reforms. His major contention was that reform was necessary in the Jewish way of life, which must adjust itself to the general way of life. Asserting that it was necessary to abrogate many of the functions assumed by the rabbis and Jewish community leaders and change them into state institutions, Mendelssohn urged divesting the *kehillah* of its authority to maintain separate courts of law and its compulsive power of excommunication.[18]

Despite these views Mendelssohn was a loyal Jew who accepted the basic tenets of Judaism and believed that performing the *mitzvot* was an integral part of the Jewish experience. Some of his disciples and successors wanted to introduce reforms designed to change the face of Judaism, while others still clung to tradition. However, scholars like Naphtali Herz Wessely (1725–1805) who wished to reform the Jewish educational system – introducing and giving precedence to general studies[19] – eventually brought about a decisive shift in Jewish outlook.[20]

A more radical impetus for reform emerged from those of Mendelssohn's disciples who ceased to observe the *mitzvot*, wishing to change the nature of Judaism according to the ideology they had developed. One of their outstanding leaders, David Friedländer (1750–1834), believed that Talmud study and the practice of *mitzvot* were unnecessary and were the major obstacle to Jews being accepted into society as citizens with equal rights. He also proposed abolishing the Jewish *kehillah* organization and all ritual or prayer linking Jews to the messianic visions of redemption in Erez Israel.[21]

During the last third of the eighteenth century many German Jews adopted Mendelssohn's innovations and the philosophy of Wessely, Friedländer and others. They subscribed to *Haskalah* literature such as the *Me'assef*, a Hebrew periodical founded in 1783 in Koenigsberg and edited by Isaac Euchel (1756–1804), who was later considered the "initiator of the *Haskalah* movement in Germany".[22] The periodical served as a voice for the *maskilim* and reached thousands of people; groups and societies of *maskilim* were established and for some time it seemed as if the *Haskalah* had swept through German Jewry. Furthermore, some of the Jews underwent a constant process of secularization. The desire to integrate into the surrounding society and the fact that some of the German intelligentsia and government leaders viewed this trend favorably (some even striving to grant the Jews emancipation)[23] motivated the *maskilim* and they adjusted their ideology accordingly. However, the *maskilim* constituted only a small percentage of the Jewish population in central and western Europe and it was some time before larger numbers adopted the principles of the *Haskalah*.

As the *Haskalah* movement in Germany expanded, its adherents began to differ in defining appropriate directions and goals for Jews and Judaism. The radicals reached the conclusion that Christian baptism would achieve their ultimate goal of total integration into general society.[24] This was the path taken by most of Mendelssohn's descendants, who converted to Christianity, as did the poet Heinrich Heine (1707–1856) who declared that "Being a Jew is an incurable disease" which one can avoid "only by baptism."[25]

However, most of the *maskilim* chose to follow Mendelssohn's example, not wishing to cut themselves off from Jewish spiritual tradition. They decided to present the richness of Judaism to the general public, in order to prove its compatibility with the principles of the European milieu. In 1819 Eduard Gans (1798–1839), together with Leopold Zunz (Yom Tov Lipmann, 1794–1886) and Moses Moser (1796–1838), founded the *Verein für Kultur und Wissenschaft des Judentums* ("Society for Jewish Culture and Science") whose purpose was to use modern scientific methods to examine the ethos of Judaism.[26]

Zunz and his colleagues maintained that if Judaism were presented in its historical perspective, using scientific methods of research, a new image would emerge which would restore to Judaism the status and respect it had lost over the years.[27]

Controversy developed among *Wissenschaft* scholars regarding ways of presenting their scientific findings. Zacharias Frankel (1801–75), one of the outstanding personalities among the German *maskilim*, believed that the Jews must continue to practice their rituals and observe *halakhah*, abolishing only minor aspects of Jewish tradition. Others, like Abraham Geiger (1810–74), wished to abolish almost all the existing systems of *mitzvot* and ritual, hoping that this would lead to a new form of Judaism.

The controversy, which was at first academic, took a practical turn when some of the advocates for change decided to implement the new ideology. In 1810 Israel Jacobson (1768–1828) inaugurated a service in the chapel of a school he had established in the town of Seesen in Westphalia (an area conquered by Napoleon), in which he introduced a new order of prayer and ritual in order to bring the Jews a step closer to their host society.[28]

A few years later a similar experiment was attempted in a private home in Berlin and in 1818 the first Reform Temple was dedicated in Hamburg. In these temples prayers were said in German, often accompanied by an organ, some sections of the traditional service were omitted (particularly those which refer to the return to Zion), and the partition separating men and women was removed. Thus the Jewish Reform movement took its first steps, hoping to reconcile Judaism with the modern world.[29]

In the 1820s and at the beginning of the 1830s it appeared that

the experiment had failed. Services in the Seesen Chapel were abandoned and in Berlin the Prussian government prohibited holding
prayer meetings in private homes. The Hamburg Temple stood
in splendid isolation, strongly opposed by the orthodox rabbinical
establishment and supported by only a few rabbis.[30] In the second
half of the 1830s, however, there was a critical turn in the history
of the Reform movement. Rabbis and intellectuals, outstanding
among whom was Abraham Geiger (sometimes called "the founding
father of Reform Judaism"),[31] sought to promote the cause of the
movement and circulate its ideology throughout Europe. They met
with considerable success. The number of new adherents increased
steadily, chiefly among the younger generation.

However, the movement encountered a number of difficulties,
since the rabbis disagreed on the nature of the changes to be made
in the customs and principles of the Jewish faith. Almost every
rabbi went his own way and sporadic attempts to achieve a unified
reform practice were of no avail. Even the more formal attempts
by the leading reform rabbis in Germany were unsuccessful.
Three rabbinical conferences on these topics, held in Brunswick,
Frankfurt and Breslau – in 1844, 1845, 1846 – bore little fruit. Sharp
disagreements about sanctioning mixed marriages, forbidding cir-
cumcision, or giving precedence to German in the liturgy divided
the participants. As a result the Reform movement was unable to
establish a recognized authority with the power to sanction changes
in the religion.[32]

Despite these difficulties the Reform movement spread throughout Germany and thence to Hungary, Austria, western Europe and
the United States. Despite the lack of uniformity, the movement
eventually developed a number of basic tenets beyond the practice of
abolishing the separation of sexes, introduction of the organ into the
synagogue, using the vernacular for most of the prayers, abandoning
Hebrew as a holy language and adopting European dress. These
tenets included new definitions regarding the universal mission of
the Jews and Judaism, whose main purpose was to disseminate
monotheism and the Jewish moral principles among the nations
of the world. Furthermore, the Reform movement maintained that
Judaism lacked an historical consciousness and it was therefore
necessary to discontinue in prayer and abandon in custom the
affinity to the messianic idea and the return to Zion.

Disagreements among the leaders of the Reform movement led
to schism and the secession of members, outstanding of whom was

Zacharias Frankel. At the Reform conference in Frankfurt, Frankel stated that the radicals' insistence on changes would probably lead the members into the arms of Christianity. He therefore suggested a middle road between Reform and Orthodox (calling the latter fossilized and unprogressive) which would retain the Jewish heritage and tradition but would add the element of critical historical study of Judaism. Frankel and his disciples founded a new party which later influenced the Conservative movement in the United States. This new party sought a synthesis between historical Judaism, with its observance of the *mitzvot* and *halakhah*, and response to contemporary needs via gradual organic reform, thus enabling the nations to accept and respect Judaism.[33]

Two new trends were added to Judaism during the nineteenth century – the Reform and the Conservative. The Reform, which from 1810 began functioning in the sanctuaries of Westphalia, Hamburg and Berlin, spreading to various centers in central and western Europe, developed during the 1860s and 70s into two established and recognized movements within the Jewish community, although their members were a minority compared with the many Jews still affiliated to the Orthodox community. Moreover, inroads made by the Reform movement in central and western Europe provoked the Orthodox community's opposition. Most of the influential Orthodox rabbis agreed with the statement of Moses Sofer (known as Hatam Sofer; 1762–1839), the rabbi of Pressburg, the most important community in Hungary: "To the extent that we wish to associate ourselves with them [the peoples of Europe] and adopt their customs, God spreads hatred between them and us."[34] This was also the stand taken by Rabbi Akiva Ben Moses Guens Eger of Posen (1761–1837), the district Rabbi of Moravia, Mordecai Banet (1753–1829), and most of the rabbis who were active in Germany and Austria-Hungary. Agreeing with the judgment of the Hatam Sofer, who upheld the Talmudic dictum that "any innovation in the *halakhah* is strictly forbidden,"[35] they forbade additions to or detractions from the *halakhah*, since all its components, they argued, are of equal status.

News of the establishment of circles for intellectuals based upon the teachings of Mendelssohn and the activities of his disciples ultimately reached the Jewish communities in eastern Europe.[36] Educated merchants and students who were in touch with *maskilim* in the west spread word of the movement, disseminating publications and manuscripts and reporting on new developments relating to *Haskalah*.[37] In the 1780s there were even a few individuals, such as Rabbi Jacob Ben Wolf Kranz (*Maggid* of Dubno; 1741–1804), Phinehas Elijah Hurwitz (1765–1821), Baruch of Shklov (Baruch Shick; 1752–1810) in eastern Europe, who advocated changes in the nature of the eastern European Jewish community, such as engaging in manual labor and introducing general studies into the educational system,[38] while nevertheless ensuring total observance of the principles of traditional Judaism. However, they were a small minority, insignificant and alien. Their philosophy was far removed from the thinking of most eastern European Jewry and after a few years of attempted activities they fell silent. Thus the circles of *maskilim* in Vilna, Odessa and Shklov, which had been founded at the end of the eighteenth century, disappeared.

There were a number of reasons for the *Haskalah* movement's failure to penetrate the Jewish communities of eastern Europe. The basic ideas of the western and central European *Haskalah* movement had not as yet been accepted as guiding principles by the Russian intelligentsia and ruling circles. These circles were also not sure how to cope with the Jewish problem since, up to the first Polish partition in 1772, the Jews, like other non-Christian religious groups, were forbidden to settle in Russia.

Moreover, the Jews in eastern Europe did not identify with the west-European *maskilim*'s desire to be recognized as part of society at large. The principle of fortifying their cultural and social uniqueness in order to protect their religion and way of life under- went no change at the end of the eighteenth century. Rather, the success of the Hasidic movement strengthened the advocates of this principle. While the Gaon of Vilna was at least aware of the dramatic changes which had taken place amongst the *maskilim* in the west,[39] the Hasidic courts preached the principles of the *sod* (the kabbalistic concept of "mystery"), i.e. interpreting the Scripture in a manner which refers the believers to the mystery of the Godhead and its hidden life and the *nistar* (the "hidden saint"); and to revel in the joy of performing the *mitzvot* – principles, which stood in opposition to the values advocated by the *maskilim* in western Europe.

Furthermore, the Jews of eastern Europe rejected the attempt by Tsar Alexander I to assimilate them into general society by compelling them to change their life-style, occupations, and educational system, as expressed in the Jewish Statute which he promulgated in 1804. The Tsar and his ministers were accused of attempting to force Jews to apostasize. Representatives of the Jewish community tried unsuccessfully to repeal or defer several sections of the Statute on the grounds that section 42, "the desire to assimilate them, with other Russian citizens," presented the possibility of an attack on their customs and religion.[40]

It was particularly during the reign of Nicholas I, when many Jews in Russia felt that the motive of the activities was to assimilate them (even to the extent of apostasy), that the *Haskalah* movement developed in Russia, one of its major goals being the elimination of the barriers between Jews and their neighbors. Agricultural and industrial modernization, European capital investment, which engendered a more open attitude toward Europe, and perhaps most significant, the slow penetration of *Haskalah* values amongst the Russian intelligentsia – one of the first and more dramatic manifestations of which was the Decemberist rising in 1825 – also influenced the Jews. Many more merchants than in the past crossed the border, returning to Russia with the impressions of the *Haskalah* they had encountered in Germany and other countries. Groups of *maskilim* were established in the towns on the German-Lithuanian border and in other cities in the Pale of Settlement. Outstanding among them were those in Vilna and Odessa.[41]

The first Jewish school in Russia to combine general studies and religious studies was established in Odessa.[42] In Vilna the Hebrew writer Mordecai Aaron Guenzburg (1795–1846) and the Hebrew poet Abraham Dov Lebensohn (pseud. Adam ha-Kohen; 1794–1878) tried to revive Hebrew language and literature and change the Jewish economic structure. The movement developed in the 1830s and 1840s, spreading to various places in the Pale of Settlement. Although the *maskilim* were still an anomalous minority, their growth and acceleration led the leaders of the Hasidic and rabbinic establishments to see them as an enemy, no less – and perhaps even more – dangerous than the Russian authorities.

The demands of the eastern European *maskilim* for social, economic and cultural changes differed from those of their colleagues in Germany. The latter's goal was to be accepted into German society and to eliminate the cultural barriers, while the former aspired to modernization, productivization of the Jewish economy and changes in the educational system.[43] For the east European *maskilim* the target goal for change was the Hasidic movement, whose adherents they perceived as the ideological and social antithesis to their own vision of the future.

Hasidism was defined as a deviant from Judaism and the major obstacle to Jewish social progress.[44] Perhaps the major difference between the development of the *Haskalah* movements in the east and west can be found in the forces which opposed them. Hasidism, which struck deep roots in eastern Europe, was an extremely centralized movement and therefore difficult to penetrate. The devotion to the *zaddik*, which was a principle of Hasidism, was the major factor preventing new ideas and forces from penetrating Hasidic society. The obedience demanded of the hasidim by the *zaddik* and his disciples decisively immunized them against *Haskalah* ideology. It became clear to the *maskilim* in eastern Europe that in order to overcome this major impediment they must present a more moderate alternative.

The *Haskalah* program in eastern Europe was outlined by Isaac Ber Levinsohn (Ribal; 1788–1860), the outstanding *maskil* in the 1830s and 1840s. In his activities and writings he sought to make the Jews more "useful" by means of a general education which would supplement Torah studies. Such education would include learning the language of the country and secular subjects in the humanities and sciences. Jews would be directed to productive occupations and to agricultural work. Thus "All the House of Israel will be repaired, with the aid of the Lord as aforetime with Torah and *derekh erez* ('way of the world') and they will be treasured people as in ancient times and will dwell in peace and security; they will not be convulsed nor slaughtered, and all the nations and peoples will be blessed in them."[45]

Levinsohn represented the moderate approach amongst the *maskilim* which, in order to attract the Jews to progress, proposed retaining a part of the Jewish way of life. Other *maskilim*, such as Benjamin Mandelstamm (1805–66), urged Jews toward more extreme goals such as the study of European languages instead of Yiddish ("they speak some ridiculous tongue"[46]) and a change in life-style and dress.

The different approaches amongst the east European *maskilim* did not prevent them from supporting and even justifying the radical Jewish program of Tsar Nicholas I. Thus they justified and even favored his demand that Jews serve in the Russian army, receive a general secular education in government schools and wear Russian- or European-style clothes. They also accepted his abolition of the *kahal* (autonomous Jewish community) in 1844 and the dissolution of all Jewish presses save two which were under government supervision. In their view, Nicholas's demands (some of which were proposals of the Jewish Committee he established to "determine the means for reforming the Russian Jews"[47]) were a potential means of integrating the Jews into the general society even if this were done by coercion and with the total disapproval of the majority of the Jews. For them, the fact that this would not only remove the barriers between Jews and Russians, but also advance the major objectives of the *maskilim* (education, productivization and integration with the general society) justified, in their opinion, Nicholas's edicts, even if these were perceived by many Jews as a path to apostasy.[48]

The *maskilim's* support for the regime intensified the resentment of their Jewish opponents. At first attacked for advocating innovations, they were now accused of collaboration with the authorities. Despite this opposition the number of *maskilim* circles grew, their activities in education, culture and pamphleteering greatly expanded and in time they gained many adherents.[49] The liberal climate which characterized the early years of Alexander II's reign (1856–63),[50] the large migration of Jews from the village to the city, Russia's openness to western cultural influence and the dramatic growth in trade between Russia and its neighbors were additional factors contributing to a continual increase in the number of Jewish *maskilim*. The movement developed to such an extent that in 1863 leading rabbis and *admorim* (*adonenu, morenu, ve-rabbenu* – "Our lord, master, and teacher") of both the Hasidic and *Mitnaggedim* camps convened a conference in St. Petersburg to decide how to contain it, but their attempts were of no avail.

One of the indicators for the growth of the movement in Russia was the expansion of the *maskil*-oriented educational network. To the small number of schools combining Jewish and general studies which existed in the 1850s in Odessa, Vilna, Warsaw and other places there was added a government-sponsored rabbinical seminary in Vilna and one in Zhitomir (1847), which trained teachers for the Jewish government schools.[51] The network expanded even further in the 1860s and in 1863 the *Hevrat Mefizei ha-Haskalah* ("Society for the Promotion of Culture among the Jews of Russia") was established to provide moral and material assistance for the staff of the schools, which were meant to replace the traditional *hadarim* and *yeshivot*. In the 1870s there were already tens of Jewish elementary schools with a *Haskalah* curriculum and a smaller number of high-schools. Moreover, from the 1860s many Jewish children began studying in Russian schools, gymnasia and universities. In 1880 they totalled some eight thousand (more than 10 percent of the total number of Jewish students) compared with about five hundred in 1860.[52] Another phenomenon in the development of the *Haskalah* movement in Russia was the publication of Jewish newspapers such as *Ha-meliz* (1860), *Ha-Zefirah* (1862) and *Razsvet* (1860).

The expansion in the number of *maskilim* groups, the growth of the *Haskalah* educational network and the publication of Jewish newspapers were all clear indications of the *Haskalah* movement's popularity among the Jewish public in Russia.

In the 1880s there was an accelerated process of secularization amongst the Jews of eastern Europe. Over and above the fact that the *Haskalah* movement developed beyond recognition and that every year thousands of new members joined the small band of *maskilim* who were active in the 1860s and 1870s, there was the beginning of a slow but consistent process of adopting *Haskalah* values amongst thousands of Jewish families in the Pale of Settlement. This found expression in a diminishing observance of *mitzvot*, children's education, and changes in everyday customs of dress and spoken language. The process usually began with adopting Russian cultural values such as speaking Russian,[53] followed by a change in attitude toward education; tens of thousands of Jewish children joined Jewish schools such as those supervised by *Hevrat Mefizei ha-Haskalah* or the *hadarim metukannim* (improved Jewish elementary schools) which included a curriculum of general studies, while many others entered Russian schools.[54] Jewish youth went to Russian and foreign universities, where they were exposed to general culture. There was such a dramatic increase in the number of Jewish students at universities that various groups in Russian society demanded their number be limited. In 1887 a *numerus clausus* was imposed which limited the number of Jewish students to two percent of the total student body at the universities of St. Petersburg and Moscow, and from 5 to 7 percent at all the others. Finding themselves barred from the Russian universities tens of thousands of Jewish youth left the country to study in Germany, Switzerland, Austria-Hungary, France and elsewhere.

Another widespread indication of secularization was the gradual distancing from religion and the decline in observance of *mitzvot*. Many Jews limited synagogue attendance to Sabbaths and Holy Days. Religious services were shortened, large sections being eliminated or performed in a perfunctory manner. In many instances Jews stopped wearing *tefillin* ("phylacteries"). The final stage of this process was to alter one's outward appearance, first by removing or trimming the beard and then by changing the traditional Jewish garb for European dress, whether Russian or German. Sometimes the removal of the traditional Jewish head-covering came at a later stage.[55]

While the secularization process which took hold of the Jewish population in Russia from the 1880s was related to the spread of secularization amongst the Russian and European population,[56] additional causes may be found in the gradual migration of Jews to the cities, where they underwent an accelerated process of modernization. The urbanization of eastern European Jewry expedited the break up of the traditional extended family that had existed in the villages and towns. Consequently there was less pressure on those Jews who sought cultural changes but desisted because of the social pressure from the extended family. The dissolution of the extended family also weakened loyalty to the rabbi and the hasidic *Admor* which was easier to maintain in the small intimate community of the village or town. The psychological pressure brought to bear upon the nonconformist who wished to transfer loyalty to another social group or even another hasidic court was tremendous and often unbearable. Such pressure hardly existed in the large cities where the population was dispersed and dissidents had much greater support. Thus it was that tens of thousands of Jews, who inclined toward Hasidism, underwent a process of urbanization and often found themselves cut off from their environment, and requiring service systems which were different from those to which they had been accustomed in the past. One of the consequences of this situation was the choice of loyalty to another culture, which included the process of secularization.[57]

The gentile environment in the large cities also influenced the process of Jewish secularization. During the last third of the nineteenth century, Russian society itself underwent a secularization process which included a gradual distancing from religion. It was easier for Jews to imitate their neighbors in the large city than in the village or town, particularly when they felt this would make life easier for them and that, by adopting the existing cultural values, they would appear less anomalous in their environment.[58] We shall see that in the large cities which were opened to Jewish settlement and where tens of thousands were living – chiefly in Poland and New Russia (Warsaw, Łódź, Odessa, Yelizavetgrad and

Yekaterinoslav) – the secularization process was more accelerated than in those areas where Jews had been living for many
generations.

In the traditional Jewish environment of the Lithuanian towns or
Ukrainian cities (with the exceptions of cities such as Vilna or a city
like Kiev, where a large Jewish community developed only at the
end of the nineteenth century), even if there was a considerable
increase in the number of Jews, they joined the existing traditional
Jewish districts and streets, which still protected them from adopting
new cultural traditions – although these traditions did manage to
infiltrate.[59]

On the other hand, in Odessa or Warsaw, cities where Jews lived in
new districts many of which were previously considered Christian,
Jews felt less pressured by Jewish society and more dependent upon
the gentile society – another factor which propelled them into the
secularization process.[60]

Circumstances compelled the Jews to engage in occupations
which they could adjust to their religious and cultural needs.
Thus it was that in the first half of the nineteenth century many
were employed in the manufacture and distribution of liquor
(see chapter 1). Urbanization forced them into other occupations
– a process which also accelerated secularization. In order to sell
their wares more efficiently, Jewish merchants had to adjust to the
values of the environment in dress and trading days. So too, Jewish
laborers had to adjust to their Christian employers and colleagues,
who often insisted that they change the day of rest from the Sabbath
to Sunday.

Another manifestation of the expansion of the secularization
process in eastern Europe during the last third of the nineteenth
century was the establishment of the political parties whose
platform included the struggle to improve the status of Jews, the
granting of equal rights and class solidarity. Within this context
tens of thousands of Jews joined Russian political parties whose
ideals similarly espoused improving the situation of the Russian
populace.

In the 1870s a small group of Jewish intellectuals began preaching
socioeconomic revolution amongst the Jews and urging a change
in values which would raise their awareness of social issues.
Outstanding amongst these intellectuals was Aaron Samuel
Liebermann (1845–80) who, forced to flee Vilna in 1875 because
of his revolutionary activities, reached London where, in 1876,

he founded the *Agudat ha-Sotzyalistim ha-Ivrim* ("Hebrew Socialist Union"). One of the objectives of the Union was a workers' republic which would manage its own private affairs without being bound to any superior authority,[61] the reference being to the rabbinical establishment. However, his proposals were less extreme than those of his colleague on the Union, George (Hirsh) Saper. Liebermann still believed in retaining Jewish customs, particularly the major festivals, and maintained that the "human goal," not just the Jewish one, was the only relevant factor[62] – in other words one must abandon Jewish values for more general ones. Nevertheless, both agreed on the principle that Jewish allegiance should be to the socioeconomic class and not to religion and customs.

Jews were among the founders of the Russian Social Democratic Workers' Party in the 1880s.[63] Pavel Borisovich Axelrod (1855–1941) and Leo (Lev Grigorsyevich) Deutsch, and other Russian exiles, founded the first Russian Marxist party. A decade later their successors in the Pale of Settlement advocated a violent revolutionary struggle against the authorities.[64] The Bund (General Jewish Workers' Union in Lithuania, Poland and Russia) was founded at a secret convention in Vilna held on 7–9 October 1897 and attended by a small group of delegates.[65] Their platform called for the "organizations of the Yiddish-speaking proletariat in the western districts of the Russian empire" and protection of the interests of Jewish workers in those districts.[66] The Bund became an organized workers' movement which at its peak in 1901–5 had about 30,000 members.

From its inception the leaders of the Bund had two ideological principles. One, cosmopolitan-revolutionary: to strive for a proletarian revolution which would overthrow the tsarist regime, bring the proletariat to power and serve as a bridgehead for a world-wide proletarian revolution. The second, national-cultural: the Bund leaders called for the establishment of an autonomous Jewish national-cultural entity. At its fourth convention in Bialystok (May 1901) the organization undertook to fight for Jewish autonomy,[67] the aims of which were the establishment of schools where Yiddish was the language of instruction and of an educational network for the "working masses"; the development of a network of newspapers and publication of books in Yiddish, and above all replacement of the existing Jewish communal leadership by a secular proletarian one "which would concern itself with deepening its identification with the Jewish worker."[68]

The Bund leaders, with their demands and actions, were in fact (though often unwittingly) strengthening the secularization trend amongst the Jews. This could be deduced both from the elimination of traditional education and from the struggle for a sociocultural way of life which would replace the traditional religious one.

The fact that the Bund had so many devotees (and possibly would have had many more members were it not for persecution by the authorities) is another clear indication of the extent of the secularization process. Indeed Jews may have been more motivated to join the Bund because of the secularization process than out of a desire to ameliorate the situation of the Jewish proletariat. In the Pale of Settlement and in Poland after World War I, the Bund was perceived as a party representing the secular segment of the population. Leaders such as Arkadi Kremer (1865–1935), Joseph Solomon Mill (1870–1952), Vladimir Kossovsky (1867–1941) and others, served the Jews of eastern Europe as symbols of their rapid secularization – even more extreme than the secularization represented by those who joined other political movements, including Zionism.

Even the ideas of the leaders of the *Hibbat Zion* ("lovers of Zion") movement founded in 1881, and their successors in the Zionist Organization sixteen years later, were to a large extent related to the secularization process which spread amongst the Jewish populace.[69] However, many leaders of the movement, including secularists such as Moses Leib Lilienblum (1843–1910), saw a connection between national independence for the Jews and the vision of Israel's prophets.[70] This connection resonated strongly in the religious *Haredi* (Heb.: orthodox religious Jew) Zionist wing led by rabbis such as Samuel Mohilever (1824–98), Mordecai Eliasberg (1817–89), Isaac Jacob Reines (1839–1915) and their successors, who saw the fulfillment of Zionism (i.e. the establishment of a national home for Jews) as a religious *mitzvah* the performance of which was an obligation equal to any of the 613 *mitzvot*.[71]

Moreover there were those among them who saw Zionism as the first stage of redemption. These included Rabbi Mohilever and Rabbi Abraham Isaac Kook (1865–1935; from 1919 the first Ashkenazi chief rabbi of Erez Israel) and the latter's heirs in *Gush Emunim*[72] 60 years later. However, amongst the Zionists this was a minority view, the majority perceiving Zionism as a movement which propelled Jews to secularization. This was the stand taken by the great rabbis of the end of the nineteenth and beginning of the twentieth centuries.

Hasidic *admorim* such as Isaac Dov Baer Schneorsohn (1826–1910; head of the Habad Hasidim in Lyady from 1880) and Torah scholars such a Rabbi Elijah Hayyim Meisel (1873–1912) of Łódź viewed Zionism as a profanity.[73] Their campaign against the movement and its ideology was based on religious arguments of which the main one was that nothing must be done to hasten the redemption. For these rabbis Zionism represented a movement away from Jewish religion and tradition to another form of belief, in which Jewish nationalism rather than religion was the central focus. Their contention was confirmed by the ideology expounded by Ahad Ha'am (pseudonym of Asher Ginsberg; 1856–1927) who, while not negating the need to retain religion and *mitzvot*, nevertheless maintained that Judaism "in its old form" had become ossified over the generations. The goal of the *Hibbat Zion* movement was to give Judaism a modern character which would eventually lead to Jewish nationalism.[74] It is hardly surprising that such ideas roused the ire of many Orthodox rabbis.

The claim that the aim of Zionism was to destroy religion – an accusation levelled by a wide circle of Orthodox Jews from the inception of Zionism – was categorically denied by Zionist leaders. Zionist leaders went to great lengths to disprove the religious leaders' contentions, aware that their constituency comprised Jewish masses who at the end of the nineteenth century still remained loyal to their belief and customs.

According to Theodor Herzl (1860–1904), the founder of the Zionist organization, "Zionism is first and foremost a return to Judaism, even prior to a return to the land of the Jews."[75] However, it was clear to Herzl as well as to other Zionist leaders that for many of its adherents Zionism was to a large extent a substitute for the religion they had abandoned. For secularists such as Max Mandelstamm (1839–1912) belief in the return of Jews to their historic homeland became a substitute for the religion and faith he had long since renounced. Although they were well aware of the fury they would arouse among their *maskilim* friends, Mandelstamm and his colleagues preached unequivocally that "Jews who were not Zionists – at least ideologically – were not Jews."[76]

Ahad Ha'am and his supporters during the *Hibbat Zion* period, particularly the members of the secret order of *Benei Moshe* ("Sons of Moses", founded in Russia in 1889), and members of the Democratic faction in the Zionist movement, led by Leo Motzkin (1867–1933) and Chaim Weizmann (1874–1952) during the Herzl period, proposed innovative educational methods of language teaching and the addition of science curricula to the religious studies taught in the *hadarim* and elementary schools.[77] Their attempts to implement these proposals aroused strong opposition among the Orthodox and *haredi* Zionists, who accused them of accelerating the secularization process. In the eyes of the Orthodox, Ahad Ha'am and his followers became the standard bearers of secularization.

In most European Jewish communities the secularization process was very strongly resisted by the Orthodox establishment, who succeeded in standing their ground until the 1920s. But the process did penetrate the Jewish community of the United States, which at that time had become the preferred destination for Jewish emigration, and gradually changed the social and cultural character of that diaspora. The shift began during the first wave of Jewish emigration from Germany to the United States (1820–80). By the 1880s more than 90 percent of the American Jewish population was affiliated to the Reform movement – a clear indication of the extent of the secularization process in this community. When the enormous waves of Jewish emigration from eastern Europe began to arrive, it appeared at first that the Reform community would become an insignificant minority. In the first stage of absorption, the new Jewish immigrants retained their traditional customs[78] – but not for long. Most of the second and third generation abandoned their parents' customs, and religion played an insignificant role in their lives. Except for groups of Orthodox Jews, many of whom clustered around *admorim*, the rest of the Jews underwent a rapid secularization process.

The process gained such a strong foothold because Jews were prepared to accept new cultural values after having dispensed with their old ones. The Jewish immigrants who arrived in the United States settled in the large cities, particularly New York.[79] This was one of the factors which, even in the first stage of absorption, germinated the process of cultural changes. Such changes also occurred in eastern Europe when Jews migrated from their traditional villages and towns to the large cities where urban conditions prevented their continuing to live as extended families. The nuclear family, more exposed to external cultural influences, replaced the extended one, which was better able to fend off cultural innovations.

The fact that in most cases the father of the family and sometimes also the mother spent most of their time outside the home earning a living also contributed to thrusting their children into the American environment. In order to integrate and survive the children could not make do with their native tongue, which was usually Yiddish, but were forced to learn English. This they did, quickly becoming fluent in English, while at the same time gradually forgetting their mother tongue.[80]

The overwhelming desire to survive and even to succeed in the new country, caused most of them to discard cultural values such as language. The next stage was to send the children to public schools, which were usually free and which, in the American ethos, were the first stage on the road to success. The vision of ultimate success compensated for the lack of a Jewish education, which U.S. law forbade in public schools. Although the few parents who still wished to give their children a Jewish education were able to do so at institutions founded for that purpose, some of which were open on Sunday, the majority resigned themselves to a lack of Jewish education. Their prime goals were to survive, to succeed and, if possible, to integrate into American society.[81] While the Americanization of the Jews, particularly the second and third generation, drove them to adopt the basic values of American society, there were some attempts to preserve Jewish cultural elements, with the addition of local cultural nuances.

Thus, a widespread Yiddish culture developed which included cultural institutions; the Yiddish theater in New York blossomed as never before.[82] Choosing Yiddish culture was a definite indicator of the secularization process which the Jews in the United States were undergoing, a process so accelerated that it was clear to all that the cultural identity of the children and grandchildren of the eastern European Jewish immigrants would undergo a dramatic change.[83]

There were, however, a substantial number of Jews who wished to halt the erosion caused by secularization. One method of doing so was to establish communal institutions exactly like those which had existed in eastern Europe, thereby disassociating themselves from the American culture and perpetuating a life-style similar to the one they had known in eastern Europe. However, the organizational capabilities of the Orthodox communities could not meet the demands of the steady flow of immigration which marked the beginning of the twentieth century. The community was composed of small congregations which sprang up only to be fragmented shortly afterwards. Torah study was conducted in dark, unsanitary basements. The sale of ritual objects, which were of such great importance for the Orthodox communities, was abused by unscrupulous jobbers and merchants and there were many irregularities in *kashrut* supervision. Various attempts to organize Orthodox Jewry in the United States were unsuccessful.[84]

The failure of Orthodox Judaism to reconstruct the eastern European way of life and tradition was a factor in the emergence of the Conservative movement. The Americanization of eastern European immigrants and the fact that there was no likelihood of their joining the Reform movement provided the impetus for men such as Jacob Henry Schiff (1847–1920), Cyrus Adler (1863–1940), Louis Marshall (1856–1930) and others who sought an alternative which would enable Jews to preserve the basic Jewish values but at the same time bring about an Americanization of the Jewish religion. For this they needed a charismatic leader and they found him in rabbinic scholar Solomon Schechter (1847–1915), who was a true example of those who did not wish to found a new faction, but rather "to crystallize an old faction . . . which would be faithful to Torah, tradition and the customs and modes of Israel but would at the same time introduce sermons in English, adopt modern educational methods . . . and bring decorum to the synagogues."[85]

While the Conservative movement was less successful than the Reform movement and attracted fewer members, it was an indication of the dramatic cultural-social change undergone by Jews in America, particularly those who came with the mass immigration after 1881. While these Jews did not want to cut themselves off entirely from their past, they desired above all to integrate into American society. Adopting new, secular, cultural values, most of which stood in opposition to those of their ancestors in eastern Europe, they contributed to the impetus and acceleration of the secularization process.

A similar secularization process burgeoned in Europe, particularly in Russia and Poland, accelerated by the movement of hundreds of thousands of Jewish refugees to central Russia as a result of the fighting in World War I (see chapter 1) and the migration of thousands to Moscow and St. Petersburg. Separation from their former community and urbanization, combined with the unrelenting battle waged by the Soviet establishment against all religions, further hastened the secularization processes. Lenin expressed his views on the negative social aspects of religion even prior to the Bolshevik revolution and from 1918 the Soviet regime implemented an anti-religious policy.[86] The Jewish institutions established by the Soviets, and particularly the *Yevsektsiya*,[87] fought religion and the Jewish religious educational network. Stalin exacerbated the conflict from the beginning of the 1930s in the framework of Sovietization which he forced upon the masses. A law promulgated on 8 April 1929, which restricted the activities of religious institutions to a minimum, was used by Stalin to persecute religious establishments in general, including the Jewish ones.[88] In 1926 about 13 percent of the Jewish population defined themselves as religious and believing,[89] but by the end of the 1930s all Jewish educational institutions and the entire Orthodox rabbinical establishment had been eliminated, leaving but a small minority who still retained their religious belief. Most of the Jews in the Soviet Union willingly or unwillingly underwent a secularizing cultural revolution.

The secularization process was less radical in Poland, where, after World War I, the other half of eastern European Jewry was concentrated. Unlike the Soviet Union, Poland did not practice religious repression. Moreover, between 1920 to 1937 the Jews were given almost total educational autonomy.[90] An indication of the absence of a rapid secularization process may be found in the results of the 1927 general elections: the Orthodox establishment led by Agudat Israel, the world organization of Orthodox Jews, received about 33 percent of the Jewish vote and the Mizrachi, the religious Zionist movement, received 9 percent. Ten years later the electoral strength of the two parties had declined only by one-quarter.[91]

In other words, up to World War II between one-quarter and one-third of Polish Jewry were still religious. These parties represented the whole range of Orthodox and *haredi* factions. If we assume that, in contrast with the supporters of the secular parties, a large number of Orthodox Jews abstained from voting at all, we can say that in Poland between the two world wars the secularization process spread slowly. Another indication of this situation was children's education. In 1934 and 1935 about one-quarter of Jewish children (132,000 out of a total of 596,000) were studying at educational institutions run by the Orthodox establishment.[92]

Until the beginning of the 1880s, the Jewish *yishuv* in Erez Israel could be characterized as Orthodox. Most of the inhabitants still lived off the *halukah* (distribution of money collected in the diaspora for support of the poor in Erez Israel) which they received for maintaining the Jewish presence in Erez Israel.[93] The character of the *yishuv* remained unaltered even while the secularization process was under way amongst the Jews of Europe. Only when the new immigrants from the First *Aliyah* arrived in the 1880s and some settled in *moshavot* built outside the holy cities did the secularization process amongst the Jewish population begin. In 1883 the leaders of the *haredi* establishment in Jerusalem accused the settlers of trying to change the character of the *yishuv*.[94]

Two years later the settlers in Gederah were accused of libertinism. In 1889 the *Hovevei Zion* were accused of desecrating the name of the Lord after they refused to comply with the demand of the *haredim* that the settlers in the *moshavot* observe the *halakhic* laws of the *Shemitah* (Sabbatical Year).[95] The attacks reached a climax in the 1890s as the secularization process intensified. Various groups in the *yishuv*, led by the secret order *Benei Moshe*, supported Ahad Ha'am's ideas and established schools in Jaffa for both boys and girls which included subjects of a nationalistic and even secular character in the curriculum.[96]

The failure of *haredi* efforts to close the schools in Jaffa was an indication that even in Erez Israel it would be difficult to arrest the secularization process. The immigrants of the Second *Aliyah*, who arrived between 1903 and 1914, proved this point. They were so much more extreme than their predecessors in their pronouncements, actions and secular *weltanschauung*, that even the previous generation of immigrants saw them as profligates and unbelievers.[97] Indeed, with the exception of personalities such as Aharon David Gordon (1856–1922), many of the immigrants held salient anti-religious views. The most radical was the writer Joseph Hayyim Brenner (1881–1921), who resented the notion that the Jewish religious perception was superior to that of other religions, particularly that of Christianity.[98] In 1906 the Herzlia Hebrew Gymnasium was opened in Jaffa and despite the fact that its curriculum included many secular subjects it was supported by the Zionist Organization. Jaffa with its 5,000 Jewish residents and later Tel Aviv became secular centers, in clear contrast to the holy cities, particularly Jerusalem.[99]

The immigrants who arrived in Erez Israel in the 1920 and 1930s strengthened the trend toward secularization. Those who came in the Third *Aliyah* (1919–23) were openly anti-religious,[100] and their successors in the Fourth *Aliyah* (1924–28) and the Fifth (1929–39) followed in their footsteps. The leadership of the Labor party, which had become the predominant political power in Erez Israel, tended to be secular.[101] During this period the religious and *haredi* elements in Erez Israel found themselves under an ever-growing threat from the secularists. During the 1880s and 1890s they had been strong and confident, but in the 1920s and 1930s and particularly in the 1940s they felt a weakening in their ability to combat the spread of secularization.[102] A further indication of the relative weakening of the religious and _haredi_ groups in Erez Israel was the comparative decline in the number of parties which represented these groups in the elections for the _Asefat ha-Nivharim_ ("Elected Assembly"; an elected body which was to conduct all the communal affairs of the _yishuv_) and the _Va'ad Le'umi_ ("National Council"; the executive organ of the _Asefat ha-Nivharim_).[103]

Even taking into account the fact that, for either _halakhic_ or political reasons, many _haredim_ abstained from voting in the elections for the Elected Assembly, it is clear that there was a growing gap between them and the secular public. In the 1920 elections to the first _Asefat ha-Nivharim_ the religious bloc received about 40 percent of the votes. Ten years later this declined to about 25 percent and in the 1940s to 15 percent.[104] Another indicator for the relative and absolute decrease in the religious and _haredi_ population was the enormous increase in the number of pupils attending schools which had a definite secular tendency. This figure grew from about 20 percent of the total student body in 1918 to 40 percent in 1921, and approximately 60–65 percent in the 1930s and 1940s. A distinction must be made between the different secular schools such as the Alliance Israelite Universelle and the German Jewish Ezra Association, and even schools in a number of _moshavot_ whose policy was to provide a curriculum that had a religious character. It is also necessary to distinguish between the character of the _heder_ and _talmud torah_ schools of the Mizrachi movement,[105] and those of the _Eda Haredit_ (Haredi Community) and Agudat Israel. The leaders of Agudat Israel viewed the education that children were receiving in the Mizrachi schools as bordering on desecration of the sacred and their criticism of the heads of these institutions was often sharper than that directed against the secular ones.[106] There is no doubt that from the 1920s on, the educational system became steadily more secular, a factor which, more than anything else, confirmed the acceleration of the secularization processes between the end of World War I and the establishment of the State of Israel.

The secularization process in the Jewish community within the State of Israel underwent significant changes in the 1950s and 1960s. The desire to ensure equality of all (Jewish) citizens forced the leaders of the state (who were ideologically secularist[107]) to devote

more thought to the question of the rights of the religious minority
and to attempt to unite the religious and secular populace despite
the dissension between them. The Labor party's parliamentary
dependence upon the religious parties and the government's
desire to prove to the world and the Jewish diaspora that the
State of Israel was Jewish in character led the government to
placate the Orthodox and *haredi* minority in a variety of ways.
In 1953 the State Education Law established two types of schools,
state and state religious, both under the supervision of the Ministry
of Education.[108] The state religious schools provided a curriculum of
religious studies, inculcating religious values and practice into that
segment of the population which sought a traditional but not *haredi*
education. The Israel Defence Force was obliged to accept certain
general *halakhic* religious principles such as the observance of *kashrut*
and the Sabbath. Gradually the Jewish community in Israel took on
a sociocultural aspect that differed from that of the pre-state period.
During the latter there was a deliberate attempt by the leaders of the
Zionist Organization and the Jewish Agency to disassociate religion
from their political activities, but after the establishment of the State
there was a distinct counteraction to this trend.

The mass immigration from the Islamic countries strengthened
the more traditional tendencies. Hundreds of thousands of immigrants from Yemen, Iraq, North Africa and other Islamic countries
increased the proportion of the population which had a traditional
religious-cultural orientation.[109] However, this orientation did not
influence the Jewish residents of Israel to change their patterns of
voting for the Knesset or their educational preferences. There was
no difference between the percentage of supporters of religious
parties before, during or after the mass immigration (an average
of about 14 percent between 1955 and 1992), and no perceptible
increase in the percentage of pupils studying in the state religious
and *haredi* schools (an average of 22 percent). This phenomenon can
be explained both by the social and economic pressure which the
dominant Ashkenazi élite in Israel exerted on the newly-arrived
immigrants and by the slow but growing secularization process
amongst the immigrants in their Islamic countries of origin, particularly in the large cities. The fact that some of them were already
inclined towards secularization[110] made it much easier for them to
succumb to the pressure. Furthermore, during the 1960s and 1970s
there was a slow movement of pupils whose parents came from
Islamic countries from the state religious schools to the secular

ones, a clear sign of growing secularization. At the beginning of the 1980s, more than one-third of the population (and their offspring) who came from Islamic countries declared themselves traditional – either Orthodox or very Orthodox – but few sent their children to religious institutions and only a minority voted for religious parties.[111] They preferred their children to attend state schools and usually voted for secular parties such as Herut, or its successor, the Likud.[112]

In short, while the secularization phenomenon was temporarily arrested in Israel from 1950 to 1960, partly due to government policy and partly because of the mass immigration from the Islamic countries, the secularization process which years earlier had spread amongst the Jews of eastern Europe and the United States also took hold of the immigrants from Islamic countries and their children. Not only was the secularization process unchecked from the 1960s on but it accelerated in the years that followed.

The Agudat Israel movement was founded in May 1912 in Kattowitz, Silesia; it brought together a number of Orthodox trends from Germany, Poland, Lithuania and Hungary[113] in an attempt to unite the European Orthodox community to combat the advances made by assimilation and the secularization inherent in the growing strength of Zionism, the Bund and other Socialist organizations. For 35 years the leaders of Agudat Israel fought fiercely and with no small measure of success against their political opponents. However, the tragic outcome of the Holocaust and the establishment of the State of Israel dictated a change in tactics. Representatives of Agudat Israel joined the *Mo'ezet ha-Am* ("People's Council"), the provisional legislature which became part of the provisional government of the independent State of Israel. The leader of Agudat Israel, Yitzhak Meir Levin (1894–1971), served as Minister of Social Welfare in the provisional government headed by Ben-Gurion which functioned from 15 May 1948 until 10 March 1949. In the election to the first Knesset (25 January 1949) the United Religious Front (National Religious Party, Agudat Israel, and Po'alei Agudat Israel) received 12.2 percent of the votes, gaining sixteen seats to become the third largest bloc. In the subsequent governments there was limited cooperation between Agudat Israel and the leaders of the Zionist institutions but the concern that secularization might increase in their ranks caused the Agudah to keep this cooperation to an absolute minimum.[114]

In 1977 there was a change in the trend. The leaders of Agudat Israel reached the conclusion (which the Mizrachi leaders had reached at the beginning of the twentieth century) that cooperation with the secular sectors would be much more beneficial for the interests of *haredi* society than separatism.

One of the images which the government of Menahem Begin tried to project was that it represented the traditional society of Sephardi Jews from Islamic countries. This made it easier for Agudat Israel to cooperate with the government,[115] and in fact during the 1980s the government allocated considerable sums of money to the *haredi* sector, something it had not done for many years.[116] Educational institutions were established with government funding and the educational network was expanded.[117] The number of exemptions from compulsory military service for *yeshiva* students also increased.[118]

The founding of the Sephardi-Haredi Shas party in 1984 increased the *haredi* participation in government administration. Rabbi Ovadiah Yosef (1920–), the spiritual leader of Shas, and the other leaders of the party represented the Sephardi constituency in the *haredi* populace. They participated fully as ministers and deputy ministers in various government coalitions. The relatively high birth rate amongst the *haredi* population compared with the secular population, and the fundamentalism which spread amongst the religious sector, accounted for the relative increase of the *haredi* population. This expressed itself in the increase of voters for the *haredi* parties in the Knesset elections from 4.7 percent in 1955 to 10.7 percent in 1988[119] and 8.4 percent in 1992, with a concomitant increase in influence on public administration.

Another symptom of increased *haredi* strength was the extensive publicity given to the *Ba'al Teshuvah* (literally "Master of Repentance") movement which reached its peak in the 1980s. For the first time in the last hundred years there was a wave of repenters, and although small in number (in 1980 it was estimated at about 3,000 throughout the world) it caught the attention of the Israeli public. However, it seems that this phenomenon had little affect on the secularization process amongst Jews.[120]

The empowerment of the *haredi* community and their enhanced status amongst the Israeli public was not the result of a regression in the secularization process but rather came from their own ranks. The relative strength of the Orthodox and *haredi* population, which represented about 20–25 percent of the total population from the early period of statehood, did not change until the end of 1988. Since then it has declined to under 20 percent as a result of the immigration of 450,000 Jews from the Soviet Union. On the other hand, during the first two decades of the State the proportional relation between the Orthodox and *haredi* population (according to the number of their representatives in the Knesset) stood at 2:1 in favor of the Orthodox, but in the 1980s the tables were turned to 2:1 in favor of the *haredim*.

*   *   *

To sum up: from the 1880s world Jewry underwent a sociocultural revolution at the center of which was the secularization process. A society in which most members inclined toward religious belief and Jewish tradition became secular. The secularization process was a continuation of the Enlightenment movement, on whose sources it drew. The sociocultural upheaval amongst the Jews resulting from the spread of secularization was dramatic and unprecedented.

Until the advent of the Enlightenment it appeared that Hasidism, particularly in its early version, would create a cultural and social revolution amongst the Jews. However, in retrospect it would seem that the changes wrought by Hasidism were not as dramatic as they were once thought to be. The final outcome was that the hasidim became an integral part of the Orthodox establishment. This fact became obvious when the Enlightenment movement began to expand amongst the Jewish communities of eastern Europe. In 1863 in St. Petersburg, leading rabbis and *admorim* in Russia, from various trends, declared a united front in the struggle against the Enlightenment movement; evidence that Hasidism had not only become an integral part of the *haredi* sector but was now its leading faction. This did not alter the traditional conflicts between the *Mitnaggedim* and the hasidim and at a later period between the Orthodox and *haredi* sectors. However, it was clear that the growth of secularization united all the religious elements to act as a counterforce.

Religious society, particularly the *haredi* element, was unsuccessful in its attempts to arrest the secularization process, which continues to gain ground today. The religious establishment in Israel tried to prevail upon the political establishment to act in every possible way – including legislation – to contain the secularization process. The secularization phenomenon in Israel is very similar to that in Jewish communities all over the world. The Orthodox constituency in the United States is decreasing and is currently the smallest *vis-à-vis* the other trends;[121] between 1980 and 1986 mixed marriages amongst world Jewry, excluding Israel, were an average of about 30 percent compared with 15 percent for the previous decade;[122] only a minority of Jews in the former Soviet Union, mainly in Russia and Ukraine, including the 520,000 who emigrated to Israel between 1988 and 1994, are affiliated with an Orthodox or *haredi* trend;[123] the Orthodox and *haredi* trends are insignificant in the Jewish communities of France, Great Britain, Canada, Argentina, Brazil and South Africa;[124] and in Israel there has been a gradual decline in the relative size of the Orthodox and *haredi* population, which for the last twenty years has hovered around 20–25 percent of the population,[125] compared with 60–80 percent at the beginning of the twentieth century.

4

Anti-Semitism

No sensible person disputes the existence of Jew-hatred, whose origins some trace back as far as the third century BCE,[1] but few are able to account for the phenomenon. There are as many disagreements as there are interpreters of the subject.[2] Some historians have identified anti-Semitism as part of the pagan-Jewish, and more especially the Christian-Jewish[3] religious and social confrontation through the ages. Others set it within the context of the innate human hatred of the different, the alien;[4] various researchers have adduced explanations related to the human need to find a scapegoat, particularly during periods of social, economic or cultural crisis;[5] and some analysts have seen it as a problem in the realm of social psychopathology.[6] Economic explanations have been offered,[7] and in some cases the blame has been pinned on the Jews' singularity within European society since the sixth and seventh centuries.[8] The debate over the causes of anti-Semitism gave rise to a separate controversy about its continuity. Some have found historical continuity among the totality of the manifestations known as Jew-hatred;[9] others believe the events connected with Jew-hatred are distinctive manifestations, related to a specific time and place;[10] and a third group, taking an intermediate position, conceded that certain elements showed continuity, but insisted that there was a difference (in some cases a great difference) between each separate event.[11]

The controversies over Holocaust-related issues which have exercised historians since Germany's surrender at the end of World War II are a measure of the complexity of those issues and perhaps still more of their emotional intensity. A case in point is the debate that raged in the 1970s over how to interpret the rise of the National Socialist Party in Germany. Scholars who emphasized the political structures and processes that led Hitler and his cohorts to the "Final Solution" in effect rejected the approach that finds continuity in the phenomenon (the "functionalists," as their colleagues dubbed them). The proponents of the contrasting position (the "intentionalists") held that the "Final Solution" was the realization of an old ideological program of Hitler's, already outlined in his *Mein Kampf* (1925), in which the mass murder of Jews was built-in. Implementation of the ideology awaited only the Führer's decision that the time was ripe.[12]

Another historiographic debate over anti-Semitism and its causes which showed how emotionally charged the issue was, and therefore how difficult to explain, erupted in June 1986. The dispute, which concerned the very essence of the Holocaust, was triggered by an article written by the German historian Ernst Nolte, "A Past that Refuses to Disappear,"[13] and the response of Jürgen Habermas, "A Type of Payment for Damages: The Apologetic Tendencies in the Writing of Contemporary History in Germany."[14] The reverberations of that widespread controversy were still being felt in 1994.[15] Nolte and others of the same school, such as Joachim Fest,[16] sought to prove that the Germans' murder of six million Jews "was not an unexampled or an unprecedented phenomenon." The Holocaust, they held, was comparable to other historical manifestations, such as the crimes of Stalin.[17] Most Holocaust historians rejected this viewpoint out of hand.[18] Jew-hatred, they maintained, was a unique historical phenomenon, and they charged that the true purpose of Nolte and his colleagues in claiming historical equivalents for the Hitlerian genocide was to exculpate the Germans.

Even a subject, such as the roots of National Socialist ideology and the early activity that brought the party advocating it to power, is free of fierce scholarly polemics. The majority view is that the foundations of Nazi ideology and of the political activity of the National Socialists lie in the nineteenth century.[19] Proponents of this approach argue that the emancipation granted to the Jews in most of Europe, with the exceptions of Russia and Romania (see chapter 2), combined with various events that occurred in the course of the century – pogroms, persecution of Jews, the establishment of anti-Semitic parties – contributed to the rise of Nazi ideology and to its transformation into a legitimate political instrument. Some scholars, however, disagree. Thus Richard S. Levy raises numerous questions concerning Nazism's continuity with the political anti-Semitism that existed in Germany 55 years before Hitler, which he views as a self-contained development and not as an episode in a continuing sequence.[20] The same question will concern us here as well: Is the phenomenon of Jew-hatred in the modern era, particularly as it emerged in the 1870s, characterized by continuity, or should we view subsequent events, notably the emergence of the Nazis and the Holocaust they unleashed, as divorced from those earlier manifestations?

The Jews' emancipation in Austria-Hungary (1867) and in Germany (1869–70), and perhaps even more tellingly their social and economic integration in Europe (see chapter 1), paradoxically contributed powerfully to the intensification of processes detrimental to their well-being. Even before the 1870s Jews were reeling under the onslaught of pogroms and attempts by hostile populations to impede their development. Cases in point are the so-called "Hep-Hep" riots of June and July 1819 in Bavaria, Würzburg and Baden,[21] and the anti-Jewish unrest throughout Germany during the period of revolutionary upheaval known as the "Springtime of the Nations" (1848–49).[22] Pamphlets and books vilifying the Jews that were published in this period, as well as trials and plots, most notably the Damascus blood libel (February 1840) in which Jewish dignitaries and rabbis were accused of murdering a Capuchin monk for ritual purposes[23] – an incident which had reverberations that affected Jews in France and elsewhere – were symptomatic of the enmity against Jews and of the singularity of the phenomenon in European society.

In the 1870s, and more especially in the following decade, anti-Jewish attacks were stepped up. The word "anti-Semitism," coined by the Jew-baiting propagandist Wilhelm Marr (1819–1904), became part of the sociopolitical jargon. Anti-Semitic agitators, while continuing to invoke allegations dating to medieval times, in which the Jews were accused of murdering Jesus or of being innately corrupt, also made claims related to the modern era, concerning the negative impact of the Jews' involvement in the European economy, their national separateness and their racial distinctiveness.

Anti-Jewish diatribes of a religious-Christian character declined in intensity in the nineteenth and twentieth centuries, as compared with earlier periods. The temporary ascendancy of rationalist philosophy and liberal ideology in Europe, and the vision of human equality propounded by the architects of the French Revolution, brought about a considerable diminution in the force of religion-based arguments. Still, the European world view remained fundamentally religious. Theological studies were a major field in the schools. The Jews' guilt in the murder of Jesus remained a conceptual pillar in every lesson dealing with the genesis of Christianity. Thus religion-based, anti-Jewish indoctrination was deeply embedded in the popular consciousness. Indeed, some scholars maintain that even though Hitler's anti-Semitic ideology may be traceable to an ostensibly rational point of departure, he was nevertheless exposed to Christian indoctrination in his formative years.[24] This was equally true of other Nazis.[25]

A different type of agitation was based on the Jews' economic activity. They were accused of exploiting every opportunity to accumulate capital and use it to seize control of economic assets, their ultimate ambition being nothing less than to utilize their wealth to achieve world domination. By means of "a handful of bankers and Semitic procurors"[26] (Wilhelm Marr), "the Elders will make their own puppets into presidents . . . In the place of the [ruling] aristocracy they have set up plutocracy or the rule of gold; and the gold is controlled by them"[27] (*The Protocols of the Elders of Zion*). The bulk of the accusations against the Jews stemmed from the wealth of a few individuals and families such as Perier in France, Guenzburg and Polyakov in Russia, but especially the Rothschilds. The astounding success of the family's patriarch, Amschel Mayer (1744–1812), and even more prodigiously of his five sons, in building a financial empire in the capitals of Europe – Paris (James, 1792–1868), Naples (Carl, 1788–1855), London (Nathan, 1777–1836), Vienna (Salomon, 1744–1855) and Frankfurt (Amschel, 1773–1855) – created a myth around the family: they became known as the kings of the Jews. Through their endeavors, the anti-Semitic journalist Edouard Drumont (1844–1917) wrote, "half of the capital in circulation throughout the entire world belongs to the Jews."[28]

But the demonic image foisted on the Jews in the nineteenth century, and particularly in its second half, was bound up not only with the wealth amassed by individuals and families, but also with the accusation that the Jews were the progenitors of the European bourgeoisie and had it under their collective thumb. The image that pervaded the writings of declared anti-Semites like Marr and Drumont was perceived as credible by intellectuals who vigorously denied that they harbored any anti-Jewish prejudice. Thus Karl Marx (1818–83) in the 1840s:

What is the Jew's foundation in our world? Material necessity, private advantage. What is the object of the Jew's worship in this world? Usury? What is his worldy god? Money . . . Thus we recognize in Judaism an anti-social element . . . The Jew has emancipated himself in the Jewish fashion not only by acquiring money power but through money's having become (with him or without him) the world power and the Jewish spirit's having become the practical spirit of the Christian peoples.[29]

Similar utterances were voiced by a socialist like Pierre Joseph Proudhon (1809–65) in the 1840s ("the Jews are the geniuses of commerce, the eternal exploiters of humanity"),[30] or an anarchist like Mikhail Bakunin (1814–1876) three decades later ("the Jews' driving force lies in that lust for trade which is one of the main features of their national character").[31] Even if by the 1890s socialists were fiercely condemning anti-Semitism, Friedrich Engels (1820–95) said (1890) that it "serves reactionary goals."[32] The notion that the wealth accumulated by capitalists was controlled by the Jews, whose ambitions and actions left their imprint on the shape of the world and affected the destinies of millions, would remain a staple of the European world view.[33]

Anti-Semites also seized on arguments related to nationalist ideology, as it evolved in the nineteenth century, to demonstrate that the Jews were alien to European society. For the most part they drew on theories propounded by the likes of Johann Herder (1744–1803) or Johann Gottlieb Fichte (1762–1814), who tried to show that a people's national distinctiveness, expressed in a shared historical past, as well as in language, folklore and other cultural elements, was marred if that people mixed with other nations. This was the conclusion drawn in the 1850s by the brilliant German composer Richard Wagner (1813–88). The works of Jewish composers (or those of Jewish extraction), such as Meyerbeer or Mendelssohn, or of poets like Heine and Boerne, harmed German culture, Wagner claimed.[34] In the 1870s and 1880s variations on this theme were at the center of the thought of anti-Semites across Europe. At the University of Berlin the historian Heinrich von Treitschke (1834–96) urged the fostering of the German national consciousness. The Jews in Germany, that "tribe" from the east, were "alien to the European essence, the German in particular"; the presence of the Jews and their "foreign nature" blocked "the development of an organic German culture."[35] Nevertheless, demagogues like Treitschke still demanded that the Jews "be Germans, feel themselves to be, simply and genuinely, Germans . . . "[36] Other anti-Semites, such as the Christian preacher

Adolf Stoecker (1835–1909), argued that only the removal of the Jew ("the cancer from which we suffer")[37] from German society would enable the perfect establishment of the "Christian-German nation." "The Jews remain a nation within a nation, a state within a state, a separate tribe within a race that is alien"[38] and had no place in the German nation.

Stoecker pointed to the religious dissimilarity between the Jews and the Germans as the cornerstone of the national differences between the two peoples and the cause of their inability to intermix. In the same connection other anti-Semites stressed the elements uniting the German people, such as the urgent need for the country's unification, and the Jew's inability to integrate into the German state. In his book *The System of Morals* Friedrich Paulsten wrote:

> Whoever is proud that he does not belong to the German people, but to the people of Israel, has no right to complain that the German people do not want him . . . To remain a perfect Jew and to be a perfect German, to be both at the same time, perfectly a Jew and perfectly a German, is impossible . . .

A different form of anti-Jewish agitation in the last third of the nineteenth century was based on scientific theories propounded earlier in the century. As early as the 1840s Comte Arthur de Gobineau (1816–82) developed a doctrine derived from studies in anthropology, linguistics and history. Gobineau's objective was to build a complete intellectual edifice in which racial criteria would account for everything in the past, present and future: "The basic organization and character of cultures are equal to the traits and the spirit of the dominant race."[39] Having classified the races, Gobineau chose the white race as the ideal and as innately superior, as compared with the yellow and black races.[40]

As the century wore on Gobineau's ideas were refined by racist anti-Semites who adopted the theory advanced by Charles Darwin (1809–82). They sought to apply the central Darwinian idea of a constant struggle in nature between stronger and weaker species to human society, which was said to consist of more highly developed races, such as the Aryan-German, and less developed such as the Semitic. Their clear and unequivocal conclusion was that the presence of the Jews was harmful to European society and to the superior Aryan race. This theory was taken to its limits by Houston Stewart Chamberlain (1855–1927), who cited two principles: the common blood ties of the Aryan race, and the Aryan ideal type whose qualities made him superior to other races. The Jews were likened to "the devil who wishes to erase those superior traits." In contrast to the German race, "the savior of mankind, successor of the Greeks and the Romans . . . destined to wage bitter battles against its foes in order to fulfill its cultural mission,"[41] the Jews are an "Asian people" bent on maintaining its racial purity and "waging a vicious war against the Aryans." "The outcome of the battle between these two races will determine . . . whether the ignoble spirit of the Jews will overcome the Aryan soul and drag the world into the abyss with it,"[42] or whether the Germans will be able to protect their race against "the stain, the Jewish devil." The vanquishing of the Jews would enable "the soul of the Aryan race to rule in the world"; victory "will forge a vision of redemption through culture."[43]

Race theory was more amenable than other anti-Semitic explanations to the mood in turn-of-the-century Europe. It rested, ostensibly, on scientific foundations, rather than on religious and nationalist ideas that derived from faith, culture, morality or variable economic factors. Race theory, based on scientific and social evidence and on biological criteria, and buttressed with scientific systems like anthropology and linguistics, had determined the Jews' negative traits for all time. It is not surprising, then, that these racist motifs were adopted by Hitler and his cohorts and invoked by Nazi agitators.[44]

Still, religious, nationalist and especially economic arguments were often cited, beginning in the last third of the nineteenth century, by those wanting to strengthen the racist case. Indeed, propounders of these theories had reached the same conclusions: race theory claimed that the Aryan race faced extinction because the very presence of the inferior Jew, the Semite, jeopardized the Aryan's superiority; while economic theory held that the Jew endangered European civilization by his attempts to seize control of its economic assets and through them dominate society. The mutual reinforcement of the racist and economic doctrines was clearly discernible in the most widely disseminated of the anti-Semitic pamphlets, *The Protocols of the Elders of Zion*. The racist approach was reflected in the negative descriptions of the Jews' leaders as originating in the "race of David," as "people with depraved passions" who "directed their goals at the apex of government." The economic arguments were underscored in the *Protocols'* accusations that the Jews aimed to gain control of international capital in order to achieve their political objectives.

By the end of the nineteenth century expressions of Jew-hatred could be found not only in pamphlets and books published by writers, philosophers and eccentrics of various stripes, or in incidents of anti-Jewish violence; anti-Semitic elements were now incorporated into the platforms of political parties. The preacher Adolf Stoecker was among the first to employ anti-Semitic propaganda in this manner. Stoecker's Christian Socialist Workers' Party never became a true political force, even though he himself was repeatedly elected to the Reichstag, serving for more than twenty years beginning in 1881. But he was able to transmit his ideas to other political groups in Germany,[45] Austria-Hungary and even France. Politicians who embraced those anti-Semitic ideas were elected to parliaments all over Europe. In 1893 anti-Semitic conservative parties in Germany achieved their peak representation in the Reichstag (16 of 397 seats). The Jew-baiter Karl Lueger (1844–1910), head of the Christian-Social Party, was elected mayor of Vienna (1896) over the vehement objections of Emperor Franz Joseph, who initially refused to confirm his appointment. The emperor finally gave in after Lueger was elected a third time, in 1897; one of the most popular politicians in Austria,[46] Lueger held office for more than ten consecutive years.

In the century's final two decades, then, movements that adopted anti-Semitic programs seemed to be amassing considerable political power, and appealed to a substantial section of public opinion in Germany and in Austria-Hungary. Anti-Semitic gatherings held in Germany, notably in Dresden (1882) or in Bochum (1889), attracted public attention and resulted in the election to parliament of more anti-Semitic delegates. In the Hungarian parliament the successes of anti-Semites such as Viktor Istoczy (1845–1915) and Ivan Simonyi (1841–99) led to the formation of several dozen anti-Semitic societies. They were heartened by the anti-Jewish blood-libel scandal in the Hungarian village of Tisza-Eszlar (1882). Although the case, in which Jews were accused of ritually murdering a Christian girl, was finally thrown out by the court as a malicious fabrication, the year that elapsed until the formal acquittal was exploited by Istoczy and his supporters to further their purposes.[47] In Austria, too, the leader of the pan-German faction, Georg Ritter von Schoenerer (1842–1921), made inroads. The subsequent formation of several dozen anti-Semitic leagues was probably instrumental in Karl Lueger's election as mayor of Vienna.

Anti-Semitism increased even in France. Although a number of parties espousing an anti-Semitic line failed, a tremendous success was scored by the anti-Semitic propaganda of the journalist Edouard Drumont, in his newspaper *La Libre Parole* and more resoundingly in his book *La France Juive* (1885). The paper sold several thousand copies every week, and the book ran through numerous editions. But it was in the Dreyfus Affair that France's anti-Semites showed their true strength. The trial and conviction of the Jewish captain, Alfred Dreyfus (1859–1935), on the charge of espionage on behalf of Germany (December 1894), had powerful reverberations throughout France. Dreyfus, who was sentenced to life in prison, became the focal point of a struggle between loyalists of the French republic who believed in his innocence and supporters of the army who insisted that the traitor had been given his just deserts. The intervention of leading public figures, notably the writer Emile Zola (1840–1902), forced a re-trial, resulting in a mitigation of sentence (1898) and finally in Dreyfus's full exoneration (1906). Still, the affair showed that even in a country considered a bastion of the rule of law, reactionary anti-Semitic forces could tip the scales of justice in their favor.[48] Ironically, the Dreyfus Affair signaled the decline of the anti-Semites' success in France; their political strength decreased and until the 1930s they remained on the extreme fringes.

The enfeeblement of anti-Semitic political forces at the turn of the century extended well beyond France, encompassing conservative groups in central Europe. Although Lueger did well in Vienna, anti-Semites fared poorly in parliamentary elections and in other public institutions in Germany, Hungary and Austria. In retrospect it is clear that this was a temporary phenomenon, and that the thesis advanced by the contemporary historian, Simon Dubnow, and later embraced by many modern historians – that anti-Semitism in central and western Europe in the final third of the nineteenth century was a major factor in Jewish history – was viable.[49] True, these historians argued, political anti-Semitism failed; but the ideas voiced by its proponents were absorbed by broad sections of the public and by many non-party organizations, such as economic circles, youth movements and sports clubs.[50] Some historians, as we saw, disagree. They find no connection between the relative success of late-nineteenth-century political anti-Semitism and the rise of National Socialism in the 1930s. Manifestly, a synthesis between the two concepts would better explain the historical developments. The seeds of Nazi anti-Semitism were sown in central and western

Europe in the 1880s, but special conditions were required, such as existed in 1930s Germany, before those ideas could ripen and be absorbed by German society.

In Russia, too, anti-Semitism was on the rise during the nineteenth century. Some trace its roots to the traditional enmity toward outsiders dating from the fifteenth and sixteenth centuries, which meant that in theory not a single Jew could reside in Russia until the eighteenth century. Others point to the hatred of Jews and the negation of Judaism that existed within Russian ruling circles without its members ever having encountered the Jewish people.[51] Whatever the root causes, the historical fact is that the division of Poland (1772–95) brought about the annexation to Russia of about a million Jews, half the world's Jewish population, forcing the rulers to seek ways to integrate them into the society. The Romanov tsars generally followed a dualistic, contradictory policy, on the one hand demanding that the Jews abandon their traditional avocations and integrate themselves culturally and socially, but on the other hand refusing to emulate the rest of Europe and grant them legal emancipation.[52]

Signs of Jew-hatred are discernible among the clergy of the Russian Orthodox Church. In contrast to the situation in western and central Europe, in Russia the religious establishment, in the form of the Orthodox Church, exercised a powerful influence on the ruling circles. In terms of importance, the minister responsible for the church (the Procurator of the Holy Synod), who was also in charge of the educational system, was on a par with the Prime Minister and the Interior Minister. In 1881 the Procurator of the Holy Synod, Konstantin Pobedonostsev, was quoted as saying that the "Jewish problem" would be resolved only if a third of the Jews remained in Russia, a third were killed and a third disappeared. The Jews, Pobedonostsev railed, had assumed tremendous economic power and wanted to eradicate the old nobility, lower the value of the large estates and get control of the Russian press.[53] Such ideas reflected a widespread anti-Jewish frame of mind in Russian society, which was affected by two cultural currents. One originated in the distant past, while the other had surfaced in the nineteenth century, but both viewed the Jews negatively. One social-cultural current was fostered primarily by ruling factions bent on preserving the distinctiveness of the Russian people; to this end Orthodoxy was a central element in Russia's social and cultural life. The second current was similar in essence but different in origin. It arose from ideas that had infiltrated Russia from western and central Europe, particularly in the mid-nineteenth century, around the time of Alexander II's accession to the throne. The proponents of this line of thought were mainly groups from the Russian intelligentsia who wanted to ground their society in modern European principles, while adapting them to parallel values in the Slavic society. What they had in mind were nationalist concepts which had been adduced in Germany in the first half of the nineteenth century. At bottom, they formulated a theory of "romantic" nationalism which viewed every people as a single organic entity possessing a distinctive and uniform cultural tradition and a shared historical past. Therefore, whoever wished to belong to the Russian nation would have to accept the Russian Orthodox faith and become an integral part of the general society.[54]

The hallmark of nineteenth-century Russian society was a stringent autocracy whose conservative world view derived from the Orthodox Church. Tsar Nicholas I noted, pithily, that Russia rested on three foundations: religion, autocracy and fidelity to the national tradition. It followed that "one of the essential conditions for the strength projected [by Russia] externally" was an "absolute, unconditional spiritual unity which tolerates no deviations, not even the most minuscule, of the Russian people. Everyone must be imbued with it, from the highest noble to the lowliest peasant." Here too lay the source of the national society's attitude toward the Jews. The faith they professed and their national singularity meant that the Jews could not be assimilated into Russian society, and all attempts during the reign of Nicholas I, and thereafter as well, to bring about their social and religious integration, even by coercion, failed.

The same world view guided the Russian minorities' attitude toward the Jews. The Ukrainian intelligentsia, for example, led by Nicholas Kostomarov, endeavored to arouse local nationalism by launching a campaign to foster the native language and encourage the study of Ukrainian history.[55]

A prominent figure among the Russian intelligentsia in the latter part of the 1850s was Ivan Aksakov, the editor of a number of Slavophile journals. Espousing the organic view of the Russian-Christian-Orthodox state, Aksakov fulminated against the Jews and Judaism. He likened the Jews to uninvited guests: treat them with respect but by no means allow them to start running the house. Although not seeking to impinge on the Jews' human rights,

Aksakov was skeptical as to whether they could obey general laws founded on Christian tenets:

> Since the Jews do not wish to forgo their religion, they cannot obey the general law; we consider that we have shown quite convincingly why the harm caused by the Jews is not a characteristic personal trait of each individual among them, stemming from personal corruption, but is a national quality with historic roots, grounded in their national-religious self-consciousness . . . [56]

Kostomarov and Aksakov each represented a different facet of the ideology of Jew-hatred as it manifested itself in Russia from the late eighteenth century until the twentieth. A third aspect of anti-Semitism is embodied in the major nineteenth-century Russian writer Fyodor Mikhalovich Dostoevsky. His work is redolent with enmity toward the Jews, whom he depicted with revulsion and avid hostility. His attitude is apparent in character sketches and passing allusions in his novels, and in offhand remarks in his articles and private correspondence.[57]

Expressions of Jew-hatred in Russia were not confined solely to propaganda pamphlets, articles in the press and books (such as *The Book of the Kahal,* published in 1869 by the Jewish convert to Christianity Jacob Braffmann, which became a standard reference work for anti-Semitic writers in Russia and elsewhere); they also took the form of deeds. Russia was the last country in Europe to grant the Jews full equality of rights (1917). During the nineteenth century and into the early part of the twentieth the Jews' legal status actually deteriorated: 1881 can therefore be seen as a watershed in Jewish history.[58] Suffice it to point out that under the reign of Alexander III (1881–94) sixty-five anti-Jewish laws were promulgated, while under Nicholas II (1894–1917) the month of June 1914 alone witnessed the enactment of fifty laws, ordinances, bills and decrees limiting the Jews' civil rights, restricting their state service and affecting their education.[59]

On 27 April 1881 widespread anti-Jewish pogroms erupted in six provinces of southern Russia. Reactionary circles close to the throne immediately turned the riots to their own advantage, even helping to fan them, in order to influence the new tsar, Alexander III. For months on end thugs left a trail of devastation as they rampaged through more than two hundred Jewish communities. Although there were relatively few deaths, the events were traumatic for Russian Jews. They were appalled by the government's impotence and its refusal to protect them. They became frantic when it began to emerge that the pogromists came from circles close to the authorities and enjoyed their support. The conspiracy was revealed through a group known as the Sacred Fraternity; one of its members, Count N. P. Ignatiev, was appointed Minister of the Interior following the riots. Declaring itself to be the "upholder of Orthodox Christianity," the Sacred Fraternity preached an ideology based on national-religious elements, emphasizing the superiority of Russian society, the Russian Orthodox Church and Slavic culture. They wanted to rid Russia of outsiders and blamed the Jews for all the tribulations of the Russian people. They held the Jews responsible for the assassination of Tsar Alexander II, an event which occurred about a month before the outbreak of the pogroms. The Sacred Fraternity was in league with groups that urged absolute Russification throughout the country.[60]

Neither during nor after the riots was there any solid evidence that the Sacred Fraternity had been directly involved in planning the pogroms. But the presence of some of its members, who had arrived from Moscow and St. Petersburg, in locales where the riots erupted, led to the suspicion that the "high circles" in those two cities, with which the extremist group was associated, were behind the disturbances. The authorities' inaction during the riots and their half-hearted efforts to apprehend the rioters only confirmed these suspicions in Jewish eyes. The fact that some of those who were apprehended turned out to have close ties with radical religious groups – ties which were greatly strengthened during the reign of Alexander III and his close associate Pobedonostsev – furnished additional proof that the pogroms were the handiwork of reactionaries who enjoyed support from the highest levels in the Russian government.[61]

The "Southern Storms," as the pogroms of 1881 came to be known in Jewish historiography, were the portent of a wave of riots that would batter Russian Jewry for nearly forty years, until 1917. Alexander II's assassination intensified the reactionary tendencies within Russian ruling circles. Some of the committees that were set up to find solutions for the Jewish problem recommended that the Jews be granted certain rights, but the majority urged that they be kept on a short leash. The upshot was the promulgation of regulations to protect "the inhabitants against Jewish exploitation." The livelihood of many Jews was affected: they were forbidden to settle in villages or to lease estates and farm land; they were barred from joining the public service and had to obtain special permits in order to practice the liberal professions, such as law; Jewish students seeking entry to institutions of higher education faced quotas, and some institutions were closed to Jews outright. In 1891, 20,000 Jews were expelled from Moscow in order "to cleanse the historic sacred capital."[62]

Conditions did not improve Under Tsar Nicholas II, who acceded to the throne in 1894. The fruits of growing anti-Semitic agitation were seen in Kishinev, capital of Bessarabia, where a vicious pogrom erupted in 1903. This followed an inflammatory campaign conducted by Pavolaki Krushevan and his anti-Semitic newspaper in connection with a blood-libel in the town of Dubosari. Some accused the Ministry of the Interior, headed by V. K. Plehve, of stirring up anti-Semitic feelings in order to provide an outlet for the rage the local residents harbored against the authorities. Forty-nine Jews were killed and hundreds were wounded and tortured in the Kishinev pogrom.[63]

Progressive public opinion in Russia and worldwide was shocked by the 1903 rioting, and an active struggle began to end such persecution. The world press covered the issue extensively and protest rallies were held in a number of countries. The Jews themselves, defying the authorities' orders, set up local self-defense organizations, and their national awareness was heightened.

More anti-Jewish rioting broke out in 1904, during the Russo-Japanese War. This time the pretext was that the Jews were disloyal and were shirking military service. Pogroms flared up again during the Revolution of 1905, and thousands of Jews were murdered. To dampen the revolutionary fever the government formed "patriotic organizations" of Russians and Ukrainians whose task was to eradicate revolutionaries and Jews. Prominent among these gangs of hooligans was the Black Hundreds organization. Its members raided Jewish residential and commercial areas, but met organized Jewish resistance that claimed the lives of many of the rioters. In the reactionary aftermath of the 1905 Revolution army and police personnel were directly involved in pogroms; Jews who were caught while engaged in armed self-defense were tried and imprisoned as rebels against the kingdom.[64]

The riots that erupted during the abortive revolution gave the Jews common cause with the insurgents and sparked the hope that the Jewish question would be resolved by means of a radical change in the regime. In October 1905 the Tsar gave in to the demand to convene a legislature and issued a proclamation granting political rights to citizens (the October Manifesto). This was greeted by demonstrations of support by the majority of the population, though opposition groups were also organized. In the volatile atmosphere discipline in the military broke down and the security forces occasionally lost control. Disturbances broke out, with Jews as their main target. Nevertheless, many Jews believed that this sequence of events was an interim stage on the way to their integration into the state. In contrast to 1881, the radical forces did not perceive the riots as a means by which the masses could vent their justified rage against the authorities. On the contrary, the rioters could be identified with the Tsar and the Jews seen as victims of a despotic government. The Jews thus seemed to become part of a common front of all the forces that were fighting absolutism: revolutionaries, liberal bourgeoisie and minorities' liberation movements. The general view, then, was that the pogroms were instigated by the government and by right-wing elements that exploited the primitive instincts of backward groups among the populace in order to combat the forces of progress.

There was something of a lull in the anti-Jewish riots following the suppression of the 1905 Revolution, but within a few years the hatred burst out again. In Kiev (1911) a Jew named Mendel Beiliss was accused of murdering a Christian boy for ritual purposes. The Minister of Justice and his staff took charge of preparing the testimonies and Beiliss was brought to trial. Local and world public opinion saw the trial as part of the struggle between the government and the opposition, and a protest movement arose in some European countries and in the United States. Beiliss was finally acquitted for lack of evidence after a three-year trial which was one of the high points in the public struggle around the "Jewish question" in Russia.[65]

In Germany and Austria the turn of the century witnessed a reduction in the use of anti-Semitism by political parties and organizations to further their interests. The public seemed less receptive to anti-Semitic agitation. But in the early 1920s, particularly in central Europe, anti-Semitic propaganda re-emerged with undiminished virulence in the form of slogans flaunted by public and political organizations. The Jews were held to blame for Germany's catastrophic defeat in World War I, for the humiliating terms of the peace agreements and for the deteriorating economic situation. At the height of its popularity the German Popular

Defense League, which voiced such slogans, claimed some 220,000 members. Although it was smaller than other extra-parliamentary groups, it was still large enough to command public attention.[66] The National Socialist Party (re-formed in 1925) was no more successful than the League. In the Reichstag elections of 1928 the Nazis returned only twelve delegates, about 3 percent of the total. In the 1920s, then, anti-Semitic sloganeering had only a limited impact on the mass public. *Der Stürmer*, the anti-Semitic paper which began to appear in 1923, had a relatively low circulation in its first years.

But beginning in 1929 a dramatic change is discernible in the impact of anti-Semitic propaganda in the German political arena. Most striking was the meteoric rise of Adolf Hitler's Nazi party. By 1932 it was the largest single party in the Reichstag (230 seats, about a third of the total), and within two more years Hitler was appointed Chancellor and the party had seized control of the state bureaucracy (30 January 1933–August 1934). Karl Dietrich Bracher suggests four reasons for the Nazis' success: the grave economic crisis, in which unemployment soared from 1.3 million in 1929 to about 6 million when the Nazis took power; the frequent crises experienced by the Weimar government, which led growing numbers of Germans to lose faith in the democratic regime; the national polarization in Germany and the ability of Hitler and his cohorts to pass themselves off as the epitomes of German patriotism; and the diversified and extraordinary propaganda methods employed by the National Socialists.[67] In his monumental work *The German Dictatorship*, Bracher does not single out anti-Semitism as a paramount reason for Hitler's success; but other scholars, including Sigmund Neumann,[68] Walther Hofer,[69] Leni Yahil[70] and Lucy Dawidowicz[71] have stressed the crucial importance of anti-Semitism in the Nazis' efforts to drum up popular support. The Nazis accused the Jews – who comprised 0.76 percent of the country's population in 1933 – of being a major cause of the economic and social crisis gripping the country. The Jews were held responsible, as Hitler put it in his *Zweites Buch* (1928),[72] for Germany's economic collapse, the atomization of its political system and the enfeeblement of its people.

On 1 April 1933, four months after Hitler's assumption of power, the National Socialists declared a boycott of Jewish shops and businesses. Thus the Nazis set out on the path that would culminate in the most devastating tragedy in the history of the Jewish people. At that stage the anti-Jewish campaign was run by an organizing committee led by Julius Streicher. However, it was not long before the Reichstag enacted a series of government-sponsored laws aiming to annul the Jews' emancipation, discriminate against them and, in the next stage, to usurp their property and isolate them from German society. The first such legislation passed by the Reichstag was the "Law for the Restoration of the Professional Civil Service." This stipulated the retirement of non-Aryan, low-level officials and the dismissal of more senior officials.

In September 1935 the "Nuremberg Laws" were promulgated, annulling the emancipation, defining a Jew (anyone with at least three full Jewish grandparents, *Volkjüdisch*, by race) and building racism into the German legal system. Marriage between Aryans and Jews was forbidden and the Ministry of the Interior (in coordination with the Führer and the Ministry of Justice) was authorized to formulate legal and administrative decrees required to complete the laws. Within three years the racial legislation was given its final shape. The Jews were set apart from German society and removed from all branches of the economy; their property was nationalized and a new stage began which further aggravated their situation: enforced expulsion and physical ostracism.[73]

The public humiliation and mockery of the Jews began as soon as Hitler took power. Physical persecution, burning of books written by Jews and assaults on Jewish-owned property became routine. As time went on, harassment increased. The institutions of the German state, through its police branches, particularly the SS (Schutzstaffel, or Defense Corps), headed by Heinrich Himmler (1900–45), assumed responsibility for the persecutions. By 1938 several thousand Jews had been incarcerated for offenses related to the Nuremberg Laws. In 1938 about 17,000 Jews who were Polish nationals but had long resided in Germany were deported. On the 9th and 10th of November, gangs of Nazis murdered more than 90 Jews, destroyed more than 7,500 businesses, and torched and plundered 101 synagogues. Five days after *Kristallnacht* ("Night of Broken Glass") Jews were barred from entering public institutions and all Jewish children were expelled from educational institutions. On 28 November a decree was issued empowering the state authorities to arrest any Jew without trial. That same day, an order was issued removing the Jews from German economic life and commanding them to pay a fine of one billion marks on account of their "hostile attitude" toward "the German Volk and Reich."[74] In other words, by the end of 1938 the first phase of the Nazis' scheme against the Jews had been completed: the Jews were ostracized, stripped of their rights, their property was nationalized and they were increasingly being removed from German soil.

Until late in 1938 the Jews generally reacted with restraint to the Nazis' actions. The majority, who deeply identified, emotionally and intellectually, with the German homeland and its culture, hoped for a return to normalcy once the storm abated: they would resume their former way of life and anti-Semitism would melt away. In the meantime German Jews (aided by Jewish institutions abroad) formed relief and welfare organizations that provided urgent help for the needy and helped establish alternative educational and cultural institutions to replace those now closed to Jews. About half of Germany's Jews and two-thirds of the Jews in Austria (which was annexed to Germany in March 1938) emigrated between 1933 and 1939. The others, among them the majority of the community's leaders, thought it prudent to wait patiently until the Nazis were ousted. *Kristallnacht* put an end to their delusions. The Jews finally grasped that no turnabout was imminent. But neither was there an alternative to Germany. Nine hundred German Jews who left the country aboard the luxury liner *St. Louis* (May 1939), bound for Cuba, were forced to return to Europe. No one wanted them, not Cuba and not the United States.[75]

On 24 January 1939 Hermann Goering (1893–1946), the commander of the German Air Force, chairman of the Council of Ministers and the Führer's successor-designate, sent a memorandum to the highest officials in the Reich asserting that henceforth the Jewish question would be dealt with exclusively by his office. The reason for concentrating the anti-Jewish efforts in a single government office (until then they had been dispersed among the Ministry of the Interior, the Ministry of Justice and the armed forces) was clear: the desire to streamline – and conceal – the Jews' physical liquidation in Germany and Europe. Here was a new stage in Nazi anti-Semitism, the portent of the "Final Solution." At the same time Goering took several measures to reduce the Jewish population: thousands were forcibly sent to concentration camps at Dachau, Buchenwald and Mauthausen, while others did forced labor under the constant threat of expulsion and arrest.

The last stage of the Final Solution was launched with the Germans' invasion of Poland (1 September 1939) followed by their conquest of large areas of Europe. Hitler's self-proclaimed "new world order," to be established in the image and form of Nazism, had no place for the millions of Jews residing in the occupied lands.

Speaking in the Reichstag on 30 January 1939, Hitler declared his intention to annihilate the Jewish race in Europe. When the Nazis overran vast areas of the continent, bringing more than 10 million Jews under their control, Hitler moved to implement his plan. What remained to be decided was method and pace. Not all the details had been worked out, but the Nazis were determined to launch their death drive as soon as possible.

In the first stage the Germans stripped the Jews of their human rights in every locale they conquered. Jews were forbidden to travel and to engage in economic activity, and they were everywhere subjected to humiliation, assault and murder. For easier identification they were forced to wear a yellow star. Beginning in the fall of 1939 the Nazis herded the Jews of Poland into ghettos. Special areas were cordoned off in the large cities – Łódź, Warsaw, Cracow, Lublin, Radom, Lvov and others – where the Jews were concentrated, cut off from the outside world. The immediate purpose of the ghettoization process launched by the Nazis, beyond the fact that it dovetailed with their racist ideology, was to enable them to better exploit the Jews for forced labor; and, in the second stage, to let the extermination machinery run more smoothly. Additional benefits to the Nazis were the removal of the Jews from the general economy and the unhindered confiscation of Jewish property left behind outside the ghetto.

In the spring of 1941 Himmler issued an explicit order to begin the systematic murder of Jews in the German-occupied countries. True, the Nazis had declared this intention on more than one occasion in the past – Hitler's January 1939 statement has already been cited – but in practice, as a systematic policy, the decision to exterminate the Jews was made about a year and a half after the war began. The Germans' initial crushing victories throughout Europe gave Hitler and his cohorts confidence in their insane plan to make the Third Reich (which was to last for "a thousand years") a racially pure Aryan state, as outlined years earlier in Hitler's *Mein Kampf*.

On 20 May 1941 the German authorities formally prohibited the emigration of Jews from all occupied countries, "in view of the imminent final solution of the Jewish question."[76] At the same time the commanders of the special SS killing squads known as *Einsatzgruppen* were ordered to execute by shooting all male Jews (as well as all Communist functionaries, "second-class Asiatics" and gypsies) in order "to solve the Jewish question by any means and with all decisiveness." By decree of Reinhard Heydrich (1904–42),

Himmler's deputy and head of the United Police Arms (SS) in the Reich, local residents were given a free hand to carry out pogroms against Jews.[77] In a meeting held three months later Hitler told some of the regime's leaders (among them Goering, Rosenberg, Keitel and Bormann) that the optimal method to bring about "pacification" in the east was "by shooting dead anyone who even looks askance."[78]

Yet, even in this period there was no comprehensive program to systematically annihilate the Jews. On 31 July 1941 Goering directed Heydrich to submit an overall plan, noting the "organizational, substantive and material" measures necessary in order to implement the desired solution of the Jewish question. That solution was put into practice when the remaining German and Austrian Jews were mass-transported to the east (beginning in October 1941). The Jews were driven into ghettos and thousands were executed daily. But until early 1942 the annihilation proceeded sporadically, without an all-encompassing design.

On 20 January 1942 fifteen senior Nazi officials met at Interpol headquarters on Lake Wannsee in Berlin to work out how to mobilize all government resources for the implementation of the Final Solution. Heydrich (appointed by Goering to oversee the preparations for the Final Solution) chaired the meeting; those present included Adolf Eichmann (1906–62) and Heinrich Mueller (b. 1896). At the order of Himmler ("over-all director" of the program) they decided on the extermination of Europe's 11 million Jews. The aim was to finish them off quickly and, as Mueller noted, "wherever we meet them and wherever possible."[79] All the Jews were to be concentrated in death camps. Some would be put to work in the Nazis' war effort, the others would be put to death in gas chambers. Mass killing of Jews by gas in trucks had been successfully attempted a month before the conference. About 150,000 Jews in Łódź had been slaughtered in this way. Now the method was to be applied against the whole of European Jewry. Mass killing in gas chambers at death camps – Belzec, Sobibor, Majdanek, Treblinka and, the largest of the charnels, Auschwitz-Birkenau – began in March 1942. By the summer of 1944 about 3.5 million Jews had perished in the gas chambers, and another 2.5 million by other means.

Every conceivable method was used to conceal the genocide. Camps were set up near large industrial plants with Jews supposedly being "resettled" nearby for the benefit of "the factories' manpower needs." Government institutions kept the mass murders a closely guarded secret. The killings were perpetrated with astounding efficiency, involving coordination among numerous government departments. Jews were transported from ghettos that were located close to the death camps and from communities throughout Europe. Many had been incarcerated in concentration camps scattered through the occupied territories, which at their peak (early 1945) held more than 700,000 people. Passenger trains were used for the mass transports. Most were killed upon arrival at the death camps. The rest were exploited for the German war effort, only to face the same fate after being worn down by starvation and cold. The genocide was carried out by all levels of the SS, aided by certain elements of the German administration, primarily the army (Wehrmacht). The Germans also used local residents and even Jews in the annihilation campaign.

The rate of extermination increased constantly after the winter of 1942, reaching its peak in 1944. In the Germans' allocation of resources the murder of Jews had indisputable priority. Even if the war effort put a tremendous drain on manpower, nothing was more important than killing Jews. "Alone for reasons of camouflage one must work as quickly as possible," Himmler said; "so that we don't get stuck in the middle," another Nazi official added near the end of the war.[80]

The Nazis' systematic murder of six million Jews; the harnessing of the entire German bureaucratic apparatus to implement the Final Solution; and the nearly flawless execution by Nazi officials of Hitler's orders – these elements set the Holocaust apart as a single and singular event in human history. The Holocaust was not unleashed by a group of revenge-crazed individuals, nor was it the madness of a single person who envisaged mass murder while languishing in prison 25 years earlier; it was not a logical consequence of the war, a way to terrorize, intimidate and deter large populations. The annihilation of Jews was built into Nazi ideology. The genocidal campaign was a corollary to the logic of racism which, as the Nazis grasped with appalling simplicity, calls for the elimination of the race that is considered inferior, parasitic and harmful by the superior race, which feels itself in mortal danger. The same logic dictated the techniques and methods of the Final Solution: the utter eradication of every Jew (as defined by the Nuremberg Laws), without possibility of escape. At the Wannsee Conference it was decided in one breath (and in one statistical table) to kill one hundred Jews in Albania, along with five million Jews in the Soviet Union. Moreover, the Nazis were punctilious murderers. They thought nothing of transferring Jews from every corner of Europe, utilizing their vast range of resources in order to carry through their scheme of murdering as many Jews as possible; and most horrific, even knowing that the war was lost they pressed ahead. Thus, in November 1944, when Himmler ordered the cessation of the gassings, fearing detection by the Allied forces that were approaching Berlin, the Nazis began evacuating Jews from the camps by foot; untold thousands perished in these "death marches."[81]

*   *   *

In Russia the equality of rights granted the Jews on 22 March 1917 and the advent of the Communist regime, with its doctrine of egalitarianism (and its large number of high-ranking Jewish bureaucrats), did not put an end to anti-Semitism. Nor did the legislation promulgated by the new regime outlawing the phenomenon make a difference. In the Civil War (1917–21) thousands of Jews were killed and wounded in pogroms perpetrated by Ukrainian Army soldiers and by other units. Some estimates place the number of Jews killed in this period at 75,000,[82] though others cite lower figures.[83] Whatever the exact number, Jews continued to suffer because of their religious distinctiveness even after obtaining legal equality of rights.

In an anti-Semitic wave that began at the end of the 1920s, the Soviet ruler Joseph Stalin invoked anti-Jewish terminology to excoriate his enemies in the leadership who were Jewish (Lev Trotsky, Lev Kaminev, Grigori Zinoviev, Karl Radek, Grigori Sokolonikov, and others). Anti-Semitic invective accompanied the great purges and political show trials held in the Soviet Union from 1936 to 1939, in which many of those in the dock were Jews.[84] Yet overall, comparatively speaking, the 1920s and the first half of the 1930s witnessed a reduction in the number of anti-Semitic incidents. Frequently the authorities took a hand; anti-Semites were prosecuted and Stalin denounced anti-Semitism publicly as "an extreme form of racist chauvinism."[85]

Nevertheless, Stalin's centralist policy, particularly in the second half of the 1930s, and the harnessing of the entire gamut of institutions and organizations comprising Soviet society in the service of the regime, harmed Soviet Jewry's social and cultural status. A vigorous anti-religious campaign was launched, and although the

anti-Semitic lexicon was generally not invoked, Jewish culture was
seriously affected. Nearly all Yiddish-language publications were
shut down and most of the schools in which Yiddish was the
language of instruction were closed. The Jews were compelled
to adapt themselves to Russian society and take an active part
in its transformation. In other words, in the 1930s the Soviets
endeavored (with no small success) to intensively assimilate the
Jewish community, with its distinctive culture, into the general
population.[86]

On 23 August 1939 the foreign ministers of Germany and the
Soviet Union, Ribbentrop and Molotov, signed a mutual non-
aggression pact. This was a portentous event for Soviet Jewry.
The signing of the agreement and the Soviet occupation of eastern
Poland in mid-September meant that two million more Jews had
come under Soviet control, bringing the total to five million. The
Jews quickly felt the brunt of a new anti-Semitic onslaught, overt
and covert, including persecution and attacks.[87] Undoubtedly this
was related to the impact of Nazism and the legitimization of
the Führer's actions by the Soviet leadership in the form of a
non-aggression pact. Yet, the treaty's abrogation upon the German
invasion of the Soviet Union (June 1941) resulted in increased
Soviet anti-Semitism. The historic anti-Jewish tradition, the origins
of which lay in ancient Muscovy and which was deeply embedded
in popular, Orthodox-Christian elements of the population, was
rekindled during the war. Stalin and the Soviet apparatus ordered
the eradication of anti-Semitism, as they had in the 1920s and 1930s,
but in practice the administration usually turned a blind eye to
anti-Semitic manifestations, which had the effect of encouraging
their perpetrators.

The leadership's desire to contain the phenomenon was dictated
by the effort to mobilize all the country's resources against the
Germans. They feared that playing up the struggle against
anti-Semitism while the Nazis and their slogans were popular
among various European minorities in the Soviet Union (notably in
Ukraine, Poland and the Baltic states) could trigger a reaction against
the government.[88] Some scholars believe that anti-Jewish feelings
were deeply rooted in Stalin himself and that if previously he had
suppressed such tendencies, he vented them with a vengeance in
his later years. Another view is that Stalin exploited anti-Semitism
to further his own political and ideological purposes.[89] In any case,
anti-Semitism assumed alarming proportions in the post-war Soviet

Union in the period from 1948 to 1953, corresponding with the final years of the Soviet dictator's life.

During the war the sharp tension generated by anti-Semitism between Jews and their neighbors sometimes erupted into sporadic attacks and even pogroms against the Jewish population.[90] In Nazi-occupied areas local collaborators colluded with the Germans in the persecution and murder of more than a million Jews. Everywhere, including areas not reached by the Germans, anti-Semitism was rife and unchecked. It spread to broad sectors of the population, including the army and workplaces. The process was unaffected by the authorities' creation of the "Jewish Anti-Fascist Committee." Its task was to enlist the support of Jews in the English-speaking countries on behalf of the Soviet Union's struggle against the Nazis. It had no mandate to combat anti-Semitism, and was silent in the face of its manifestations.

When the full scale of the Nazis' atrocities was revealed after the war, Soviet Jews believed the government would take vigorous measures to quell anti-Semitism. Yet, it was in the war's aftermath, from 1948 to 1953, that anti-Jewish agitation reached new levels, so much so that this period came to be known as the "black years" of Soviet Jewry. In the Soviet press and in journals and books the Jews were branded "rootless cosmopolitans" who rejected Soviet values, were disposed toward western culture, fawned over the imperialists and despised the Russian people. The Jews were said to harbor "chauvinistic tendencies," to be Zionist sympathizers,[91] and to support American imperialism so unreservedly that Jewish physicians had conspired to murder Soviet leaders under the guise of giving them medical treatment (the "doctors' plot").[92] Other national and religious groups were similarly targeted, but not as virulently as the Jews.[93] Thousands of Jews were exiled to the eastern Soviet Union, to be incarcerated in gulags; leading figures of the Jewish intelligentsia, including some from the Jewish Anti-Fascist Committee – writers, poets, artists and journalists – were executed. Jews lost their jobs and were physically assaulted in the streets. Only the death of Stalin (5 March 1953), who some claimed had been planning, in his last days, to expel the Jews from European Russia, put an end to this dark period in the annals of Russian and Soviet Jewry.

Many explanations have been adduced for the anti-Jewish campaign launched in Stalin's final years. Some link the campaign to his personality and to his anti-Semitic proclivities that increased with age. Another explanation is that Stalin and his associates saw the harassment of Jews as an element in the fight against American imperialism and the superpower struggle for hegemony during the Cold War. The stereotypical perception cultivated by the Soviet leadership held that American Jews were an integral part of the establishment there and served the regime at all levels. To denounce the Jews, then, was tantamount to denouncing the Americans. As we saw, Soviet stereotypes (originating in prejudices that developed in the nineteenth century) also depicted the Jews as "cosmopolitans" without true roots, as a fifth column that would stop at nothing to unseat Communism.

Hence the Cold War connection. But whatever the actual motivation, Stalin in his final years became one of the Jewish people's most brutal enemies.[94]

*   *   *

The struggle between Jews and Arabs for Palestine, beginning at the end of the nineteenth century,[95] the growth of the Arab-Jewish conflict and the establishment of the State of Israel (see chapter 5) were further causes of anti-Semitism, particularly in the second half of the twentieth century. The reverberations of these anti-Semitic manifestations, which originated in the Middle East, were felt in Europe, Asia and Africa. Conflict fanned anti-Semitism: the Jews' capture of large areas of Palestine in the 1948–49 Israeli-Arab war, including much of what had been designated by the United Nations in November 1947 as the area of the Arab state; the emergence of the Arab refugee problem; Israel's conquest of the West Bank and the Gaza Strip in the 1967 Six Day War; and Israeli victories in the wars of 1956 and 1973 – all contributed to the spread of anti-Semitism.[96]

In the Muslim society of the Islamic lands, however, as distinct from Europe, anti-Semitism was not a deep-rooted phenomenon.[97] True, the Jewish-Muslim encounter produced enmity and incitement, but such phenomena were relatively infrequent as compared with parallel periods in Europe. Anti-Semitic feelings increased in North Africa in the late nineteenth and early twentieth centuries[98] as a result of European influence, but these feelings never approached the intensity they had achieved in Europe itself. It was the heightened level of the Arab-Jewish conflict in Palestine from the 1920s and 1930s on that brought about a rise of anti-Jewish propaganda.

The meaning of "anti-Semitism" within the context of the Arab-Jewish conflict is undoubtedly problematic. Any power struggle can foment hatred and give rise to stereotypical motifs which cast the enemy in non-human terms. Patterns of hatred for the other side are clearly discernible on the part of both Arabs and Jews in the Middle East, as they are in other national conflicts. For the Arabs, the struggle against Israel became part of an ideological struggle against European imperialism. With the backing of about a hundred states, Zionism was defined by the United Nations General Assembly (1974) as a racist movement. Implicitly, then, anti-Zionism was legitimized by the nations of the world, according to criteria determined by the international community (until the resolution's repeal in the summer of 1991).

A perusal of the anti-Zionist propaganda produced in the Arab states and elsewhere, particularly in the Soviet Union and the Communist bloc states in eastern Europe[99] – in articles, books, pamphlets and other material – shows indisputably that anti-Semitic elements were injected into an ostensibly legitimate struggle. Since the 1920s Zionism and, later, the State of Israel, were frequently depicted as part of an international Jewish conspiracy aiming to achieve world domination through Jewish money;[100] while in literature, the press and cartoons the Jew was portrayed in a manner identical with anti-Semitic material produced in Europe.[101] Typical anti-Semitic stereotypes, such as the "international Jewish plot" (from *The Protocols of the Elders of Zion*[102]), or certain alleged physical traits (long nose, beard, repulsive features), became part of the standard repertoire of writers, artists and caricaturists. In short, anti-Semitism was often disguised as anti-Zionism. In the Arab states, especially those directly involved in the confrontation with Israel – Lebanon, Syria, Jordan, Egypt and Iraq – anti-Semitic motifs were widespread, particularly during and after wars.

In certain ways, however, Arab anti-Semitism differed from the European variety. Since it was often enlisted in the cause of the anti-Zionist struggle, it assumed a political-ideological character and became an integral part of the campaign against Israel. In contrast to Europe, Arab anti-Semitism originated largely with the ruling circles and the literary and political élites, and less from the ordinary strata of society.[103] Its themes were for the most part directed against Israel rather than against Jews as such: in other words, its target was not the Jewish People, but Jewish culture and history.[104] Moreover, owing to the distinctive character of Arab anti-Semitism, its anti-Jewish propaganda usually came in waves and was often connected with particular developments in the Arab world. Thus the Arabs' attitude toward the Jews and Zionism was often determined more by internal events – the expulsion of the British, or the contest for power between Islamic fundamentalists (such as the Muslim Brothers) and secular movements (such as the Ba'ath organizations in Syria and in Iraq) – than by events directly related to Israel or to Jews. In other cases, notably in World War II, anti-Semitism was generated by *ad hoc* political alliances. Anti-Semitic incitement also increased during periods of internecine Arab strife. Hatred for Israel and the Jews seemed to unite the Arab world. Hence also the infrequency of anti-Semitism in its brutal, overt, direct form in the Arab world. Jews were permitted to emigrate to Israel from most of the Arab states, and with a few exceptions – pogroms in Baghdad and in various towns in Algeria and Morocco, public hangings of Jews in Iraq (also explained as part of the Arab-Israeli conflict) or the persecution of Jews in Syria (said to be an internal Syrian matter) – the Jews who remained in Arab lands experienced long periods of friendly relations with their neighbors. Indeed, this was something that anti-Zionist propaganda in the Arab states rarely forgot to mention.

*   *   *

In conclusion, Jew-hatred has been an integral element of Jewish history, perhaps from as far back as the third century BCE. A historic watershed occurred in the 1870s and 1880s. If until then anti-Jewish feelings focused primarily on Jews' negative traits, their calumnies, and above all on their sin of murdering the son of God, the late nineteenth century saw the emergence of two types of anti-Semitism. The granting of emancipation to the Jews, combined with the industrial, social and scientific revolutions that changed the face of Europe in the nineteenth century, had the effect of transforming the Jews, in the eyes of their denigrators, into an imagined society seeking to achieve world domination through its riches; a group that was baneful to its host-nations, ruling out the possibility of integration with its neighbors and adversely affecting other nations' distinctiveness and their "natural traits."

The advances in the biological and social sciences in the nineteenth century had a radicalizing effect on anti-Jewish vilifications. Until then Jews could convert to Christianity in order to atone for their sins, but from the 1870s and 1880s their guilt was absolute and irremediable. The racists said the Jews were engaged in a campaign to dominate the Aryan race in Europe. In this clash of the races, of which the model was a simplistic reading of Darwinian theory, there would be only one victor. Jew-hatred was comprised of these new elements and given a new name – anti-Semitism. At the same time the phenomenon became a political tool. Political parties introduced anti-Semitic themes into their platforms. The anti-Jewish struggle was integral to the ideology of the radical right.

Anti-Semitic movements had relatively little impact in the last third of the nineteenth century. Some anti-Semitic incidents had widespread reverberations – the pogroms in Russia in 1881–82, 1903 and 1905, the Dreyfus Affair in France, or the blood-libel at Tisza-Eszlar in Hungary – but overall, anti-Semitism had little effect on the general society, on the Jews' legal status or on their socioeconomic development. However, in this period the seeds were sown that resulted in the Jewish people's greatest catastrophe. A direct line can be traced between the ideology spouted by Hitler and his cohorts, and the ideological anti-Semitism of the late nineteenth century. The delegitimization of the Jews and of Judaism under the Nazi regime was the fruit of the seedlings planted by Houston Chamberlain and his ilk in the latter decades of the nineteenth century.

The Holocaust dwarfed all previous and subsequent manifestations of anti-Semitism. The murder of 49 Jews in the Kishinev pogrom of 1903 shocked the entire world. So did the "Southern Storms" (1881), the October 1905 pogroms and, later, Stalin's crimes against the Jews. But these were mere candles in the wind before the conflagration of the Holocaust.

Today, too, as the twentieth century draws to a close, anti-Semitism persists. Institutes that monitor such phenomena[105] have found that in the course of some 70 years anti-Semitism increased in Middle Eastern Arab society, as did anti-Jewish manifestations in the Soviet Union. But in the post-Holocaust era the tendency in most countries, including those locked in a bitter confrontation with Israel, is to conceal anti-Semitism, to show that the target is not the Jews and Judaism but the State of Israel, and more specifically, Zionist ideology. Overall, then, Jew-hatred with its distinctive motifs that sprang up in the 1870s and 1880s, culminating in the 1940s in the most horrific tragedy ever to strike the Jews, still exists, but as a relatively marginal phenomenon.

5

Zionism and the State of Israel

The first Jewish national movement that aspired to establish a political entity in the Land of Israel, *Hovevei Zion* (Lovers of Zion), sprang up in Russia in the early 1880s. In August 1897, Theodor Herzl wrote in his diary that at the First Zionist Congress, in Basle, he founded the Jewish state. Most contemporary intellectuals found both the activity of *Hovevei Zion* and the views of Theodor Herzl utopian. Few Jews joined the nascent Zionist movement; those who yearned for a change found the United States of America a preferable destination in every respect. Even among the movement's leaders and rank-and-file, no more than a small minority would have believed that Herzl's prophecy would come true within only fifty years; that the day would come when David Ben-Gurion (1886–1973), the leader of the Jewish community in the Land of Israel, would proclaim the creation of the independent State of Israel:

> the renewal of the Jewish state in the Land of Israel, which will open wide the gates of the homeland to every Jew and confer on the Jewish people the status of a nation possessing equal rights within the family of nations.

Zionism, which began as a relatively marginal social and cultural movement, soon became an extraordinarily important phenomenon in the Jewish world, eclipsing movements such as Hasidism or the Bund, which had once loomed large. What were the dynamics of this process? What was the background to the rise of Zionism and what was the significance of its triumph? These are the principal questions to be considered.

From the end of the eighteenth century, politicians, clerics, writers and eccentrics of various kinds had been drawing up programs for the creation of a state for Jews. Such a state was generally seen as a solution for the Jewish question, for Judaism, or even for all mankind.[1]

Their proposals went beyond support for the building of Zion and Jerusalem as envisaged in the Jews' holy texts across the ages. Statesmen like Napoleon Bonaparte (1769–1821), public figures like Lawrence Oliphant (1829–88), thinkers like Joseph Salvador (1796–1873), writers like Emma Lazarus (1849–87), or eccentrics like Emanuel Noah (1785–1851) sought, each by means of his or her own method, to resolve the Jewish problem through the creation of a Jewish state.[2] Rabbis, among them Nathan Friedlander (1851–83), Judah Bibas (1780–1852) and Joseph Natok (1813–92) summoned the authority of their position to preach that the establishment of a Jewish state would hasten the redemption.[3] Protestant sects believed that it would herald the Second Coming of Jesus.[4]

But no one acted to actualize the ideas and visions. The most serious activity was undertaken by the educator Hayyim Lorje (1821–70?) who in 1860 founded the "Society for the Colonization of Palestine" (Colonisation-Verein für Palastina).[5] Its purpose: to promote the "productivization" of Jews in Palestine. But his efforts were stillborn. A few rabbis and activists joined Lorje's society, but they accomplished little.[6] Among his supporters were the socialist writer Moses Hess (1812–75), whose book, *Rome and Jerusalem*, admonished Jews "to rise up and go forward," for "the ancient homeland" was calling them;[7] Rabbi Yehuda Alkalai (1798–1878), who asked the philanthropist Moses Montefiore (1774–1885) and the French politician Adolphe Crémieux (1806–80) to help the Jews "re-inherit" the "land of their forefathers";[8] and Rabbi Zwi Hirsch Kalischer (1795–1874), who maintained that when tens of thousands of Jews would settle in the Land of Israel "and pray mightily at the sacred mount in Jerusalem, the Creator bless Him shall hear and bring closer the redemption."[9] But their fervor and their readiness for action[10] could not further Lorje's ideas, and he soon gave up his activity. The same fate awaited other intellectuals and would-be activists in the 1860s and 1870s, including Yehuda Leib Gordon (1831–92), editor of the Hebrew journal *Ha-magid*, and the writer Peretz Smolenskin (1842–85). Both used their creative gifts to lobby for international recognition of the Jewish minority.[11] But theirs were voices in the wilderness.

Not until the 1880s, then, in Russia and Romania, were associations formed advocating the creation of a Jewish state, in which some members actually tried to implement the programs.[12] It is only natural to ask why the Jewish national movement came into existence just then. Earlier activity had failed, true, but the Jewish religion itself contains nationalist elements. Embedded in the Jewish faith is the aspiration to forge a national territory in Zion and Jerusalem; the Jews' language of prayer was inseparable from their historical past. Moreover, why did the conditions for the creation of the Jewish national movement emerge so many years after other national movements had sprung up in Europe – some of them quite early in the century? Among the reasons: opposition of Orthodox rabbis, on the grounds that man must not try to hasten the redemption; the thrust of the *Haskalah* (Jewish Enlightenment) movement toward assimilation in European society, a tendency that was obviously the reverse of Jewish nationalism; and, concomitantly, its demand for emancipation, again an idea inherently at odds with a Jewish national movement based on the Jews' distinctiveness within the society. The failure of two nationalist uprisings in Poland (1830–31, 1863) and the suppression of the Polish national movement by the Russians was a chastening factor for the Jews. Above all, however, the Jewish community simply lacked the political maturity that is part and parcel of a national movement.[13] Most Jews identified themselves as members of a separate religion who were organically linked with their place of residence. Until the 1870s and 1880s, very few Jews recognized that by nationality, too, they were different from their immediate surroundings.

Indeed, *Hovevei Zion* in part rode the crest of a nationalist wave in the last third of the nineteenth century, when Europeans became powerfully aware that human society was composed of separate and distinct nationalities. In Russia, then home to half the world's Jews, a plethora of nationalist movements arose. Besides the Poles, the Ukrainians, Belorussians, Lithuanians, Latvians and others created national movements.[14] In the Hapsburg Empire the same trend was visible among the Czechs, Slovaks, Magyars and other peoples. The Jews, ultimately, did not want to be left out.

A wave of anti-Semitism in Europe in the 1870s and 1880s (see chapter 4) also played a part. Jew-hatred grounded in Christian theology persisted even in an age of rapid technological progress and indeed was aggravated by the emergence of political anti-Semitism. Some of the new organizations and parties invoked modern concepts from the social sciences. Politicians whose platform was based primarily on hatred of Jews were elected to parliaments across

Europe. Anti-Jewish literature flourished. Some Jews, observing these events, were driven to conclude that emancipation, far from eliminating Jew-hatred, would, paradoxically, intensify it. One solution they proposed was the creation of a liberation movement that would seek the complete separation of the Jews from the surrounding society. Thus would anti-Semitism inevitably be eliminated.

The demographic increase of the Jews in eastern Europe, which reached huge proportions in the later part of the nineteenth century, required dramatic socioeconomic solutions. None were available. The fomentors of the Jewish nationalist movement argued that it would also help relieve the Jews' social and economic plight. The emancipation that was granted to the Jews in western and central Europe by the end of the 1860s was a further spur to the emergence of a nationalist movement. The intellectuals who had fought for emancipation could now turn their energies to the struggle for national rights.

Nevertheless, this concatenation of events did not lead large numbers of Jews to accept as self-evident the need, urged by *Hovevei Zion*, to create a Jewish state in the Land of Israel. Nor was the "Am Olam" movement, which wanted to set up an independent national entity in the United States, greeted with much enthusiasm.[15] Despite everything, the majority of Jews remained convinced that they could go on living alongside their neighbors as they had for untold generations.

Various rationales for resolving the Jewish problem by means of a national entity in the Land of Israel were advanced by the leaders of *Hovevei Zion*. The writer Moshe Leib Lilienblum (1843–1910), the movement's first secretary, represented the pragmatic current that interwove modern nationalist ideas with religious and traditional elements. The Jews needed a state in Palestine, he said, so that they could be masters of their own fate. Everywhere else their development would be stunted, owing to their alien status and the prevailing anti-Semitism. "No civilization on earth has the power to demand that a stranger should be accepted by a different family as though he were its natural-born offspring . . . We are strangers in the society around us, and strangers we shall remain." Only in the Land of Israel, "to which we have a historical claim," could Jews live in relative "peace and tranquility."[16] Similarly, the doctrine of the physician Leib Pinsker (1821–91), who led *Hovevei Zion* in its first years of existence, was based on a pragmatic nationalist ideology.

But Pinsker, in contrast to Lilienblum, urged a break with the Jewish historical past in order to concentrate on solving the Jewish problem. Like Lilienblum, he cited anti-Semitism as the major reason for the creation of a Jewish state. Emancipation, he insisted, was certainly no panacea for the Jews. Pinsker, however, thought it immaterial whether the state was in Palestine or America. The crucial thing was for Jews to control their destiny in a "secure refuge" where they would become "capable of being made productive."[17]

Rabbi Shmuel Mohilever (1824–98), from Bialystok, the most prominent of the rabbinical figures in *Hovevei Zion*, espoused a national-religious approach. As such, his reasons for wanting to establish a national entity in the Land of Israel were different from those of Lilienblum and Pinsker. Mohilever argued that the precept to settle the Land of Israel took precedence over all others, and that settlement of the land would be the first step toward redemption.[18] The "first step" idea was crucial, if one accepted – as Mohilever did – Maimonides' view that human endeavors to advance the redemption were tantamount to heresy. Thus settlement of the land at this time was only a step in that direction (not the redemption itself). "We must expect the redemption in due course,"[19] he wrote, but now was the time "to get our land and ingather our dispersions."[20]

The ideology set forth by Lilienblum, Pinsker, Mohilever and others developed against the background of the founding of *Hovevei Zion* in Russia and counterparts elsewhere, notably Bilu (Hebrew acronym for "O House of Jacob, come let us walk [by the light of the Lord]," Isaiah 2:5) in Kharkov. Its members, overwhelmingly young people and students, took action immediately after a wave of pogroms. Their activity touched a deep chord; at one point the organization had three thousand members.[21] However, the physical conditions in Palestine and the return of calm in Russia cooled their ardor. The hard-core activists realized that only a dramatic change could save their movement.

Bilu, finally, fared no better than other branches of *Hovevei Zion*. Initially fired by enthusiasm, a few of their members (including some from Bilu) made the journey to Palestine. But many left and those who remained had little motivation, aware of the futility of what they were doing. The message was not lost on the 29 leaders of the movement who gathered (18–23 November 1884) at Kattowitz, in Silesia, not far from the German-Russian border, to set up a body that would lead *Hovevei Zion*. They knew that a radical overhaul of the movement was an immediate necessity. Until then, a few dozen societies had operated inside and outside Russia with little contact or coordination between them. There was no authoritative body or leader to steer the movement toward the realization of its goals. The participants at Kattowitz were bent on remedying the situation to prevent the movement's decline.

To conceal the true purpose of the conference – to found a movement that would work to establish an autonomous center for Jews in the Land of Israel – and to ensure that the authorities did not suspect them of forming a nationalist movement to better the lot of Jews, the participants declared that their sole purpose was to set up a society for the settlement of Palestine, to be based in Odessa. Pinsker maintained that *Hovevei Zion* should found an association "to promote cultivation of the land as support for the settlers in the Land of Israel," while the larger aim was "to forge for our people a new road on which to embark in pursuit of happiness and activity that truly promotes human dignity."[22] But everyone who was familiar with Pinsker's pamphlet (*Autoemancipation*) and with Lilienblum's writings knew perfectly well that the former's declaration about creating a "settlement movement" was meant to conceal from the Russian authorities the movement's nationalist goals.

For a time the Kattowitz Conference energized *Hovevei Zion* in Russia. But there was no continuation. In the five years that followed, the movement's members did not achieve their purposes. Two subsequent meetings, held in Drugoznik (Grodna District, 1887) and in Vilna (1889), were devoted primarily to personal issues. Power struggles for control of the movement erupted between adherents of the Enlightenment led by Pinsker, Lilienblum and Avraham Greenberg (1831–1906), and the ultra-Orthodox faction headed by Rabbi Mohilever and Rabbi Shmuel Yosef Fein (1818–90). The religious bloc won and Mohilever was chosen as the movement's leader.

The movement's unproductive activity and purposeless deliberations won it few new members. Only a drastic shake-up could keep *Hovevei Zion* viable. In February 1889, Asher Zvi Ginsberg (1856–1927), an intellectual who had recently moved from Ukraine to Odessa and wrote under the pseudonym of "Ahad Ha'am" (One of the People), published an essay ("This Is Not the Way") in the Hebrew journal *Ha-melitz*, fiercely attacking *Hovevei Zion*.[23] The movement, he said, must revise its goals. It should devote itself to educating Jews about their nationhood, for in the course of their history they had lost their direction as a people and a nation. In subsequent articles, Ginsberg, or Ahad Ha'am as he was known for the rest of his life, continued to develop his themes, particularly the need for a Jewish national-cultural center in the Land of Israel.

His ideas were ardently welcomed by a number of intellectuals in *Hovevei Zion*. Seven of them, notably Yehoshua Hana Ravnitsky (1859–1944), Avraham Eliahu Lubarsky (1856–1920) and Yehoshua Eisenstadt-Barzilai (1856–1918) banded together with Ahad Ha'am to form a secret order (*"Benei Moshe"*) with the goal of actualizing his ideas.[24] In its eight years of activity *Benei Moshe* attracted some two hundred members; the intellectual élite of *Hovevei Zion*, their self-perceived mission was to instill in the Jewish people a sense of nationalism and to promote Ahad Ha'am's concept of a cultural center for the Jewish people in Palestine.

However, even with all their energy and drive, they were unable to gain control of *Hovevei Zion* or alter its goals. Two others who sought the same end were Lilienblum and Pinsker, after losing the leadership of the movement in the summer of 1889 to Mohilever's ultra-Orthodox faction. They now followed up the success of Alexander Tsederbaum (1816–93), the editor of *Ha-melitz*, who had persuaded the Russian authorities to formally recognize *Hovevei Zion* (following five years of futile efforts). On 26 April 1890, the two formed the "Society for the Support of Jewish Farmers and Artisans in Syria and Palestine" – the Odessa Committee, as it was commonly known, after the city in which it was founded. Through the new organization, which became the legal successor to *Hovevei Zion*, Pinsker and Lilienblum were able to regain leadership of the movement and oust the ultra-Orthodox group. However, not even the Odessa Committee could reinvigorate *Hovevei Zion*. Worse, in 1890–91 the committee was implicated in a fiasco in Palestine. More than eight thousand settlers, who had arrived in Palestine during a two-year period, needed a guiding hand. The Odessa Committee, which took responsibility for the project, failed disastrously. Thousands of the new arrivals who wanted to purchase land for settlement soon found that they had thrown their money away. The appointment of Vladimir Tiomkin (1861–1927) to head the "Actions Committee" in Jaffa – the body that was to implement the Odessa Committee's policy in Palestine – proved a colossal error of judgment. Tiomkin and his aides made every possible mistake. As a result of their actions the price of land soared, huge sums of money were lost, and the majority of the settlers left.[25]

The Odessa Committee's failure boosted the stock of Ahad Ha'am and the *Benei Moshe* order. They had a comparatively successful image owing to their educational and cultural activity. In 1895 it seemed momentarily that they would gain control of the leadership,[26] but the moment passed. Ahad Ha'am found it difficult to lead his group, and finally salvation came from a totally different quarter – the Jewish community in central Europe.

In the mid-1890s a Budapest-born Jew named Theodor Herzl took a different route toward implementing the ideas of *Hovevei Zion*. During a five-year stint in Paris (1889–94) as a correspondent for the important Vienna-based liberal paper *Neue Freie Presse*, Herzl was deeply affected by events involving Jews, including some cases of anti-Semitism. Episodes such as the "Panama Canal Affair," in which Jews were involved, and anti-Semitic writings by Edouard Drumont sharpened Herzl's perception of the Jews' situation in European society.[27]

The climactic episode was the "Dreyfus Affair." Allegations that a young French-Jewish officer, Alfred Dreyfus, had spied for Germany, and the atmosphere of terror and intimidation from which French Jews suffered during the trial, shocked Herzl. His conclusion: the Jewish problem was intractable, emancipation had failed, and a new approach was urgently needed.

Herzl published his ideas in the press and in a pamphlet titled *The Jewish State*. His central thesis was that anti-Semitism was ineradicable. "All the peoples among whom the Jews dwell are, whether ashamed of it or not, anti-Semitic."[28] Anti-Semitism prevented the Jews from developing economically and in all other ways. The creation of a state for Jews where they would be masters of their fate and could develop as they wished was the only real solution. Herzl went on to outline practical methods for implementing his ideas.

His first step was to ask wealthy Jews, particularly Baron Rothschild and Baron Hirsch, for financial assistance to get the project off the ground. They refused, calling Herzl's plan unrealistic. Undaunted, Herzl opted for a new tactic: he would enlist the support of the whole Jewish people by convening a national congress. He recruited a number of supporters, including intellectuals like Max Nordau (1855–1923), merchants like David Wolffsohn (1855–1914) and eccentrics like Henry Hechler (1845–1931). Herzl envisaged a forum that would serve as a kind of Jewish parliament, through which a Jewish state could be created. Like Pinsker before him, Herzl at first attached little importance to the location of the state; it might be in Argentina ("one of the world's richest countries ")[29] or perhaps in Palestine ("the unforgettable historical homeland").[30] However, he soon realized that only the latter, the Land of Israel, could inspire the Jewish people, especially east European Jews. Herzl believed that an arrangement could be worked out whereby the Jews would grant financial aid to the Turks' shaky Ottoman Empire – which ruled in Palestine – so the Turks could defray what they owed the Great Powers and partially consolidate their other vast debts, in return for which they would grant or lease Palestine to the Jewish people.

The First Zionist Congress opened on 29 August 1897, attended by 197 delegates from around the world. At the three-day meeting, a tremendous success in the eyes of its participants,[31] Herzl won support for his program. One of the resolutions adopted by the plenary was to make the Congress the supreme institution of the "Zionist Organization," which would choose the Zionist leadership and ratify its decisions. Herzl was chosen to be President of the new body, which he would lead through an elected "Actions Committee." The Congress defined the goals of Zionism, chiefly "to create for the Jewish people a home in Palestine to be secured by public law ";[32] decided to establish the institutions of the Zionist Organization; and spelled out its operative goal: international recognition of Zionism as a first step toward the creation of a Jewish state.

During the last seven years of his life, when he served as president of the Zionist Organization, Herzl created a framework through which some of his ideas began to be implemented. The Zionist Congress, the representative body of the several thousand members of the Zionist Organization, convened on five further occasions before Herzl's death. Among the projects it ratified were the creation of the "Jewish Colonial Bank," to underwrite the movement's activity; and the "Jewish National Fund," to purchase land in Palestine. Congress delegates also deliberated the political moves Herzl undertook to actualize his plans.

The Zionist movement encountered powerful opposition: Orthodox circles feared that Zionism would further intensify the trend toward secularization among Jews (see chapter 3); and intellectuals were concerned that by its very existence the Zionist Organization would furnish proof of emancipation's failure (and demonstrate that Jews could not assimilate in European society). Nevertheless, Zionism became a central political force among the Jewish people. Herzl, though, encountered serious difficulties in the pursuit of his policy proposals. Five times he went to Constantinople to negotiate with the Turks, all to no avail. They spurned the idea of a state for Jews in Palestine, refusing to issue even a mere charter for Jewish colonization in return for financial assistance. Herzl was no more successful in trying to persuade European leaders to intercede with the Turks. The Ottomans would not part with Jerusalem under any circumstances.

To Herzl, the overriding necessity was to create a state for Jews, even if this meant forgoing Palestine. He therefore cast around for other territorial options. At first he considered Cyprus and El-Arish (in Sinai) as alternatives, but when these ideas also proved unworkable, he accepted the offer of the British Colonial Secretary, Joseph Chamberlain (1836–1914), to establish a state for Jews in east Africa, specifically in areas of Kenya and Uganda.[33]

As leader of the nascent Zionist Organization, Herzl at first persuaded many of the soundness of his programs. He was particularly successful with eastern European Jews, whose support he deemed crucial. Ideas like Herzl's, it should be emphasized, had been floated in Russia since 1881. It is also of relevance that relations between Jewish intellectuals in the east and the west were vitiated by inbuilt social and cultural tensions. Still, Herzl was able to win over Jewish leaders in the east.[34] He had scored a major success at the First Zionist Congress, and membership in the Zionist Organization increased steadily. But when it became apparent that Herzl could not implement his political program, opposition groups began to emerge. Leading Herzl's opponents were the heads of the Zionist movement in Russia. Two years earlier, they had been his most loyal supporters; now they claimed his program was untenable. After he had failed to win over the Ottomans, they argued, political recognition for Zionism was out of the question in the foreseeable future. As an alternative, they demanded a "practical" policy that would revivify the policy of *Hovevei Zion* in the 1880s and 1890s – meaning gradual settlement of Palestine. That tactic – of settling in Palestine wherever possible – would also prove politically sound in the future, they argued.

Herzl's plan to create a state for Jews outside Palestine infuriated the Russian Zionists. The dispute peaked in the Sixth Zionist Congress (23–28 August 1903) when Herzl presented his program for settlement in east Africa. The ensuing rift and looming crisis in the Zionist Organization was deferred by Herzl's untimely death on 3 July 1904, at the age of 44.

The Congress that convened two years later reinstated Palestine as the Zionist goal. Herzl's successor, David Wolffsohn, who headed the Zionist Organization from 1905 to 1911, sought to follow Herzl's "political" path.[35] But having learned the lesson of the "Uganda Affair", he held talks with Turkish officials and tried to elicit recognition for Zionism among European leaders. Wolffsohn, though, was no more successful than Herzl. The Turks were even more adamantly opposed to his proposals. Not even the revolution in Turkey (1908) that brought to power a group of ambitious young officers known as the "Young Turks", who wanted to foment a social and cultural upheaval in their country, made a difference.[36] One point on which the Young Turks agreed with their predecessors was on their attitude toward Zionism.

Wolffsohn's political failure generated greater pressure by opposition groups within the Zionist Organization for a policy of "practical" action. Their leaders were Menachem Ussishkin (1863–1941), Yehiel Chlenov (1863–1918) and Nahum Sokolow (1859–1936) from Russia, and Otto Warburg (1859–1938) from Germany. In the Wolffsohn era they stepped up their pressure – and were successful. Wolffsohn and his supporters, whether out of weakness or perhaps out of understanding and assent, acceded to the opposition's demands: the Zionist organization opened offices in Palestine, a fund for settlement activity was created, and greater donations were solicited for the Jewish National Fund. The German-born sociologist Arthur Ruppin (1876–1943), who was appointed the Zionist Organization's representative in Palestine, opened the "Palestine Office" in Jaffa. Thus began a new phase in the Zionist Organization's activity, which culminated with the appointment by the Tenth Zionist Congress (1911) of an Actions Committee (headed by Warburg) of the "practical" faction, consisting of four members, all of whom espoused "practical" Zionism.

The decade between Herzl's death and the outbreak of World War I saw an exponential growth in the activity of the Zionist Organization. The movement became a key element in Jewish life. Reports made to the five Zionist Congresses held in this period (1905, 1907, 1909, 1911, 1913) showed the movement becoming a political body recognized by the world's nations. But the most crucial development was the transition to "practical" activity. The movement's central goal now became the expansion, by every means possible, of the "New" Yishuv in Palestine.

The origins of the New Yishuv (in contradistinction to the Old Yishuv, which was concentrated in Jerusalem and a few other towns) actually lie in the early 1880s.[37] Between 1881 and 1884 five colonies (*moshavot*) were created by members of *Hovevei Zion* who came from Russia and Romania. These were: Rishon Lezion, Zichron Ya'akov, Ekron, Yesud Hama'alah and Gedera. Two colonies previously abandoned, Rosh Pina and Petah Tikva, were resettled. By 1903 there were already 28 Jewish settlements with a total population of 5,700.[38] This group of settlers was later to be known as the First *Aliyah*), to differentiate them from other waves of new immigrants who followed in the early part of the century.[39] What set the First *Aliyah* apart was motivation. Its ideology went beyond the settlement of Palestine, making it the national center of the Jewish people. They were out to effect a dramatic change in Jewish society: Jews should do productive labor, they said, and in particular they should work the land.

However, owing to the severe conditions in Palestine and the settlers' inexperience in agriculture, they were on the brink of packing up and leaving a short time after their arrival. It was Baron Edmond de Rothschild (1845–1934) who came to their aid by investing a fortune to alleviate the crisis.[40] Rothschild went further: working through agents, who supervised the work of the new farmers, he expanded the existing colonies and established several new ones. Among his innovations were the introduction of vineyards and the wine industry, as well as glass-making and silk production. In time the farmers grew dependent on the Baron's agents. One of Rothschild's conditions for helping was that he be given full and complete authority over the farmers. For this he was criticized by political figures (such as Ahad Ha'am) – and by some of the farmers. While not denying that his assistance had helped the colonies survive, they complained that his conditions stultified their desire for independence. Rothschild's supporters countered by saying that without his contribution, the entire "new" national enterprise would have disappeared.

In 1899, Rothschild decided to transfer responsibility for the colonies to Baron Hirsch's Jewish Colonization Organization. The JCO's directors in Paris agreed, on two conditions: that Rothschild go on donating funds for the colonies' upkeep, and that the JCO manage the colonies in a way that would enable the farmers to stand on their own, even if this should entail financial losses or cause some farmers to leave. Rothschild's acceptance of the conditions heralded a new era for the Yishuv.

The JCO's entry proved more beneficial than the farmers and Yishuv leaders had envisaged. Within about five years most farmers were able to exist independently, while JCO officials worked to expand existing colonies and settle others. The colonies and agricultural farms that were established by the end of 1903 formed the backbone of the new Jewish national community in the Land of Israel. In retrospect, it is clear that those settlers were the vanguard who developed a distinctive form of agriculture, began to process and market their produce locally and for export to Europe, and even laid the foundations for a national Hebraic educational system.[41]

It was not only the Jewish agricultural sector that showed impressive growth in the 1880s and 1890s. The urban Jewish sector also made great strides and was a magnet for many new immigrants. Jerusalem was the town with the largest Jewish population in the nineteenth century, and its numbers increased dramatically beginning in the 1860s. The number of Jews in Jerusalem rose from 8,000 in 1860 to 35,000 at the turn of the century.[42] In 1856, the British-Jewish philanthropist and public activist Moses Montefiore conceived the idea of building a neighborhood for Jews outside the Old City wall in order to alleviate the overcrowding in the Jewish Quarter. Montefiore raised funds for his project (known as Mishkenot Sha'ananim), which was located opposite the wall, and persuaded a few people to move in, despite poor security. As his plan involved the productivity of the Yishuv, he also built a number of workshops and a flour mill for the livelihood of the new occupants. Mishkenot Sha'ananim was followed by the Jewish neighborhoods of Mahaneh Yisrael (1866), Nahalat Shiva (1869), Beit David (1873), Meah She'arim (1874) and others. Thus was the way paved for the expansion of Jerusalem's Jewish community. The extensive areas outside the wall offered the city's Jewish residents varied sources of income. Welfare and other public institutions were founded to serve the new neighborhoods. Best of all, the housing situation in Jerusalem improved.

In Jaffa, too, the Jewish community surged forward after 1880. In the next 25 years the town's Jewish population increased five-fold, from 1,000 to 5,000.[43] Every incoming Jew passed through Jaffa, the major port in Palestine, and many of them, even if they planned to settle in the colonies of the New Yishuv or join the Old Yishuv in Jerusalem or elsewhere, found lodgings or work in the town.

Jaffa had undergone rapid economic development since the mid-1890s. The port expanded beyond recognition and the town became a key junction for travelers from and to the north, south and east of the country. A commercial center sprang up; banks, including the Jewish Colonial Trust, opened branches. An increasing number of Jewish educational institutions helped make the town a cultural center that offered new and distinctive values for the emerging society in Palestine. Expansion was such that by 1906 some of the Jewish community's leaders in Jaffa saw a need for new neighborhoods, outside the town, where overcrowding would be reduced and sanitary conditions improved.

Besides Jaffa and Jerusalem, Jewish quarters developed in other towns across Palestine, both in old settlements like Hebron and Tiberias, and in locales where few Jews had lived, like Haifa. Overall, there was a continuation of the general trend which had marked Jewish settlement in Palestine since the 1880s: great increases in numbers, a developing economic life and a changing national character.

In 1903 a new wave of Jewish immigrants began arriving in Palestine, subsequently known as the Second *Aliyah*. Although some of the newcomers resembled their predecessors socially and culturally,[44] in general they were younger and espoused different values. It was a group which produced many future leaders of the Yishuv and of Israel: David Ben-Gurion, Yitzhak Ben-Zvi (1884–1963), Yosef Sprinzak (1885–1959) and Berl Katznelson (1887–1944) are a few examples. Still, what ultimately set the Second *Aliyah* apart was its far-flung activity.

At first they settled in the veteran colonies. But they quickly found that the farmers would not hire them. Their different character, secular approach and above all their inexperience in manual labor, led the farmers to hire Arabs, who had more modest demands and far greater experience working the land. The situation produced friction between the different groups of immigrants, aggravated by cultural and social differences.[45] To the newcomers, being hired by the farmers was not only necessary to make a living, it was also part of their nationalist ideology. Its slogans were: "Jewish labor" and "the conquest of labor." A. D. Gordon (1856–1922), who helped formulate the new ideology, preached that working the land was a sacred value without which the Jewish national renaissance would be meaningless and Jewish society would not be reformed. The struggle that began over the right to a livelihood became for the Second *Aliyah* a central ideological issue.

Another slogan brandished by the new immigrants was "Jewish guard duty." To hire Bedouin or Circassian guards, they argued, however faithfully they carried out their duties, was incompatible with the nationalist principles underlying the development of an independent Jewish-national community in the Land of Israel. In 1907 they formed the "Bar Giora" organization and two years later "Hashomer" (The Guard). Members of the two groups underwent training in the use of weapons and in self-defense, and were employed as guards in the settlements.

In 1909, six newcomers settled on a tract of land called "Um Juni" on Lake Kinneret. They formed a *kvutza* (literally, group), a new form of agricultural settlement based on full cooperation among the members in work and on equal profit-sharing. Degania, as it was named, was a unique model of Jewish settlement. The national institutions, and Arthur Ruppin in particular, gave the experiment their ardent support.[46] Some of the collectivist principles that inspired Degania's founders had been formulated a few years earlier by Franz Oppenheimer (1846–1943). Another group that endeavored to apply Oppenheimer's ideas founded Kibbutz Merhavia, in the Jezreel Valley, about a year later. In time, proponents of Oppenheimer's principles refined them and became more adept at putting them into practice. The underlying principles were still upheld in the *kvutza* – or kibbutz, as it is better known – that was established in the following years. These included: complete cooperation among the settlers, in labor and in wages; maintaining tenets of socialist ideology; and disseminating the principles involved in this social-economic model in the Yishuv.[47]

Underlying all these principles was the idea of creating an autarkic economy and society in the Land of Israel. These pioneers wanted to forge a Jewish economy that would be distinct from the Arab economy – in composition of work force, essence of work and form of organization. This trend was bound up with the inevitable radicalization of relations between the Jewish minority and the Arab majority. Still, from the 1890s until the advent of the Young Turks (1908), that radicalization involved mainly local conflicts between Jewish and Arab farmers over issues like land ownership or control over marketing produce.[48] But by the early 1890s there were already signs that the conflict was assuming the proportions of a national struggle. That was the view of Arab groups in Tiberias or Haifa, and it was the thesis of Ahad Ha'am. In the first years of the new century the differences between Arabs and Jews in Palestine became more acute, but there was no real rift until 1908. On the contrary, both sides expressed optimism about the prospects for coexistence. Zionist leaders from Herzl and Nordau to Wolffsohn and Warburg were confident. Their European perspective, grounded in the period's imperialistic orientation, led them to argue that the development of the Jewish community would contribute decisively to the advancement of the local Arabs (the "natives"); hence the two peoples could coexist in Palestine without friction. However, the revolution of the Young Turks sparked Arab nationalism in the Middle East. This, fueled by a parallel political awakening on the Jewish side, accompanied by an emerging chauvinistic vocabulary, formed the foundation of a developing confrontation between Arabs and Jews. Anti-Zionist feeling ran high among the Arabs, who feared that the Zionists intended to become a majority and seize possession of the land, Arab property and the holy places. More and more Arab leaders subscribed to the viewpoint that "the revival of the Arab nation" and "the Jews' covert effort to recreate, on a large scale, the ancient Kingdom of Israel," would bring about "a relentless struggle that will end . . . when one of the nationalist movements overcomes the other."[49]

The Haifa-based paper *Falistin* urged the Ottoman authorities "to do their duty and not permit the Jewish immigrants to remain in the country."[50] In the Turkish parliament (April 1914), the Arab delegate Ra'ab al-Nashashibi called for "seizing on the methods of Romania . . . and declaring the Jews foreign nationals . . . in order to spare us the harm we can expect from the Zionists and Zionism."[51] Such passionate outbursts were not confined solely to the Arab side. The Jewish journalist Aharon Hermoni, writing in *Ha-shiloah*, exhorted the Jews to fight the Arab nationalist movement before it became too strong;[52] the socialist Jewish paper *Ha-po'el Ha-tza'ir*, published in Jaffa, remarked that the Arabs (particularly the Christian Arabs) "sow hatred [of Jews] wherever they can."[53]

The exacerbation of the conflict, then, was brought about by both Jewish and Arab elements. But certainly a major contributing factor was the increasing friction between Jews and Arabs in the big cities, particularly those experiencing rapid development, such as Haifa and Jerusalem. Jaffa and its Jewish community, we have already seen, had grown by leaps and bounds since the 1890s. The Jews who felt too cramped decided to do something about it: they founded Tel Aviv.

In 1906, a group of artisans, merchants, academics and practitioners of the liberal professions formed an association with the purpose of building a new neighborhood outside Jaffa. They hoped to raise their standard of living by improving housing conditions, sanitary facilities and community life. In 1909, on a parcel of land purchased with the aid of the Zionist Organization, some sixty members of the association began building a suburb (called Ahuzat Bayit) which soon became the town of Tel Aviv.[54] By 1914 about 2,000 people resided in 139 houses. It was not long before the development became the center of Yishuv life. At the same time, new neighborhoods sprang up in Haifa, where the Jewish community numbered 3,500 in 1914. In Jerusalem, the Jewish neighborhoods developed rapidly between 1900 and 1914, their population increasing from 29,000 to 46,000. Overall, then, at the beginning of the new century the urban Jewish sector, particularly in Jaffa, Jerusalem and Haifa, experienced dramatic growth, which was closely paralleled by developments in the Arab sector. This generated friction between Jews and Arabs and as a result separate Jewish neighborhoods were established; however, a far more serious consequence was the intensification of the Arab-Jewish national conflict.

The period of the Second *Aliyah* was a dynamic era in the Jewish community. New forms of settlement were created. Greater political awareness led to the formation of political parties (Ha-poel Ha-tza'ir – the Young Worker; Po'alei Zion – Workers of Zion) and the publication of political newspapers (*Ha-po'el Ha-tza'ir, Ha-achdut*). There was a growing sense of the need to study and speak Hebrew – motivated by the nationalist conception underlying the building of an autarkic Jewish-national community in the Land of Israel. The height of the process involved a clash over the language of instruction – Hebrew or German – at the Haifa Institute of Technology (Technion). In 1913–14, the Yishuv was rocked by a "war of the languages," which was fought in the institutions of the Zionist Organization, within the group that had founded the Technion, and throughout the country's Jewish community. Hebrew finally won the day in the Technion. More significantly, Hebrew thus came to be recognized by the national institutions and by the New Yishuv as the Jewish national language. It was a period of domestic social tensions as well between different groups within the Yishuv. This was especially marked between the farmers of the First *Aliyah* and the Second *Aliyah*; and, at different levels, between the farmers and immigrants from Yemen who arrived by the thousands in the years between 1909 and 1912 (augmenting groups who had come in the 1880s);[55] and between the Ashkenazi urban community – the Old Yishuv – and the very different types who constituted the New Yishuv.[56]

World War I brought the Yishuv's development to a halt.[57] In some cases Jews who were foreign nationals were suspected by the Ottoman authorities of collaborating with the enemy and of disloyalty. Some 30,000 Jews (out of 85,000) were exiled or left the country voluntarily. Severe economic dislocations resulted, partly because a large proportion of the harvest was earmarked for the Turkish troops stationed in Palestine, and partly due to the fact that locust swarms had devastated crops. Some of the Jewish population, dismayed at the Turks' negative attitude toward the Yishuv, supported the Allied forces in the hope that they would expel the Ottomans from Palestine. In the villages of Zichron Ya'akov and Binyamina an anti-Turkish underground called "Nili" was formed whose members, led by Aharon Aharonson (1876–1914), engaged in espionage against Turkey's ally, Germany.[58] Although the group failed in its mission – providing hardly any information to the British in the few months before it was discovered and liquidated – its very existence was symptomatic of the passionate anti-Turkish feeling in sections of the Yishuv.

The leaders of the Zionist Organization, who were based in Berlin when the war broke out, declared their neutrality – a position virtually dictated by the fact that Jews were fighting on both sides. To underscore its stance, the Zionist Organization set up a liaison bureau in neutral Copenhagen, headed by Leo Motzkin (1867–1933). In Britain, however, Zionists identified openly with the Allies. The movement's leaders there, most prominently Chaim Weizmann (1874–1952), declared their support for Britain. Weizmann himself, a scientist at the University of Manchester, was co-opted to the British war effort. He and his close associates, including Nahum Sokolow, Yehiel Chlenov and Ahad Ha'am, maintained throughout the war that a pro-British policy was consistent with long-term Zionist interests. The British, they believed, were bent on capturing Turkish territories in the Middle East so that they could more effectively control the strategic crossroads of the Suez Canal and the region's oil reserves. From the very start of the fighting, Weizmann and his Zionist colleagues argued that Zionism's best hope lay in the British conquest of the Middle East.[59] During the war's first three years, the Weizmann group relentlessly pressed the British leadership to recognize Zionism. British interests, they said, corresponded with Zionist interests, and the Zionist movement was destined to become a pro-British bastion in the Middle East.

Following the appointment of Lloyd George (1863–1945) as prime minister in December 1916, and Arthur James Balfour (1848–1930) as foreign secretary, there was increasing support within the British cabinet to recognize the Zionist movement. Some of the ministers favored the creation of a Jewish state for religious reasons, but more generally it was thought that Zionism's goals would serve British regional interests. In fact, an immediate consideration was that support for Zionism would further the British war effort. British leaders hoped that their backing for Zionism would induce prominent American Jews to urge Congress and the Administration to recommend U.S. material and military aid for Britain in its war with Germany.

On 2 November 1917, the British cabinet recognized the right of the Zionist movement to establish a "national home for the Jewish people" in Palestine. Still, the "Balfour Declaration" did not fully meet the demands of the Zionist movement, particularly as regards the creation of a national home in all of Palestine. That, the British knew, was wholly unacceptable to the Arabs. Indeed, two years earlier, on 24 October 1915, the British High Commissioner in Egypt had promised that Britain would ultimately recognize the Arabs' independence in the Middle East and support the creation of a confederation of Arab states.[60] In any event, the Balfour Declaration was a decisive turning point in the history of Zionism. Herzl's aspiration was realized: Zionism had been granted political recognition by the world's greatest power.

In the spring of 1917, British forces invaded Palestine under the command of General Edmund Allenby (1861–1936). By the end of the year Jerusalem and Jaffa were in British hands and the country was under martial rule. Three years later, the Jewish statesman Herbert Samuel (1870–1963) was appointed British High Commissioner in Palestine. Samuel's authority derived from the British occupation; formally, however, he was appointed by decision of the Supreme Council of the Allied Powers which met at San Remo (25 April 1920), to give Britain the Mandate for Palestine in the spirit of the Balfour Declaration. In 1922, the Mandate was endorsed by the League of Nations. The Zionists viewed the Lloyd George government's appointment of a senior figure like Samuel as part of British policy intended to realize the Balfour Declaration.[61] The fact that the League of Nations recognized the British pledge to Zionism filled the movement – headed by Weizmann since July 1920 – with hope for the future.

The British conquest of Palestine launched a new chapter in the annals of the Yishuv. At the end of the war, the Jewish population stood at about 55,000, as compared with some 680,000 Arabs. Five years later there were 92,000 Jews, and by the end of the 1930s their number had risen to 449,000. This period witnessed three more waves of immigration: the Third *Aliyah* (1918–1922), the Fourth (1924–26) and the Fifth (1933–38).[62]

Of the 35,000 Jews who comprised the Third *Aliyah*, nearly all of them from Russia and Poland, more than 60 percent settled in Tel Aviv, Jerusalem and Haifa. The majority belonged to the middle class or below and earned their living as artisans or from commerce and business.[63] Nevertheless, the image of this group of immigrants, in both contemporary and later eyes, was, like that of its predecessor, forged by those of its members who joined agricultural settlements. Having, in part, belonged to pioneer movements back home, particularly to *He-halutz* ("The Pioneer"), they now sought to implement their ideology, which revolved around the building of an egalitarian, socialist-Zionist society in the Land of Israel.[64] Naturally, they identified with the values of the Labor movement.[65]

Tel Aviv's economic potential made it a magnet for new immigrants. Within four years (1920–23), the city's population increased ten-fold, from 2,000 to 20,000. The main sources of livelihood were in commerce, crafts and industry, especially the construction industry and its branches, which employed many of the new arrivals. The city grew quickly. The employment potential of the developing neighborhoods in Jerusalem and Haifa also attracted newcomers, though not on the scale of Tel Aviv.

Yet even this rapid urban growth was insufficient to supply the employment demands of the Third *Aliyah*. As a result, about a year after the start of the immigration influx, unemployment began to rise and grew steadily as more immigrants continued to arrive. The British administration stepped in to help. To the British, the immediate development of Palestine, particularly the extension of its road network and the expansion of Haifa port, was a paramount strategic necessity for their forces in the Middle East. This, together with Herbert Samuel's desire to assist the Yishuv, led the Mandate authorities to initiate public works on a large scale. Thousands of job seekers, nearly all of them recent arrivals, were employed by the British in building roads, laying railway lines and in the construction of public structures for the government. Others found work in subsidiary construction industries such as stone quarries and in the deepening and expansion of the port at Haifa.

The majority of those employed in relief work were young immigrants who, in Poland and Russia, had organized in socialist-oriented groups and now endeavored to preserve their ideological principles. In their eyes, relief work, especially road construction, was not only a livelihood per se, but part of an ideological approach that was bound up with building the Land of Israel, with creating a Jewish State that would be an egalitarian entity on the Soviet model.

The most prominent of the relief-work groups – it would come to symbolize the entire Third *Aliyah* – was the "Labor Battalion."[66] Its six hundred members, influenced by the Communist revolution in the Soviet Union, declared that they had abandoned Soviet Communism because of their belief in Zionism, but still upheld its ideals and especially its revolutionary principles. They aspired to transplant those values to their new land. Their self-perceived mission was to build an ideal society in the Land of Israel, which would take the form of a "general commune" of "Hebrew workers." Inevitably, there was a vast disparity between the Labor Battalion's theory and its practice. During their first two years in the country, when they did relief work – road building and some farming – they still thought they could realize their dreams in the future. But it was not long before they grasped that the situation in Palestine made this impracticable. The Labor Battalion disbanded in 1927 and a few of its members returned to the Soviet Union, believing that only there could their utopian ideas be translated into reality. But the group's melancholy end, which was aggravated by bitter personal and ideological disputes, did not erase the image of its initial success; indeed, it was held up by some of those who stayed and by the land-settlement movement as a positive symbol of the whole Third *Aliyah*.

The wave of immigration in the aftermath of World War I, combined with the return of some of the war deportees, threw the Palestinian Arabs (who even before the war had begun to fear that the Zionists were indeed going to fulfill their goals) into a state of depression. To the Arabs, the influx of immigrants was a confirmation of the seriousness of the Zionists' intentions, and more so of the British, concerning the Balfour Declaration. For a brief period in late 1918, the Arabs thought that the establishment by Britain of a semi-autonomous administration in Damascus, with French consent, would scuttle the Balfour Declaration. The resurgence of Jewish immigration rekindled their original fears. The anti-British demonstrations that erupted in Jerusalem from February to April 1920 and swept Palestine, culminating in bloody anti-Jewish riots, were a symptom of the Arabs' apprehensions and proof of their hostility toward the Zionists. Moreover, in July 1920, Feisal's regime in Damascus collapsed. Until then, the leaders of the Arab community in Palestine saw themselves as citizens of the southern section of "Greater Syria." But when the semi-autonomous Arab regime in Damascus was replaced by a French Mandatory administration, and when, in Palestine, now under civilian British rule, a senior British-Jewish politician was given the task of implementing the Balfour Declaration, the feelings of Arab nationalists, who considered Palestine their exclusive territorial prerogative, were radicalized. The struggle against Zionism now became the heart of the Palestinian Arab national experience.

A conference of the Palestinian leadership which convened in Haifa in late 1920 demanded a stop to Jewish immigration and the formation of an Arab national government. A representative body, the Arab Executive, was elected, to be headed by Mussa Kazim Pasha al-Husseini. Six months later, on 1 May 1921, anti-Zionist demonstrations were held which developed into a series of raids and lethal attacks on Jews throughout Palestine. Forty-seven Jews were killed and hundreds wounded. With this, the Palestinians effectively declared a violent and uncompromising struggle against Zionism. Symbolizing this, from May the campaign was led by the new Mufti of Jerusalem, Hajj Amin al-Husseini (1895–1974), whose fanatical anti-Zionism was well known.

The British response to the rising tension between Arabs and Jews was complex. Samuel did not disavow the mandate he had received from his government: to implement the Balfour Declaration. He sought ways to assist the Jewish community and to create mechanisms for that purpose. At the same time, he looked after the Arab community and insisted that he was being impartial. Indeed, to the Jewish leadership it sometimes seemed that Samuel was going out of his way to placate the Arabs. The Yishuv was outraged by his appointment of Hajj Amin al-Husseini as Mufti of Jerusalem and head of the Muslim Higher Council (January 1922). The British thus placed far-reaching powers[67] in the hands of one who claimed that the Islamic holy places in the country were in jeopardy because of Zionism. Husseini became the all-powerful authority in everything having to do with Muslim religious affairs in Palestine.[68] Furthermore, to demonstrate to the Arabs that there was no intention of uprooting or dispossessing them, Samuel underscored a number of pro-Arab elements in the White Paper that was issued (3 June 1922) by the British Colonial Office under Winston Churchill (1874–1965). In particular, it was stressed that the intention of the Balfour Declaration was not that the whole of Palestine should become a Jewish "national home," but only parts of it. This, together with the pronouncement that the declaration was not subject to change and that it did not apply to the areas of Palestine east of the Jordan River.

British policy drew a mixed reaction from the heads of the Zionist Organization and the Yishuv leadership. To a moderate like Chaim Weizmann, it was clear that Samuel was not trying to revoke the pledge given in the Balfour Declaration, but was taking a clear-eyed view of the situation in Palestine and giving consideration to the Arab side. Others, however, like Jabotinsky and Ussishkin, saw in Britain's moves a pro-Arab tilt, aimed at weakening its commitment to the Zionists. The arrest of Jabotinsky by the British following the bloody riots in the summer of 1921 (he was sentenced to fifteen years in prison but released after three months) proved to the activist wing of Zionism that British policy had changed for the worse.

A figure whose judicious voice was increasingly heeded, beginning in the 1920s – he leaned more toward Weizmann than toward the activist wing of Zionism, though he often expressed extreme opinions – was David Ben-Gurion. Beyond his magnetic personality, there is no doubt that his political success was intimately bound up with the growing importance of the Labor movement, the paramount political force in the country in the aftermath of the Third *Aliyah*. Already in the voting held in April 1920 for the first Elected Assembly, which represented the Yishuv *vis-à-vis* the British, the two major workers' parties garnered 35 percent of the votes, to become the largest bloc. The labor movements flexed their muscles by establishing the Histadrut, the General Federation of Labor for Jewish Workers. The most prominent political body in the Yishuv during the 1920s, the Histadrut was founded by 87 delegates, representing 4,433 workers, at a meeting in Haifa (5 December 1920).[69] Ben-Gurion, who served as the organization's general secretary for 15 years, thus controlled the body that aspired to represent all workers in Palestine. His position enabled him and the workers' party to seize the Zionist leadership and facilitated the Labor movement's takeover of the Zionist institutions in the 1930s.

Proof of the Histadrut's political strength and centrality within the Yishuv was furnished a few years after its founding, when a severe recession struck the Jewish community in Palestine, resulting from the changes caused by the immigrants of the Fourth *Aliyah*. There were some 60,000 new arrivals, the vast majority from Poland. In contrast to the preceding wave, and despite the fact that their numbers were unprecedented since the start of modern Jewish immigration, their social structure was more homogeneous. Most belonged to the middle and lower classes. They had left Poland to escape the harsh economic situation there. The middle class had been hardest hit by reforms introduced by the Polish Finance Minister, Ładisław Grabski, in 1923–24. As in the past, many middle-class Jews set their sights on America. However, as the Americans had imposed severe immigration restrictions since mid-1924, the Jewish victims of Grabski's reforms could turn only to Palestine.[70]

The first two years of the Fourth *Aliyah* had been accompanied by a tremendous economic boom, generated by the new arrivals' capital together with private and institutional investments. The new prosperity was most in evidence in the Tel Aviv area. In an eighteen-month period beginning in mid-1924, the city's population nearly doubled, from 21,500 to 40,000. Residential neighborhoods appeared and businesses, as well as small plants and a few industrial enterprises, were opened. Haifa, Jerusalem and other areas also benefited from the boom. The Histadrut joined in by establishing factories and other enterprises, soon becoming the largest single employer in the Jewish economic sector. The Zionist institutions, with the encouragement of outside elements, also contributed to the development momentum. The new town of Afula in the Jezreel Valley was envisioned as the Jewish center in the north. Private rural settlement expanded as a series of new *moshavot* were built, and cooperative settlement connected with the Labor movement increased exponentially. Everywhere in the Yishuv, the economic good times left their mark; Zionism seemed to have embarked on a new path.

But the boom quickly faded. By the end of 1925, an economic slowdown was felt. Two years later, the worst economic and social depression in memory set in. Capital imports ceased and investments ground to a halt. Tens of thousands went bankrupt. A third of the working force was unemployed. Laborers, particularly in the construction industry, faced prolonged layoffs. For artisans and capital-intensive organizations, the outlook was bleak. Worst of all for the Zionist movement, more than 15,000 veteran immigrants left the country in a two-year period (1927–28). The Histadrut sought to remedy the situation by whatever means it could. It created organizational tools such as labor bureaux and set up bodies that provided social and economic aid to help both the employed and the unemployed weather the economic crisis.[71] In so doing, the Histadrut paved the way for the workers' parties to achieve political hegemony in the Yishuv. The depression gradually began to lift in 1928 and the economy revived. This turn of events is well symbolized by the development projects undertaken at two of the country's major enterprises, the Dead Sea Works, where phosphates were produced, and the Naharayim power plant.

In August 1929, Palestine was jolted by a wave of unrest.[72] Arab gangs attacked Jews and Jewish property in Jerusalem, Jaffa, Tel Aviv, Haifa, Safed, and in many farming settlements. One hundred and thirty-three Jews were killed, about 440 were wounded, and more than 7,500 were uprooted. The worst incident occurred in Hebron, where about 60 Jews were massacred, dozens were wounded and the rest of the town's Jewish Quarter fled.[73] Shocked and outraged, the Yishuv took stock: the intensity and scale of the unrest showed that the Jewish-Arab conflict in Palestine had undergone a serious change. The shock was all the greater because in the immediately preceding years, the Arabs seemed to have accepted the existence of the Zionist Yishuv. Since 1921, when incidents broke out at the Western Wall, with Arabs accusing Jews of attempting to seize the mosques on the Temple Mount, Jewish relations with the Arab majority had been by and large peaceful. But in the early 1930s, it was obvious that those relations were a thing of the past.

That prognosis was borne out during the next decade. The height of the unrest came in the second half of the 1930s. We have already seen (chapter 1) that a central reason for the conflict's exacerbation was the tremendous increase in the Jewish population. In the 1930s, the Jewish economic sector grew dramatically. Jewish industrial output and domestic product more than tripled, the former increasing from 2.8 million Palestine pounds in 1930 to about 9 million in 1939, the latter from 1.2 million Palestine pounds to more than 4 million in the same period. In stark contrast, Arab economic indicators suggested only minor gains during the decade: industrial output went from 2.3 to 3.4 million Palestine pounds, and domestic product from 883,000 Palestine pounds to 1.4 million.[74] The huge surge in the Jewish economic sector, combined with negative Arab immigration and a rapidly increasing Jewish population, brought about a radicalization in the stand of the Palestinian Arab leadership.[75] Zionism was perceived as a growing threat which would ultimately cause the Arabs' dispossession. The Arab struggle reached new levels of violence.

The Arabs fought Zionism in two spheres. In the military struggle, armed gangs had been attacking Jews since the summer of 1929. The raids intensified during the 1930s, as the Arabs' discontent grew.[76] In the political sphere, the Palestinians tried to persuade regional Arab leaders to pressure Britain into terminating both Jewish immigration to Palestine and land purchases in the country by Zionist institutions.

Incipient signs that Arab pressure was bearing fruit were seen by the early 1930s. The British government, led by the Labor Party's Ramsay Macdonald (1866–1937), was less committed than its predecessor to the Balfour Declaration. In October 1930, the colonial secretary, Lord Passfield (1859–1947), issued a White Paper stating that there was insufficient land for more Jewish settlement in Palestine. Consequently, Jewish immigration must be halted. London's disavowal of pledges previously given the Jews was unfavorably received by British public opinion, and Macdonald was finally obliged to issue a "Letter" modifying the White Paper. Nevertheless, the British moves were a clear signal to both sides in the Middle East that the policy adopted in 1917, which the first High Commissioner had been requested to implement, was no longer in effect.[77]

The British responded sharply to the bloody clashes that erupted in 1936 and the general strike by the Arab population. With large troop reinforcements at their disposal, British commanders forcibly suppressed Arab disturbances. Palestinian leaders and members of Arab gangs were arrested. At the same time, Arab military and political pressure had its effect on British policy. From 1936, the Foreign Office maintained that the Palestine question should be considered within the context of overall British policy in the Middle East, as every development in Palestine affected Britain's regional status and its interests in the other Arab states.[78] In its initial phase, the new policy was seen by British government as the British search for a compromise that would reduce Jewish-Arab friction, but which would come at the expense of the "national home" promised the Jews. In short, to ensure its long-term rule in Palestine, Britain resorted to a more balanced policy that took into account the interests of the adversaries, tried to play them off against each other, and above all looked after the promotion of its own interests, which were based on upholding its imperial status in Palestine.[79]

As for the compromise, a commission headed by Lord Peel proposed partitioning western Palestine into a Jewish state, an Arab state and a British district. The idea was shelved after being rejected by the Arabs,[80] but again, it was proof of a new British line of thought. In the late 1930s a new factor entered the picture, which radicalized British policy further in the same direction – the rise of Hitler and the Nazi Party in Germany. Germany's growing might, its ambition to succeed Britain in the Middle East, combined with its aggressive anti-Semitism, were the major factors that caused British policy to become more extreme.[81] The fact that the senior Palestinian leader, Hajj Amin al-Husseini, expressed ardent support for the Nazis, and that the Arab leadership in Palestine pinned its hopes on German help against Zionism,[82] meant that London came under more pressure to take an unequivocally pro-Arab stand. Thus, on 17 May 1939, a new White Paper on Britain's future Palestine policy showed a pronounced retreat from the promise made to the Zionists two decades before. The White Paper called for the establishment in western Palestine of an independent Palestinian state with an Arab majority within ten years. Jewish immigration on a very limited scale would be permitted only in the first five years, to ensure the preservation of the existing demographic ratio (a 30 percent Jewish population), while land purchases by Jews would be completely halted.[83]

The Zionist Organization reacted furiously to the White Paper.[84] It seemed a mortal blow. Twenty-two years earlier, Chaim Weizmann and his associates had been certain that the day was not far when the dreams of *Hovevei Zion* and Herzl would be realized. Now those hopes were dashed. Worse, the setback from England came in the shadow of the anti-Semitic menace from Germany. To Ben-Gurion, Weizmann and other Zionist leaders, the Nazi actions and British decrees showed that Zionism was poised on the edge of an abyss.

In the early 1920s, Weizmann had foreseen Zionism's triumph. At the Zionist Conference that convened in London in July 1920, he had been able to convince his colleagues that their national goals were realistic. So optimistic was he, that he thought "political" Zionism had already done its work and that the time was at hand for a different form of Zionism, wholly directed toward implementing the movement's goals in Palestine. Few in the Zionist leadership threw cold water on Weizmann's euphoria. One who did was the American Zionist leader Louis Brandeis (1856–1941). In contrast to Weizmann, who thought that Zionism's principal goal at that stage should be to raise capital by means of national funds (such as Keren Hayesod), a notion deriving from his certainty that world Jewry would contribute willingly, Brandeis preferred a policy of decentralization. Less sanguine than Weizmann about the possibilities available to the Zionists, he wanted to strengthen the individual Zionist federations. Each such federation, and particularly the American branch, would raise Jewish (including non-Zionist) capital and invest it in the Zionist enterprise to further goals it deemed important. What the times called for, Brandeis believed, was not a great leap forward, but small, measured steps.[85]

In the ideological contest between Weizmann and Brandeis, which turned into political and personal rivalry, Weizmann emerged the victor. But beyond personality clashes, Weizmann's accomplishment reflected the optimistic mood that prevailed among Zionists in the aftermath of the Balfour Declaration. To Weizmann and his supporters, the portents were clear: the British conquest of Palestine, Herbert Samuel's appointment as High Commissioner and Britain's pledge to realize the Zionist vision. A Jewish state would soon become a reality.

That optimism faded during the 1920s. Weizmann's impassioned call to all Jews to fulfill the resolutions of the Zionist Organization went unanswered. More than in any other period, the Jews in their various dispersions identified with their host societies. Jewish autonomy in the diaspora seemed far more credible than Zionism (see chapter 2). Understanding this, Weizmann wanted to change the face of the Zionist Organization. He had reached Brandeis's conclusions the hard way. But his proposals had a different thrust. Following a stubborn, seven-year battle (1923–29) that Weizmann waged against personalities from across the Zionist political spectrum, from the Revisionist leader Ze'ev Jabotinsky to figures like Ussishkin, it was decided to create a joint body comprising the Zionist Organization and non-Zionist Jewish groups, and known since as the "Jewish Agency." Weizmann's hope was that extra-Zionist forces could help him reach his goal. The Jewish Agency was officially founded at a festive ceremony in Zurich on 11 August 1929. Weizmann was elected its first president.[86] But it was clear that a sharp turn was needed on the road along which Weizmann had led the Zionists during the 1920s. New forces were needed from outside the movement, but primarily from inside, who would assay new paths toward the Zionist goal.

Many saw in the creation of the Jewish Agency a hopeful sign. The leadership viewed the new influx of immigrants (the Fifth *Aliyah*, which of course was totally unrelated to organizational changes in the Zionist movement) and their relative success in reinvigorating the Zionist enterprise[87] as the vindication of the structural changes. In the first half of the 1930s, the Jewish economic sector in Palestine recovered strongly. The Yishuv, as we saw, developed dramatically. There was a regression, even a recession, in the decade's second half, but the expansion momentum was unaffected.[88] The Jewish population increased sharply between 1930 and 1939. Land purchased by the national bodies was settled by new immigrants: the number of Jewish settlements grew from one hundred at the start of the 1930s to one hundred and sixty in 1935, and to more than two hundred in 1934.[89] The economic revival was felt most powerfully in towns with Jewish populations, notably Tel Aviv. In the mid-1930s, Tel Aviv had more than 140,000 inhabitants, and 177,000 by 1939 – up from only 45,000 at the beginning of the decade.

In the first part of the 1930s, the economic boom was manifested in the expansion of large and small industry and in a huge growth in the services sector. Industrial output and GNP increased by dozens of percent every year. The construction boom continued unabated. The proportion of the Jewish sector in the construction industry rose from 60 percent in 1930 to 80 percent at the decade's end. The feverish activity in the credit market that developed in the early 1930s led to the establishment of some fifty new banks, the majority of which were small enterprises, within five years. The British administration also contributed its share to the intensive development. A large percentage of the taxes it collected was recycled into investment projects. The trains, along with the postal, telegraph and telephone services, were expanded, new roads were built and the Haifa port was developed.[90] Cultural and educational institutions blossomed.

These social and economic changes reverberated in the political arena. As we saw, in the 1920s the strength of the parties that comprised the Labor movement grew enormously. This was most strikingly expressed in the Histadrut's political ascendancy under Ben-Gurion's leadership. The next step was the conquest by the Histadrut of the Zionist Organization. In early 1931, the two central parties in the left-wing bloc united: Achdut Ha'avoda and Po'alei Zion now became Mapai (acronym for Land of Israel Workers' Party).[91] The new party proved itself the strongest political force in the Yishuv, receiving 42 percent of the votes cast for the Elected Assembly in January 1931.

Mapai's chief rival, then and in the years to come, was the Revisionist party founded by Ze'ev Jabotinsky. In the 1931 poll, the Revisionists, with 20 percent of the votes, became the second-largest party. Right through the 1920s, the Revisionists were in opposition to the Zionist leadership under Weizmann. The latter, with the support of the workers' parties, was able to parry Jabotinsky's biting criticism on the creation of the Jewish Agency, settlement issues, the attitude toward the Arabs, and the growth rate of the Yishuv. In the 1930s, when Weizmann's political decline began, the Revisionists became the adversaries of Mapai. Their contest was for hegemony in the Yishuv and in the Zionist Organization.[92]

The differences between them were seen at two levels. In terms of social class, the Revisionists considered themselves the representatives of the bourgeoisie and capitalism; their ambition was to create a Zionist society in the Land of Israel based on those principles. The Labor movement, in contrast, advocated the formation of a moderate socialist society in which the means of production and the ownership of land would be nationalized. A second level of dispute concerned the best tactic for establishing a Jewish state. Ben-Gurion and his colleagues wanted a Jewish political entity in which Jews would constitute the majority, whereas Jabotinsky urged the immediate creation of a Jewish state on both sides of the Jordan River – a state in which Jews would be in the majority.[93]

The political rivalry between the two movements over control of the Yishuv and Zionist movement institutions became more extreme with time. In the summer of 1933, the dispute grew heated as the Zionist Organization geared up for an election that would determine control of the movement in the post-Weizmann era. On 16 June 1933, the rivalry reached a climax with the murder of Dr. Chaim Arlosoroff (1899–1933), one of Mapai's most oustanding and brilliant young leaders. The Labor movement claimed the murder was politically motivated and pointed an accusing finger at the Revisionists. Jabotinsky and his supporters in Palestine denied the charge outright, branding it a blood libel. The radicalization showed itself in a spurt of violence, both physical and verbal, between the political adversaries. Afterwards, a semblance of calm returned, particularly after the clear-cut results of the elections for the Zionist Congress, with Mapai doubling its strength to 42 percent, twice what the Revisionists received. The new leadership of the Zionist movement included three senior Mapai figures in prominent positions: Ben-Gurion, Moshe Shertok (1894–1965) and Eliezer Kaplan.

Within a few weeks of the outcome of these elections, then, tempers began to cool. The two great rivals, Ben-Gurion and Jabotinsky, reached an agreement designed to end the contretemps between their movements and preserve a fair political-functional division of power between them in the Zionist Organization. In retrospect, that agreement seems no more than a momentary attempt to create a status quo. Ultimately, Mapai, headed by Ben-Gurion, acquired hegemony over the national institutions.[94] The Revisionists seceded from the Zionist Organization and for a long time were virtually powerless.

From 1936, the Yishuv had other matters on its mind. The Arab general strike and uprising left their imprint in the political arena. The paramount question was how to react to the Arab provocations. The majority, led by Ben-Gurion, favored restraint, in order to demonstrate the Yishuv's self-confidence and maturity. But a minority wanted to retaliate in kind against the Arab gangs.[95] Another question was how to treat the various British proposals for resolving the Jewish-Arab dispute. Should the Yishuv accept the Peel Commission's recommendation to partition Palestine, as Ben-Gurion wanted? Should it accept the British suggestion for a Jewish-Arab dialogue? In any event, the White Paper and the outbreak of World War II brought an end to this chapter in the disputes within the Yishuv and between the Yishuv and the British and Arabs.

Beginning in late 1941, the Zionist Executive began hearing rumors about the horrendous tragedy that was devastating European Jewry.[96] In consequence, and because Britain continued to espouse its White Paper policy – even though its leader, Winston Churchill, was known as a fervent supporter of Zionism[97] and considered the document the "violation of a solemn commitment"[98] – the Zionist leadership adopted a firm and uncompromising line with respect to the future of the Zionist ideal. If, until then, some of the Zionist leaders had still believed it was necessary to compromise over western Palestine and agree to slow and gradual immigration, the views now tended toward revolutionary activism. The tone was set by Ben-Gurion, who wanted to create a state and bring in two million Jews right after the war. Weizmann, however, adhered to his traditional outlook, arguing that it was best to continue with the gradual but continuous immigration of about one hundred thousand Jews each year. These differences would later be regarded as symptomatic of two distinct policies, originating in polar disagreements between the two statesmen.[99] Naturally, as time passed, Ben-Gurion in the main wanted to distance himself from Weizmann's ideas. But in historical perspective it is clear that the differences were more of tone and rhetoric than of substance. Ben-Gurion viewed the British as an enemy to be fought so that a Jewish state could be created. At the same time, he fully supported the British campaign against Germany and the Axis. Weizmann, on the other hand, still saw Britain as an ally capable of helping the Jews, as it had before. But Weizmann was sharply critical of British policy as expressed in the White Paper. To Ben-Gurion, Weizmann's approach represented a "Zionism of talk"; whereas he sided with a "fighting Zionism" in which all means were justified to achieve the end. Weizmann indeed sought a different route than Ben-Gurion's, but their goals were similar and the differences between them were more political in character – Ben-Gurion's aspiration to total leadership (without Weizmann) in the Zionist Organization.

Ben-Gurion's militancy was reflected in the resolutions adopted in May 1942 at a congress of American Zionists held at the Biltmore Hotel in New York. In attendance were the leaders of the movement in the United States, most prominently Abba Hillel Silver (1893–1963), and senior members of the Zionist Executive, including Ben-Gurion and Weizmann. The latter claimed, with much justification, that the Biltmore resolutions echoed firm views he had expressed five years earlier.[100] But there is no doubt that the spirit of the resolutions, and in particular their formulation, were influenced by the extreme views espoused by Ben-Gurion at the time. Among them: to give Britain an ultimatum to open the gates of Palestine to mass Jewish immigration; making the Jewish Agency responsible for supervising immigration and vesting it with the authority to develop the Land of Israel; and creating in western Palestine a Jewish "commonwealth" that would fit into the Arab world.

The "Biltmore Plan," formally adopted by the Zionist Executive in November 1942, is considered a watershed in the history of the Zionist movement.[101] Not only because of its demand for the immediate establishment of a Jewish state in western Palestine and other clauses, but equally because Ben-Gurion and the Zionist leadership proceeded to launch a vigorous drive to win the support of Jewish and general public opinion in the United States. In place of the dominant British political orientation, whose architect was Weizmann, the Ben-Gurion wing allied itself with the American Zionist leadership and placed their reliance on the U.S. Administration, whom they believed, with some perspicacity, was the only power that could help implement the Biltmore Plan.[102]

Ironically, this turn of events coincided with desperate efforts by the British to safeguard the Middle East against German aggression. In stark contrast to the dark night of European Jewry, the Yishuv in Palestine had enjoyed unprecedented prosperity since 1941 – all thanks to the British. To meet their war needs, the British placed large orders with Yishuv factories. As a result, net domestic product in the Jewish economic sector more than tripled in the war's first years and had quintuplicated by its end: from 20.6 million Palestine pounds in 1940 to 110 million in 1946.[103] Moreover, hundreds of thousands of Jews volunteered to fight alongside the British against the Germans. Thus, precisely during the war years, just when Ben-Gurion wanted to effect a dramatic change in Zionist policy, it seemed as if the Yishuv's identification with Britain had never been greater and that the Mandate authorities, under the duress of the new circumstances, had never assisted the Yishuv's development so intensively. Yet the White Paper policy remained in effect: Jewish immigration and land purchases were prohibited. That policy was strikingly manifested by the expulsion of the immigrant ship *Patria* after two hundred of the refugees on board had perished when the ship was scuttled (25 November 1940) by the Haganah Jewish Defense Force; and by the sinking of the immigrant ship *Struma*, with seven hundred "illegals" aboard, on the Black Sea, after it had been turned away from Palestine.[104] Support in the Yishuv for Britain was accompanied by intimations – which London did nothing to dispel – that British policy would change after the war in light of the new situation in Europe, and that the White Paper might be modified.[105]

At first, the British Army did not want to take Jewish volunteers. In the first year, few were mobilized, though large numbers volunteered. However, that policy soon changed. Jews were inducted first to reinforce service units and later into combat units, notably the specially created Jewish Brigade.[106] By inducting Jews, the British, even if inadvertently, significantly strengthened the Haganah. When it was established in the early 1920s, the Haganah was part of the Histadrut. From the outset, Haganah commander Eliahu Golomb (1893–1945) and its other leaders believed the organization's mission was to help defend the Yishuv. Nevertheless, they held Britain exclusively responsible for the civil security of the Jewish settlements. Following the 1929 disturbances, a new perception of the Haganah's role evolved. The Yishuv leadership continued to hold Britain responsible for the safety of the population, but the impotence of the authorities led to a decision to expand the Haganah's functions so that, if necessary, it could take the place of the British in defending against Arab aggression. In the summer of 1931 a national command was formed, the first step in the Haganah's reorganization.

Fundamentally, the Haganah was an underground force which initially operated under the aegis of Histadrut bodies and from 1931 was accountable to various bodies among the Zionist national institutions. Its leadership was under the influence of the workers' parties. The result was that from the early 1930s, Haganah members were engaged in political disputes as to the tactics to be adopted in defending – and fighting – against the Arabs ("*haganah*" is Hebrew for "defense"). In April 1931, the disagreements brought about a split in the Haganah, ultimately leading to the creation of a rival underground force – the National Military Organization ("Etzel" in the Hebrew acronym). In 1941, the Haganah underwent another organizational upheaval.[107] Fear of a possible German invasion and a desire for cooperation with the British at any price induced the Haganah to increase its ranks and build up its matériel. From its beginnings as an underground force, the Haganah grew to a military body whose existence could no longer be concealed. In the early 1930s, the Haganah had a few hundred members, and a few thousand by the end of that decade – but by 1942 it numbered thirty thousand, of whom some 70 percent carried weapons. Two years later, the Haganah numbered thirty-seven thousand members, equipped with weapons and combat matériel.[108] From the summer of 1942, when reports began to appear about the tragedy of European Jewry, the Haganah high command extended the organization's goals: in addition to defending Jewish settlements from Arab marauders and defending the Yishuv against a possible German invasion, the Haganah committed itself to building a force that, in due time, would help bring the Jewish State into being. Here is another explanation for the Haganah's cooperation with the British in the fight against the common German enemy. The Haganah leadership took heart at the formation of independent Jewish units within the framework of the British forces. This was considered crucial to building a defense force that would one day have to cope with attacks by Palestine Arabs and by Arab states. Haganah policy toward the British was thus ambivalent. On the one hand, the Haganah considered itself the partner of the British in the campaign against the Germans, but at the same time it viewed them as a potential enemy whom they might one day have to fight.

Etzel leaders, who had bolted from the Haganah in the 1930s owing to political and tactical disagreements, generally assented to its policy in the war's first years as dictated by the dual attitude toward Britain. Indeed, Etzel commander David Raziel (1910–41) was killed while on a British intelligence mission in Iraq. But the Etzel policy toward Britain split Etzel. In July 1940, a few of its members resigned and formed another underground group, known as "Lehi" (an acronym for Israel Freedom Fighters), headed by Avraham Stern ("Yair," 1907–42).[109] The Stern group struck at the British relentlessly, not letting up even when Britain stood alone against Nazi Germany. Britain, in Lehi's view, was the enemy which was preventing the creation of a Jewish State and thereby increasing Jewish suffering in Europe. Lehi's terror tactics forced the authorities to crack down, resulting in Stern's murder by the British (February 1942) and the incarceration of about one hundred and fifty of his comrades.

The end of 1943 witnessed a change in Etzel's policy regarding the British. The initiative came primarily from its commander, Menachem Begin (1913–92). Begin's rationale was that with the British defeat of the Germans at El-Alamein (October 1942), the danger of a German invasion of Palestine no longer existed, hence there was no reason why a Jewish state should not be established at once. An added urgency was the horrific fate of Europe's Jews. As the English stood in the way of a Jewish state, Begin asserted, the truce between Jews and the British was at an end. It was necessary to fight Britain to the bitter end in order to achieve the Zionist goals. In early February 1944, Begin's "revolt" was activated. Etzel members, about a thousand strong, launched an intensive wave of terror against Britain.[110]

The terrorism perpetrated by Etzel and Lehi generated great tension in the Yishuv. The leadership, headed by Ben-Gurion, objected to the activity of the two undergrounds as detrimental to the national cause, and tried to prevent it by all possible means. Terrorist activity at this stage, they insisted, would scuttle negotiations with the British and play into the hands of the Palestine Arabs. Lehi's assassination, in Cairo, of the British Minister of State in the Middle East, Lord Moyne (6 November 1944), exacerbated the situation. The Yishuv institutions ordered Etzel and Lehi to desist immediately from their war against the British. When they refused, the Haganah denounced them. They were arrested, tried, and punished; many were exiled to the British colony of Eritrea.[111]

The Yishuv, then, was split badly regarding the tactics to be employed in fighting for the creation of the Jewish state. Only the conclusion of the war, and the fact that the British continued to pursue their former policy in Palestine, brought an end to the bloody internecine quarrel. Two major developments – the failure of the Yalta Conference (February 1945) of the victorious Powers to change the status of Palestine, as the Zionists had hoped; and the fact that the new British foreign secretary, Ernest Bevin (1881–1951), adopted a policy that upheld many of the White Paper principles – united the entire Yishuv in a joint struggle against the British.

The Yishuv's disappointment at the policy of the newly-elected British Labor government was intense. The Nazi atrocities exposed by the Allies at the war's end and the thousands of displaced persons (DPs) who eagerly awaited an opportunity to reach Palestine induced Yishuv leaders to unite in their demand for a change in British policy.[112] But that change did not come. Indeed, British government resolutions at best emulated and in some cases worsened formulations proposed to the Zionists in the late 1930s. In reaction, Ben-Gurion called for an armed struggle against the British and invited Lehi and Etzel to form, with the Haganah, a joint command. In October 1945, the "United Resistance Movement" was formed. In the months that followed it carried out numerous acts of sabotage against British installations, causing casualties and material damage.[113]

If the point of the guerrilla actions was to pressure Britain to revise its Middle East policy, stronger and more effective pressure on the English probably came in the form of the thousands of Jewish DPs scattered in refugee camps across Europe whose sole desire was to get to Palestine.[114] The most insistent pressure in this regard came from Washington, and dependence on American aid obliged London to soften its position.[115] In December 1945, the two countries formed a joint commission to investigate the Palestine question. The British hope was that through the commission the Americans could be made to see that the Zionist solution was out of the question owing to the Arab states' vigorous objections. But the majority of the commission remained unconvinced. Its report, issued 1 May 1946, recommended the immediate entry into Palestine of one hundred thousand DPs and the annulment of the land laws that were detrimental to the Jews.[116]

The British, then, were engaged in a three-front struggle against the Yishuv. On one front, the battle against the Jewish undergrounds; British activity reached a peak in the early summer of 1946, with the arrest on a single day of some three thousand Jewish activists, among them Yishuv leaders ("Black Sabbath," 29 June 1946).[117] The Haganah renounced underground activity, but this had no effect on the extremists: Etzel and Lehi continued to strike at British personnel and British public structures until the Mandate's termination.

On a second front, the British operated to prevent Jewish immigration. After the war, Yishuv institutions set out to bring immigrants into the country in defiance of the British prohibition. The British tried to prevent this in the country of departure; failing that, they tried to intercept the ships at sea; and, as a last resort, they used force to prevent the immigrants from coming ashore on the Palestine coast. Thousands of aspiring immigrants were thus either sent back or incarcerated in detention camps. Nevertheless, thousands of others on more than sixty-five ships made it ashore, evading British obstacles and quickly blending in with the rest of the population.[118]

The third front was the political and diplomatic arena. Here, the Zionists made use of their connections with American politicians, most prominently President Harry Truman (1884–1972). Overall, the administration had tended to support the Zionists' aspirations since the end of the war. But American officials were at loggerheads on the issue of a Jewish state and support for the partition plan.[119] Some officials tried to persuade their superiors to back the British. However, Truman, along with the majority in both Houses of Congress, leaned toward the Zionists. And, as mentioned, American pressure on Britain was effective because of the latter's dependence on aid from across the Atlantic.

Ultimately, a series of factors induced the British to change their stand on the Palestine issue: American pressure; depleted resources, which ruled out increasing the number of troops in Palestine to enable them to cope with the underground movements; and a dramatic reversal of outlook concerning Britain's need for overseas territories (as reflected most conspicuously at the time by the granting of independence to India). In February 1947, the government in London decided to pull out of Palestine and transfer responsibility to the United Nations.[120]

Post-war Zionist policy had a clear purpose: the establishment of a Jewish state in western Palestine in accordance with the Biltmore Plan. But the Zionist camp continued to wrangle over which tactic would best serve that end. A consensus seemed to have been reached with the formation of the United Resistance Movement. Everyone then was committed to an armed uprising against the British. But within six months, in the summer of 1946, as Jewish terrorism intensified and brought harsher British retaliation, demands were voiced for a policy revision. At that time, the leaders of the Zionist movement thought the Biltmore Plan was unworkable because of Washington's opposition. Their greatest fear was that President Truman would revoke his support if they did not agree to a compromise with Britain and accept partition. The Yishuv leadership came around to the same view following Washington's outraged reaction to Etzel's bombing of the King David Hotel in Jerusalem (22 July 1946), where senior Mandate personnel had offices and British Army HQ was located. The 91 fatalities (17 of them Jews) and 59 wounded were reason enough to put a stop to the united resistance.[121] Ben-Gurion and his associates, who disavowed any responsibility for the blast – even though the order to proceed was given by Haganah commander Moshe Sneh (1909–27) – said a new stage had been reached in the struggle, and that political conditions were not ripe for establishing a Jewish state according to the Biltmore Plan. It followed that the Yishuv should accept partition.

A new phase in the Zionist struggle for the Land of Israel began in April–May 1947. The U.N., convening in extraordinary session to debate the Palestine issue, decided to set up a commission of inquiry. The members of UNSCOP – U.N. Special Commission on Palestine – arrived in the country in the summer of 1947 to collect information and hear testimonies. The ongoing terrorist actions and an increase in the flow of illegal immigrants to Palestine put pressure on the commission to effect a change in the status quo. The most dramatic event in this period was the arrival of the ship *Exodus* in July, carrying 450 would-be immigrants, who were sent back to Europe following violent clashes with the British.[122] In the event, the majority report was consistent with the Zionists' demands: termination of the Mandate, creation of a Jewish state alongside an Arab state, and internationalization of Jerusalem. On 29 November, the U.N. General Assembly ratified the commission's report. Both the United States and the Soviet Union voted in favor. In practice, this meant the establishment of a Jewish state in most of western Palestine.

The Zionists welcomed the decision enthusiastically. With the exception of Revisionist circles, who demanded the enlargement of the proposed state, the Yishuv leadership saw the U.N. vote as a historic achievement. The fact that Jerusalem was to be outside the new state and that a few dozen settlements were to be in the Arab state did not put a pall on the spontaneous outburst of delight in the Yishuv at international recognition of the Zionists' goals. But the Arabs rejected the decision out of hand and declared all-out war.

The day after the U.N. vote, Palestinian Arabs, organized in military units, began attacking Jewish targets. Their target-date was 14 May 1948, when the last British troops were to leave. No area was safe from the Palestinians, and in March 1948 the Yishuv seemed to be reeling, particularly as the Palestinians had succeeded in blocking key roads. Jewish convoys trying to reach Jerusalem, the nearby Gush Etzion settlements and Kibbutz Yehiam in the Galilee were wiped out. However, the Haganah, which had expanded its ranks tremendously in the eight months preceding the war, soon showed its mettle. From mid-April, forces made up almost completely of Haganah units, joined by a few from Etzel, launched a concerted series of attacks which consolidated Jewish positions across the country. The siege of Jerusalem was lifted and key towns which had an Arab majority – Haifa, Acre and Tiberias – were captured.[123]

Tens of thousands of Arabs fled or were forced out of their homes in towns and villages taken by the Israeli forces, becoming homeless refugees. Their flight was sparked by faith in the assurances of the Palestinian Arab leadership and of Arab states that the Jews would soon be defeated and they would be able to return; and by the dread that seized the Arabs in the face of Jewish military might, especially following a massacre perpetrated by Jewish forces in the village of Deir Yassin on the outskirts of Jerusalem (9 September 1948) and in other villages. When the Israeli army forcibly expelled Arabs, it was due to concern that a hostile population would impede their combat goals. In other cases, Arabs were driven out of their homes by local commanders who wanted to "cleanse" the country of them, although the army high command never harbored any such intentions.[124]

As a result of the successful Jewish counter-offensive in April and early May 1948, and the mass Arab flight, military forces from a Jewish population of 650,000 were able to hold a continuous area, stretching from Metulla on the Lebanese border well into the south, where more than a million Arabs had been living. True, in Jerusalem and the Negev area there were Jewish enclaves, but the Jewish leadership under Ben-Gurion undoubtedly now felt more confident about their ability to meet an all-out Arab invasion. On 14 May 1948 the last British soldier left Palestine, and on 15 May, Ben-Gurion proclaimed the creation of the State of Israel. The declaration of independence was a calculated risk on the part of the Zionist leadership. To Ben-Gurion and his provisional government it was clear that the Arab states would see the act as a deliberate provocation and invade. Nevertheless, they went ahead, heartened by recent military victories and believing that the Jewish armed forces could do the job. They also assumed that the Great Powers, with the United States in the forefront, would recognize the fledgling state and prevent its conquest. Still, no one could be absolutely certain that Washington would recognize Israeli independence, especially as the U.S. administration had withdrawn its support for the partition plan some months earlier, proposing instead a trusteeship regime under U.N. auspices.[125]

On its first full day of existence as a state, Israel was invaded by the armies of the four neighboring countries – Egypt, Syria, Jordan and Lebanon – and Iraq. However, within a few months the IDF

(Israel Defense Forces, created 31 May 1948) had not only managed to contain the five armies, but had conquered new areas. With the exception of the West Bank (including east Jerusalem), which fell to Jordan's Arab Legion, and the Gaza Strip, conquered by Egypt, by 1949 Israeli forces controlled all of western Palestine.

Among the reasons for the IDF's victory in the War of Independence were the highly motivated fighting forces, who knew they had no viable alternative; the intensive training which some arms of the IDF, the Palmach commando squads in particular, had received since the start of World War II from both the British and local commanders; efficient utilization of forces; the ability of the command level to concentrate large forces for various offensives (such as Operation Nahshon to open the road to Jersualem, Operation Yiftah in the Galilee and Operation Horev in the Negev); reserve forces in the form of incoming new immigrants and volunteers from abroad; local fund-raising and contributions from overseas; a regular supply of weapons seized from British armories or acquired in massive purchases of World War II surplus, but above all a major procurement from Czechoslovakia, with the Soviet Union's assent; and the successful enlistment of the Jewish economic sector in the war effort to supply the IDF's immediate needs. A full explanation of the IDF's victory must also take into account the reasons for the failure of the Arab armies and Palestinian forces. These included poor training (with the exception of the Jordanians), the Arab forces' inability to mass their troops for a concerted offensive, and internecine strife.

The final chapter in the saga of Zionism began with the Declaration of Independence which created the State of Israel. Zionism, on that occasion, was triumphant. The calls for the establishment of a state for the Jews which were voiced at the end of the nineteenth century but went largely unheeded, became an irrevocable reality. On 15 May 1948, the State of Israel became the national center of the Jewish people. True, that center is, at this writing, far from realizing Herzl's vision of liquidating the diaspora. In fact, it bears a greater resemblance to Ahad Ha'am's concept of a national-cultural center in the Land of Israel. Still, the dynamics of the process, as they have evolved in the past 46 years (1948–94), point unequivocally to the gradual termination of the diaspora and immigration to Israel. Theory is becoming practice.

The history of Israel's development is beyond the scope of this work. The Arab-Israeli conflict and the wars it has generated, the absorption of immigrants, the changes in Israeli society, the development of education and culture – all these are weighty issues which demand a different type of study. Basic research on these matters is still in the nascent stage, few subjects have been satisfactorily treated, and therefore it is still impossible to present a synthesis which will shed light on all aspects of the topic. But there is no doubt that at this stage of Israel's development, Zionism, far from losing its senior status as a central phenomenon in the Jewish world, has become considerably stronger. But there are cracks which ultimately could topple the entire edifice. A number of phenomena pose a permanent threat to the future of Zionism: the rifts in Israeli society between Right and Left; between religious and secular; and between Jews and Arabs both inside and outside Israel. Lastly, and perhaps the greatest long-term danger, is the assimilatory tendency in Europe and America. Only the future will tell whether Zionism will continue on its successful road as a major phenomenon in Jewish life.

Conclusion

"It all began in the eighties." This paraphrase of the pithy comment by the great scholar of the French Revolution, François Furet ("It all began with the French Revolution"[1]), is well suited to the historic processes that began among the Jewish people in the 1870s and 1880s: a seminal period of revolutionary developments perceived, in historical perspective, as "the beginning of modern times in Jewish history." Our aim was to demonstrate that central historical processes in Jewish history – emigration, emancipation, secularization, anti-Semitism, Zionism – originated in that period (more precisely, in the last third of the nineteenth century) and have played themselves out in our time.

It is indisputable that well before the last three decades of the nineteenth century Jews wandered in their masses within Russia, from there setting out for central Europe and the United States; that they were granted full civil rights in France in 1790, a generation later in Britain and Holland; that secularization was widespread in Germany by the late eighteenth century; and that Zionism, in some views, has its origins in the 1840s or 1850s, perhaps even earlier. But in the decade of the 1880s all these processes became *dynamic*. The marginal historical developments of which incipient signs were discerned in the mid-seventeenth century by Salo Baron and Shmuel Ettinger, and by others in the eighteenth century – its beginning (Ben Zion Dinur), its middle years (Heinrich Graetz) or its latter stages (Simon Dubnow)[2] – gathered into powerful, indeed irreversible, currents by the eighties of the nineteenth century.

Thus with emigration: Jews had been on the move by the thousands from the 1820s. In certain periods hundreds of thousands made their way from Lithuania, Belorussia and the Polish hinterlands to Ukraine, the new Russia and the cities of Poland. Simultaneously Jews crossed the borders of Austria-Hungary and

Germany on their way to the large cities in Europe, before they set their sights on New York. No fewer than 150,000 Bavarian Jews crossed the Atlantic Ocean in search of a new home. Yet, in retrospect, such phenomena are marginal in comparison with the huge movement of Jews from Russia to the United States which began in the 1880s, continued unabated for more than 40 years, and ultimately encompassed 2.5 million Jews who sought a brighter future in the New World; and, also beginning in that decade, the emigration of more than 2 million Jews from Europe and Islamic lands to Palestine. The waves of migration set in motion a process which dramatically reduced the size of the Jewish community in eastern Europe (Russia and Poland), the world's largest at the end of the nineteenth century. Two-fifths of that population wandered eastward or westward, half were murdered by the Nazis. Concurrently, the Jewish communities in the United States and Palestine flourished, becoming the new centers of the Jewish people in the modern era.

Thus with emancipation: French Jews were granted full civil rights by the end of the eighteenth century. Dubnow identified this development as the start of a new chapter in Jewish history. But only a small minority of Jews benefited. More than 90 percent of the Jews had to wait many years more for emancipation: 1.5 million Jews in Austria-Hungary and Germany until the end of the 1860s, and more than half the Jews in the world, who lived in Russia, for 50 years after that. Even then, it was a short-lived equality. The laws promulgated in Nuremberg in 1935 undermined the basic principles that gave Jews equality with the surrounding society; and in the ensuing world war the Germans deprived the majority of the world's Jews not only of emancipation but of the right to life. Paradoxically, it was the Nuremberg laws and the Germans' attempt to apply them, 150 years after the French Revolution (Dubnow's starting point for the modern era in Jewish history), that constituted the turning point in the emancipation of the Jews. The horrific consequences of those laws served as an object lesson to the enlightened world.

Some date the genesis of the social-cultural revolution to the later part of the eighteenth century, when the teachings of the Ba'al Shem Tov spread through the Jewish world and his Hasidic movement became the largest religious-social movement the Jews had known. Perhaps the roots of the social-cultural revolution go back a century earlier, as Scholem claimed, to the Sabbatian upheaval. Hasidism, in any event, became an integral element of religious Orthodoxy

during the nineteenth century, making it an unlikely candidate for
the progenitor of the cultural shocks experienced by the Jews since
the last third of that century. Graetz and his followers pointed to
the thought of Mendelssohn and the cultural-social activity of the
maskilim in the first half of the nineteenth century as the starting
point for "modern times" in Jewish history. But Graetz was well
aware that the aspiration of Mendelssohn and his disciples to remain
Jews in their homes while blending with the surrounding nation
outside was accepted by only a small minority of Jews, most of
whom resided in central and western Europe. The others remained
faithful to the various branches of Orthodox Judaism.

In contrast, the 1870s and 1880s witnessed the start of new processes that would utterly transfigure Jewish society. Within a few
generations secularization brought about a cultural-social revolution
that impinged on every facet of Jewish life. True, it was a relatively
slow and gradual revolution. Observance of religious precepts, for
example, a reliable indicator of the depth of secularization, was
still part of the experience of most Jews until World War I, and of
a smaller proportion afterward. Undeniably, however, a dramatic
change had occurred in the basic approach of the majority of Jews
toward their religion; since the 1880s it played a diminishing part in
their lives, and the attachment of increasing numbers to Judaism was
grounded more in sentimentalism and nationalism than in religious
faith as such. Symptomatic of the trend were developments in Jewish
education. No longer was the diligent Torah student held up as the
educational ideal; the new paragons were the intellectuals and the
practitioners of the liberal professions. Moreover, from the end of
the nineteenth century two new streams in Judaism – Reform and
Conservatism – loomed larger within Jewish society. The Reform
movement in particular, at first a small, marginal minority, soon
made considerable inroads. Although even at the height of its
strength, in the mid-twentieth century, Reform never claimed
the allegiance of more than 10 percent of the Jewish people, its
relative success was a stark reflection of secularization's penetration.
Moreover, the numbers professing affiliation with Orthodoxy (in all
its branches) were no greater than those of Reform. The true gauge
of the impact of the secular revolution which began in the last third
of the nineteenth century is the fact that since the 1920s most Jews
have defined themselves as "secular" or "traditional."

The origins of anti-Semitism lie in the distant past – in the third
century BCE, according to some. But in the last third of the nineteenth

century anti-Jewish ideology was radically transformed. The new generation of Jew-haters drew on modern doctrines. Nationalism, economic and social developments, scientific advances – all were grist to the mill of anti-Semitism's new brand of theorizing. Terminology too was radically revised. Jews were now an "inferior race," a "pernicious sect." The very name of the phenomenon was altered: "Jew-hatred" gave way to "anti-Semitism." Hitler and the Nazis adopted the new vocabulary, race theory in particular, and translated it into the murder of six million Jews.

As for Zionism, three times a day Jews across the ages prayed for Zion and Jerusalem. However, not until the 1880s did a national movement arise with the goal of creating a Jewish political entity in the Land of Israel. In 1897 Theodor Herzl transformed his ideas into practice by founding an organizational body to implement Zionism. The Zionist movement subsequently became the most important organization of the Jewish people in the modern era. The Declaration of Independence of the State of Israel, proclaimed by David Ben-Gurion on 15 May 1948, embodied the goals yearned for by *Hovevei Zion*, Herzl and their successors.

In this book I have tried to show that the genesis of the modern era in Jewish history lies in the last third of the nineteenth century. However, this should not be construed as an attempt to refute the wisdom of others. Shmuel Ettinger's historical acuity needs no elaboration. His contention that "Jewish history in the modern age" had its "beginnings in the seventeenth century" is grounded in the hypothesis adduced by F. Grayton (in Volume I of the *Cambridge Modern History*)[3] that modern history has its origins in a period when past and present intermingle *knowingly and unknowingly*. Ettinger, like other distinguished historians cited in the text, indicated his genesis of the phenomenon or its harbingers in terms of his own era. However, the changes that affected the Jewish people in the past 120 years – demographic development, mass migration and the establishment of new centers in the United States and Israel; the vicissitudes of emancipation; a secularization process that radically altered the Jews' social and cultural structure; the new anti-Semitism; and the emergence of Zionism – lead, inexorably, to the conclusion that past and present intermingled in the history of the Jews, beginning in the last third of the nineteenth century. And that *that history* was the beginning of Jewish history in modern times.

Appendix

Table 1: The increase in world Jewish population from 1880 to 1990

Year	Number of Jews
1800	2,500,000
1850	4,700,000
1880	7,660,000
1900	10,660,000
1914	13,500,000
1925	14,800,000
1939	16,600,000
1945	11,000,000
1960	12,161,000
1970	12,824,000
1980	13,028,000
1990	12,887,000
Estimate	
2000	12,431,000

Source: see chap. 1, note 3.

Table 2: Distribution of Jews according to continents, 1800–1914

	1800 Absolute number	%		
Europe	2,730,000	83.2		
(of which Russia)	(1,600,000)	(48.8)		
North America	10,000	1.0		
(of which the United States)	(8,000)	(0.2)		
Asia	300,000	9.2		
(of which Erez Israel)	(8,500)	(0.2)		
Africa	240,000	7.3		
Australia	1,000	–		
Total	3,281,000	100.0		

	1850 Absolute number	%	1880 Absolute number	%
Europe	4,127,500	86.6	6,771,500	88.4
(of which Russia)	(2,599,363)	(54.5)	(4,228,770)	(55.2)
North America	65,000	1.4	250,000	3.3
(of which the United States)	(120,000)	(2.5)	(240,000)	(3.1)
Asia	320,000	6.7	350,000	4.5
(of which Erez Israel)	(13,600)	(0.3)	(24,000)	(0.3)
Africa	250,000	5.3	280,000	3.6
Australia	2,000	–	12,000	2.0
Total	4,764,500	100.0	7,663,500	100.0

	1914 Absolute number	%	1900 Absolute number	%
Europe	9,100,000	67.5	8,690,500	82.1
(of which Russia)	(5,900,000)	43.7	(5,190,000)	(49.0)
North America	3,500,000	26.0	3,175,000	11.0
(of which the United States)	(3,388,951)	(25.0)	(1,500,000)	(14.1)
Asia	500,000	3.5	420,000	3.9
(of which Erez Israel)	(85,000)	(0.5)	(50,000)	(0.6)
Africa	400,000	3.0	300,000	2.8
Australia	10,000	–	17,000	0.2
Total	13,510,000	100.0	12,602,500	100.0

Source: see chap. 1, note 25.

**Table 3: Waves of Jewish immigration to,
and emigration from, Erez Israel**

Waves of immigration	Number of olim	Waves of immigration	Total number of emigrants
1881–1882	4,500	1885–1890	1,500
1883–1886	7,000		
1890–1891	9,000		
1895–1903	13,000	1892–1894	7,000
	33,500		8,500
Total number of Olim	25,000		
Second Aliyah (1903–1914)			
1903–1914	39,500	1906–1914	31,000
Total number of Olim in the Second *Aliyah*	8,500		

Source: see chap. 1, note 25.

**Table 4: Dispersion of Jews in Russia and the Soviet Union
from 1897 to 1939 (in areas which were retained by the Soviet
Union from 1918 to 1939)**

District	1897	1914	1923	1939
Ukraine (including modern Russia), parts of Lithuania and Belorussia which remained with the Soviet Union after World War I, and Asiatic Russia	2,260,000	2,450,000	1,987,000	2,072,000
Central Russia	40,000	50,000	624,000	948,000
Total	2,300,000	2,500,000	2,611,000	3,020,000

Source: see chap. 1, note 42.

**Table 5: The number of Jews in eastern Europe
(excluding the Soviet Union) from 1920 to 1939**

Country	1920	Percentage of Jews in relation to total number in the world of 14.3 million	1939	Percentage of Jews in relation to total number in the world of 16.6 million
Poland	2,855,318	20.0	3,325,000	20.0
Rumania	834,344	5.8	850,000	5.1
Hungary (1921)	473,355	3.3	504,000	3.0
Czech. (1935)	354,342	2.5	357,000	2.1
Yugoslavia	64,221	0.4	71,000	0.4
Bulgaria	45,600 (1923)	0.3	48,565	0.3
Baltic States:				
Lithuania	157,527 (1925)	1.1	150,000 (1935)	0.9
Latvia	95,675 (1922)	0.7	93,479	0.6
Estonia	4,566	–	5,100	–
Total number of Jews in eastern Europe (exclud. Soviet Union)	4,884,948	34.1	5,404,144	32.4

Source: see chap. 1, note 51.

Table 6: Aliyah to Erez Israel from 1919 to 1939

Years	Number of olim	The Jewish population in Erez Israel	
1919–1923	35,183	(1923)	84,000
1924–1926	62,133	(1926)	115,000
1927–1931	19,480	(1931)	174,606
1932–1936	191,224	(1936)	404,000
1937–1939	56,499	(1939)	445,000

Appendix

Table 7: Jewish world population from 1939 to 1948

Country	Number of Jews: 1939	Percentage of Jews in relation to total	Murdered by the Nazis (1945)	Number of Jews after the war	Percentage of Jews / relation to total no. in world
U.S.	4,975,000	30.0		5,000,000	45.4
Poland	3,325,000	20.0	(Poland, Sov. Union and States)	88,000	0.8
Soviet Union	3,020,000	18.2	4,565,000	2,000,000	18.2
Romania	850,000	5.1	60,000 (excluding Transylvania)	380,000	3.5
Hungary	504,000	3.0	402,000	174,000	1.6
Germany	359,000	2.2	170,000 (including Austria)	153,000	1.4
Palestine	445,000	2.7	–	716,000	6.7
North Africa (Morocco, Algeria, Tunisia, Egypt and Libya)	401,000	2.4	–	562,500	5.1
Czech. (1931)	357,000	2.2	277,000	42,000	0.4
Grt. Brit.	300,000	1.8	–	345,000	3.1
Argentina (1936)	275,000	1.7	–	360,000	3.3
France	260,000	1.6	107,700 (incl. Belgium, and Luxembourg)	235,000	2.1
Baltics (Lithuania, Latvia, Estonia)	248,000 (1931)	1.5	(included in Poland)	(included in USSR)	
Balkans Yugoslav., Bulgaria, Greece)	201,000	1.2	125,000	63,500	0.6
Canada	155,000	0.9	–	180,000	1.6
Other	924,000	5.5	Italy, the Netherlands, Norway, 114,260	701,000	6.2
Total	16,600,000	100.0	5,820,960	11,000,000	100.0

Source: see chap. 1, note 58.

**Table 8: The ratio of Jews to Arabs in Palestine and Israel
between 1947 and 1988**

Year	Number of Jews		Non-Jewish population	Percentage non-Jewish population
1947	630,019		1,340,345	59.9
1948	649,600		141,900	19.4
1961	1,932,357		221,373	11.3
	State of Israel		*Conquered territories*	
September 1967	2,373,885	491,200	954,898	37.8
1980	3,282,700	639,000	1,146,000	35.2
1988	3,659,000	718,000	1,424,000	39.3

Source: see chap. 1, note 73.

Table 9: Emigration of Jews to Israel 1948 to 1993

Period	Number of Jews	Average per year
1948–1951	686,739	189,184
1952–1954	54,065	18,022
1955–1957	164,936	54,979
1958–1960	75,487	25,162
1961–1964	228,046	57,012
1965–1968	81,337	20,334
1969–1973	227,258	45,452
1974–1975	52,007	26,004
1976–1989	195,125	13,937
1989–1993	420,000	94,000
Total	2,185,000	

Source: see chap. 1, note 77.

Appendix

Table 10: Jewish world population 1948 to 1988

Country	1948	Percentage of Jews in relation to the total number in the world	1967	Percentage of Jews in relation to the total number in the world	1980	Percentage of Jews in relation to the total number in the world	1988
United States	5,000,000	45.4	5,447,000 (1979)	40.6	5,860,000	45.0	5,510,000
			(1970)				
Soviet Union	2,000,000	18.2	2,151,000 (1970)	16.1	1,811,000	13.9	1,370,000
Israel	750,000	6.8	2,436,000	18.1	3,283,000	25.2	3,717,000
North African Countries (Morocco, Algeria, Tunisia, Egypt and Libya)	562,000	5.1	61,500	0.5	30,000	0.2	12,500
Romania	380,000	3.5	100,000	0.7	42,000	0.3	19,000
Argentina	360,000	3.3	500,000	3.7	242,000	1.9	218,000
Great Britain	345,000	3.1	410,000	3.1	450,000	3.5	320,000
France	235,000	2.1	535,000	4.0	535,000	4.1	530,000
Canada	180,000	1.6	275,000	2.1	308,000	2.4	310,000
Hungary	174,000	1.6	80,000	0.6	20,000	0.1	58,000
Germany	153,000	1.4	32,000	0.2	30,000	0.2	35,000
South Africa	70,000	0.6	90,000	0.7	102,000	0.7	115,000
Brazil	46,700	0.4	240,000	1.8	80,000	0.6	100,000
Others	744,300	7.8	1,042,500	7.8	235,000	1.8	289,800

Source: see chap. 1, note 78.

Table 11: Jewish Occupations in Poland – 1897 to 1931
(in percentages)

Occupations	1897	1921	1931
Commerce, finance, haulage, transportation	42.6	44.8	41.4
Industry and crafts	34.3	34.0	42.1
Day laborers, apprenticeship	8.3	1.4	0.7
Liberal professions, public administration	5.3	5.0	6.4
Agriculture	2.5	5.8	4.3
Unspecified	7.0	9.0	5.4
	100.0	100.0	100.0

Source: see chap. 1, note 53.

Notes

Introduction

1. Heinrich Graetz, "The Structure of Jewish History," was first published in Zacharias Frankel's periodical *Zeitschrift fuer die religiosen Interessen des Judentums*, vol. 3 (1846).
2. B. Dinur, "The Modern Era in Jewish History: Its Diagnosis, Essence and Image," in B. Z. Dinur (ed.), *At the Turning Point of the Generations* (Jerusalem, 1965), 19 (Hebrew). Cf. M. A. Meyer (ed.), *Ideas of Jewish History* (New York, 1971), 1–41.
3. H. Graetz, "The Structure of Jewish History"; Y. Baer, "Symposium on Historical Periodization," *Proceedings of the Fourth World Congress in Jewish Studies*, I (1967): 57–60 (Hebrew).
4. S. Dubnow, *Letters on Old and New Judaism* (Tel Aviv, 1936), 52–55 (Hebrew); S. Dubnow, *History of the Jewish People* (Tel Aviv, 1972), 34–37 (Hebrew).
5. R. Mahler, *History of the Jewish People in Recent Generations*, 1, 1, (Merhaviah, 1961), 9–10 (Hebrew).
6. G. Scholem, "Redemption Through Sin" (Hebrew), *Knesset*, 2 (1937): 66–67.
7. S. Baron, *A Social and Religious History of the Jews*, vol. 2 (New York, 1937), 164–65; S. Baron, *A Social and Religious History of the Jews*, vol. 1 (New York, 1965), iii–ix; S. Ettinger, *History of the Jewish People in the Modern Era* (Tel Aviv, 1969), 17–22 (Hebrew).
8. B. Dinur, "The Modern Era in Jewish History," 19–68.
9. Cf., for example, M. A. Meyer, "From When Should We Date the New Era in the History of the Jewish People?" *Gesher*, 21, 2 (1975): 53–62 (Hebrew).
10. B. Dinur, "The Modern Era in Jewish History"; J. Barnai, *Historiography and Nationalism* (Jerusalem, 1995), 27, 36, 42,

71–76, 81–84, 94–95, 120–21 (Hebrew).
11. Ibid., 26.

Chapter 1: Migration

1. "Introduction," in A. Shanan (ed.), *Emigration and Settlement in Israel and Other Countries* (Jerusalem, 1985), 16 (Hebrew).
2. The definition of who is a "Jew" is problematic, consequently the statistics about the number of Jews are controversial. I have used the definition proposed by U. O. Schmelz and S. Della Pergola of the Institute of Contemporary Jewry, The Department of Demography and Statistics, The Hebrew University of Jerusalem, which appeared in: M. O. Schmelz, S. Della Pergola, "World Jewish Population, 1989," *American Jewish Year Book* (1990): 514–32. In this article the figures refer to the core Jewish population. The "Core Jewish population includes all those who converted to Judaism or joined the Jewish group informally. It excludes those of Jewish descent who formally adopted another religion, as well as those individuals who did not convert-out but currently refuse to recognize their Jewishness."
3. Regarding the demographic changes among Jews see: R. Bachi, *Population Trends of World Jewry* (Jerusalem, 1976); U. O. Schmelz, *World Jewish Population: Regional Estimates and Projections* (Jerusalem, 1981); S. Della Pergola, *La Transformazione demografica della diaspora ebraica* (Turin, 1983); U. O. Schmelz, S. Della Pergola, "World Jewish Population, 1989."
4. Estimate according to S. Della Pergola, *La Transformazione*.
5. Ibid.
6. In eastern Europe it reached more than 300 percent because the demographic increase of the Russian population was about 120 percent. Compare W. Eason, "Population Changes," in E. Black (ed.), *The Transformation of Russian Society* (Cambridge, 1960), 75; Y. Talmon, *Romanticism and Revolt* (Tel Aviv, 1973), 197 (Hebrew).
7. J. Lestschinsky, "Die Umsiedlung und Umschichtung der Juedischer Volkes in Laufe des letzten Jarhunderts," *Weltwirtschaftliches Archive*, 31 (July 1929): 132; B. Pinkus, *The Jews of Russia and the Soviet Union – The History of a National Minority* (Jerusalem, 1986), 70 (Hebrew).

8. R. Bachi, *Population Trends of World Jewry*, 46.
9. The beginning of the phenomenon occurred already in the first half of the nineteenth century. Compare: *The New Cambridge Modern History*, vol. 10, "The Zenith of European Power, 1830–1870" (Cambridge, 1960). Another comparison: an analysis of a similar phenomenon at the beginning of the twentieth century, A. M. Carr-Saunders, *World Population* (Oxford, 1936). To a certain extent there is a considerable similarity between the demographic development of the eastern European Jews in the nineteenth century and that of the Palestinian Arabs between 1881 and 1947. Compare G. Gilbar, *Trends in the Demographic Development of the Palestinians, 1870–1987* (Tel Aviv, 1990), 7 (Hebrew); for demographic developments in developing nations compare R. Bachi, *Population Trends of World Jewry*, 13–21.
10. A. Ruppin, *The Social Structure of the Jews*, vol. 1 (Tel Aviv, 1932–34), 148–49 (Hebrew).
11. U. O. Schmelz, "World Jewish Population in the 1980's, A Short Outline" (Occasional Paper, 1989–1990), The Institute of Contemporary Jewry, The Hebrew University of Jerusalem, 1990.
12. *Sbornik Materialov ob ekonomicheskom polozhnii evreev v Rossii* (Petersburg, 1904), xiv–xlvi. "The Berdichev Jewish Community from 1789 to 1918," *Bleter far Yidishe Demografie Statistik und Economic* (Berlin, 1923), 37 (Yiddish).
13. B. Garnazarka-Kedari, *The Jewish Contribution to the Development of Industry in Warsaw and Łódź, 1816–1914* (Tel Aviv, 1985), 261–93 (Hebrew).
14. Ibid., 118.
15. Ibid.
16. Regarding Odessa see S. J. Zipperstein, *The Jews of Odessa: A Cultural History, 1794–1881* (Stanford, 1985), 129–56.
17. There is no correlation between the statistics of Ruppin, *The Social Structure of the Jews*, vol. 1 and those of Lestschinsky, *Economic Situation of the Jews in Eastern and Central Europe* (Tel Aviv, 1935), 66–72 (Hebrew). Compare also S. Dubnow, *World History of the Jewish People* (Tel Aviv, 1962), 105 (Hebrew); Y. Goldstein, *Between Practical and Political Zionism: The Beginnings of Zionism in Russia* (Jerusalem, 1991), 18–19 (Hebrew).
18. L. P. Gartner, "The Mass Migration of European Jews" in A. Shanan (ed.), *Emigration and Settlement in Israel and Other*

Countries (Jerusalem, 1985), 343–83 (Hebrew). For a general
bibliography see ibid., 360–61. M. Wischnitzer, *To Dwell in
Safety: The Story of Jewish Migration Since 1880* (Philadelphia,
1949); J. Lestschinsky, "Jewish Migrations, 1840–1956" in
L. Finkelstein (ed.), *The Jews: Their History, Culture and Religion*,
vol. 2, (Philadelphia, 1960), 1536–96; A. Goren, Y. Venkart
(eds), "The Great Jewish Emigration and Consolidation of
American Jewry," in *Topics in Jewish History*, vol. 5 (Jerusalem,
1977) (Hebrew).
19.   On anti-Semitism in Germany in the last third of the nineteenth
century see P. G. Pulzer (ed.), *The Rise of Political Anti-Semitism
in Germany and Austria* (New York, 1964); P. W. Massing,
Rehearsal for Destruction (New York, 1967); U. Tal, *Christians
and Jews in Germany – Religion, Politics and Ideology in the Second
Reich, 1870–1914* (Ithaca and London, 1969). In Austria: W. O.
McCagg Jr., *A History of Habsburg Jews, 1670–1918* (Bloomington, 1989), 161–222; R. S. Wistrich, *The Jews of Vienna in the Age
of Franz Joseph* (Oxford, 1990); P. G. Pulzer, *The Rise of Political
Anti-Semitism*; S. Almog, *Nationalism and Antisemitism in Modern Europe* (Jerusalem, 1985), 53–59 (Hebrew). In France: S.
Almog, *Nationalism and Anti-Semitism in Modern Europe*, 63–67;
R. F. Byrnes, *Antisemitism in Modern France* (New Jersey, 1950).
20.   On the rate of emigration see the above sources (note 18)
and D. Sulzberger, "The Growth of Jewish Population in
the United States," *Publication of the American Jewish Historical
Society*, 4 (1987): 141–49.
21.   S. W. Baron, J. L. Blau (eds), *The Jews of the American Jewish
Historical Society* 3 vols (New York, 1963); L. P. Gartner, "The
Formation of American Jewry," in *Topics in Jewish History*, vol.
5 (Jerusalem, 1977), 9 (Hebrew); B. Koren, *The American Jewish
Community During the Period of Its Invigoration* (Jerusalem,
1971) (Hebrew); M. Davis, *Beit Yisrael in America: Studies and
Sources* (Jerusalem, 1970), 31 (Hebrew). Statistics from A. M.
Carr-Saunders, *World Population*, 49.
22.   Compare M. Meyer, *Between Tradition and Progress* (Jerusalem,
1990), 261–303 (Hebrew).
23.   S. Baron, *The Challenge of Freedom* (Tel Aviv, 1977), 156–62
(Hebrew); L. P. Gartner, "The Mass Migration of European
Jews; L. Hirsch, "Jewish Emigration to the United States,
1899–1925: A Demographic Analysis," in *Topics in Jewish History*, vol. 5 (Jerusalem, 1977), 25–74 (Hebrew); S. Joseph, *Jewish*

Immigration to the United States from 1881 to 1910 (New York, 1910).

24. S. Baron, *The Challenge of Freedom*, 168–88; B. D. Weinryb, "The Adaptation of Jewish Labor Groups to American Life," *Jewish Social Studies*, 8 (1946): 219–44.

25. S. Della Pergola, *La Transformazione*, 44, 49; J. Lestschinsky, "Die Umsiedlung und Umschichtung der Juedischer Volkes in Laufe des Letzten Jahrhunderts," 123–56; A. Ruppin, *The Social Structure of the Jews*, vol. 1, 68ff; B. Pinkus, *The Jews of Russia and the Soviet Union – The History of a National Minority*; R. Bachi, *The Population of Israel* (Jerusalem, 1974), 4–8, 367–68; A. Tartakower, *The Jewish Community*, vol. 2 (Tel Aviv/Jerusalem, 1959) (Hebrew).

26. *Ha-Maggid* 39, 6 October 1881.

27. A. Menes, "The Am Olam Movement," *Yivo Annual of Jewish Social Science* 4 (1949): 9–33; H. Turtal, "The Am Olam Movement," *He-avar* 10 (1963): 124–43 (Hebrew).

28. For various details about *Hibbat Zion* see D. Vital, *The Zionist Revolution*, vol. 1 (Tel Aviv, 1978), 61–178 (Hebrew); Yisrael Klausner, *The Movement to Zion in Russia*, vols 1–3 (Jerusalem, 1962–1965) (Hebrew).

29. Y. L. Pinsker, *Autoemancipation (Road to Freedom)* (New York, 1944), 31.

30. The articles of association of the Petah Tikvah Company, 18 December 1881, *Documents Relating to Hibbat Zion and the Settlement of Erez Israel*, vol. 1 (compiled and edited by Alter Druyanow: [1919–1932], new edition edited by S. Laskov) (Tel Aviv, 1982), 133 (Hebrew).

31. R. Bachi, *The Population of Israel*.

32. Regarding the difference between *hagirah* (emigration) and *aliyah* (immigration to Erez Israel) much has been written. There are those who feel there is an intrinsic difference between the two concepts. For example A. Tartakower says that for the Jewish people *aliyah* symbolizes an act for the "general welfare" of Erez Israel while *hagirah* is for "personal welfare." *Aliyah* is *hagirah* to Erez Israel. A. Tartakower, *The Jewish Community*, 81. For a further discussion on the subject see A. Tartakower, *The Wandering Man* (Tel Aviv, 1954) (Hebrew). In my opinion the difference is purely semantic.

33. G. Gilbar, *Trends in the Demographic Development of the Palestinians, 1870–1987*; K. H. Karpat, "Ottoman Population

Records and the Census of 1881–1882–1883," *Islamic Journal of Middle East Studies*, 9 (1978): 262–71.

34. R. Bachi, *The Population of Israel*, 6.

35. Regarding the entire *yishuv*, see Moshe Lissak, Gavriel Cohen (editors-in-chief), *The History of the Jewish Community in Erez Israel, The Ottoman Period*, ed. Y. Kolatt (Jerusalem, 1990), 419–502 (Hebrew).

36. Y. Kaniel, *Continuance and Permutation* (Jerusalem, 1982), 310.

37. T. Herzl, *Der Judenstaat* (Vienna, 1896), 37–38.

38. H. Avni, *Argentina "the Promised Land"* (Jerusalem, 1973), 285.

39. B. Pinkus, *The Jews of Russia and the Soviet Union – The History of a National Minority*, 115–16; S. Baron, *The Russian Jews under Tsars and Soviets* (New York, 1976), 159.

40. Gessen minimizes. Y. Gessen, *Istoria evreiskovo naroda v Rossii*, 1 (Leningrad 1925), 153. S. Dubnow maximizes when he estimates the number of Jews forced to leave their villages at half a million. S. Dubnow, *History of the Jews in Russia and Poland*, vol. 3 (Philadelphia, 1916), 326.

41. Even this figure is controversial. There are those like I. M. Aronson who minimize (estimating about 20,000 were expelled), see his *Russian Bureaucratic Attitudes towards Jews, 1881–1894* (Ph.D. diss., Evanston, 1973), 37. There are others who maximize (claiming about 30,000) like Pinkus; compare B. Pinkus, *The Jews of Russia and the Soviet Union – The History of a National Minority*, 114.

42. The sources are from *Sbornik Materialov ob ekonomicheskom polozhnii evreev v Rossii*; B. Garnazarska-Kedari, *The Jewish Contribution to the Development of Industry in Warsaw and Łódź, 1816–1914*; A. Ruppin, *The Social Structure of the Jews*, vol. 1; B. Pinkus, *The Jews of Russia and the Soviet Union – The History of a National Minority*; L. Greenberg, *The Jews in Russia*, vol. 2 (New Haven, 1951); S. Baron, *The Russian Jews under Tsars and Soviets*.

43. Regarding the Birobidzhan Plan, see Y. Levavi, *The Jewish Settlement in Birobidzhan* (Jerusalem, 1965) (Hebrew).

44. A. Ruppin, *The Social Structure of the Jews*, vol. 1, 1; S. Della Pergola, *La Transformazione*, 49; E. Mendelsohn, *The Jews of East Central Europe Between the World Wars* (Bloomington, 1983), 11–83.

45. R. Katznelson, *L'Immigrazione degli ebrei in Palestina nei tempi moderni* (Napoli, 1930).

46. A. Tartakower, *The Migration of Jews in the World* (Jerusalem, 1947), 121 (Hebrew); A. Tartakower, *The Jewish Community*, vol. 1, 75.
47. E. Mendelsohn, *The Jews of East Central Europe Between the World Wars*.
48. M. Ben Hillel Hacohen, *The Wars of the Nations*, vols 1–2 (Jerusalem, 1981–1985) (Hebrew); N. Efrati, *The Jewish Community in Erez-Israel during World War I (1914–1918)* (Jerusalem, 1991), 34–44 (Hebrew); M. Eliav (ed.), *Siege and Distress, Eretz Israel during the First World War* (Jerusalem, 1991), 97–110, 248–61 (Hebrew).
49. Y. Porat, Y. Shavit, *The Mandate and the Jewish National Home (1917–1947), History of Erez Israel*, vol. 9 (Jerusalem, 1982), 106–37.
50. Y. Mezer, *National Capital for a National Home, 1919–1921* (Jerusalem, 1979), 18 (Hebrew).
51. R. Bachi, *Population Trends of World Jewry*, 4–5; S. Della Pergola, *La Transformazione*, 49. A. Ruppin, *The Social Structure of the Jews*, vol. 1, 49ff; Y. Slutzki, *The Haganah*, vols 2, 3 (Tel Aviv, 1975–1976) (Hebrew).
52. Y. Arazi, *The Book of the Third Aliyah*, vol. 1 (Tel Aviv, 1964), 8–9, 14.
53. D. Giladi, "Urban Absorption – The Story of the Fourth Aliyah," in A. Shanan (ed.), *Emigration and Settlement in Israel and Other Countries*, 249–54.
54. Y. Gelber, *New Homeland* (Jerusalem, 1990) (Hebrew).
55. D. Giladi, *The Yishuv During the Fourth Aliyah* (Tel Aviv, 1973), 193–230 (Hebrew).
56. S. Reichman, *From a Foothold to a Land of Settlement* (Jerusalem, 1979), 169–225 (Hebrew).
57. B. Pinkus, *The Jews of Russia and the Soviet Union – The History of a National Minority*; S. Della Pergola, *La Transformazione*, 43, 49; S. Baron, *The Russian Jews under Tsars and Soviets*; E. Mendelsohn, *The Jews of East Central Europe Between the World Wars*; R. Bachi, *Population Trends of World Jewry*, 4–5, 79; S. Baron, "Population," in *Encyclopaedia Judaica*, vol. 13, 884–902.
58. B. C. Pinchuk, *Soviet Jews in the Face of the Holocaust: Research Regarding the Problems of Banishment and Evacuation* (Tel Aviv, 1979), 130–37 (Hebrew); B. C. Pinchuk, *Shtetl Jew Under Soviet Rule* (London, 1990).

59. M. Abitbol, S. Ben-Asher, Y. Barnai, Y. Tubi, *History of the Jews in the Islamic Countries*, vols 1–3, ed. S. Ettinger (Jerusalem, 1986) (Hebrew).
60. K. D. Bracher, *The German Dictatorship* (New York, 1970).
61. Y. Bauer, *Flight and Rescue: Brichah* (New York, 1970).
62. R. Bachi, *Population Trends of World Jewry*, 86.
63. M. Abitbol *et al.*, *History of the Jews in the Islamic Countries*, 466–68.
64. For the beginnings of the government's cooperation with the Jewish Agency, compare A. Tartakower, *The Wandering Man*, 182ff with Y. Eilam, *The Jewish Agency: The First Years* (Jerusalem, 1990) (Hebrew).
65. M. Lissak, "Aliyah Policy in the 1950's – Some Organizational Aspects and their Social Implications," in A. Shanan (ed.), *Emigration and Settlement in Israel and Other Countries*, 255–90. Additional publications about *aliyah*: S. N. Eisenstadt, *The Absorption of Immigrants* (London, 1954); S. Smooha, *Israel: Pluralism and Conflict* (London, 1978); S. N. Eisenstadt, *The Transformation of Israeli Society* (London, 1985).
66. M. Lissak, "Aliyah Policy in the 1950's – Some Organizational Aspects and their Social Implications." For further information on the cultural and social differences according to statistical variables, see: U. O. Schmelz, S. Della Pergola, U. Avner, *Ethnic Differences Among Jews: A New Look* (Jerusalem, 1991), 37–78
67. Compare, for example, statements by the sociologist A. Tartakower, which give even harsher expression to this reprehensible opinion. Tartakower tried to prove that there was "a low level of culture" amongst the Jews from the Islamic countries. Also compare A. Tartakower, *The Wandering Jew*, 40–41, and other such statements. For the change in self-image and in that of the environment of the immigrants from Islamic countries, see: E. Ben Rafael, "The Changing Experience, Power and Prestige of Ethnic Groups in Israel: The Case of the Moroccans," *Studies in Contemporary Jewry* 5 (1989): 39–58.
68. G. Gilbar, *Trends in the Demographic Development of the Palestinians, 1870–1987*; *Israel Statistical Year Book* 1961, 1964, 1981, 1987; R. Bachi, *The Population of Israel*, 5, 399. Regarding the cultural gaps, see for example, Y. Peres, *Ethnic Relations in Israel* (Tel Aviv, 1971) (Hebrew); C. Herzog, *Political Ethnicity: Image and Reality* (Tel Aviv, 1986) (Hebrew); M. Inber, C. Adler, *Ethnic Interactions in Israel* (New Brunswick, 1977).

Notes to pp. 23–28

69. The statistical information is from M. Sikron, *Emigration to Israel 1948–1952*, parts 1–2 (Jerusalem, 1957) (Hebrew).
70. I. Ro'i and R. O. Freedman (eds), *Soviet Jewry in the Decisive Decade, 1971–1980* (Durham, 1984); M. Altshuler, *Soviet Jewry Since the Second World War* (Westport, 1987).
71. Compare *New York Times*, 3 December 1990; *Washington Post*, 10 September 1991.
72. *Israel Statistical Year Book* 1990, 1991, 1992; *Ha'aretz*, 2 December 1991; *Ma'ariv*, 23 December 1993.
73. Figures from *Israel Statistical Year Book* 1950, 1960, 1965, 1968, 1969, 1981, 1987; G. Gilbar, *Trends in the Demographic Development of the Palestinians, 1870–1987*.
74. D. Bensimon, S. Della Pergola, *La Population Juive de France* (Jerusalem and Paris, 1984).
75. S. Goldstein, *Tefutzot Yisrael* 4 (1980): 65–69 (Hebrew); *New York Times*, 3 December 1990.
76. U. O. Schmelz, "Jewish Population Until the Year 2,000," *Tefutzot Yisrael* 4 (1980): 147–67 (Hebrew); U. O. Schmelz, *Aging of World Jewry* (Jerusalem, 1984).
77. R. Bachi, *Population Trends of World Jewry*.
78. U. O. Schmelz, S. Della Pergola, "World Jewish Population, 1989," *American Jewish Year Book*; S. Della Pergola, *La Transformazione*, 49; R. Bachi, *Population Trends of World Jewry*; S. Baron, *The Russian Jews under Tsars and Soviets*; I. Rosenwaike, "A Synthetic Structure of American Jewish Population Movement Over the Last Three Decades," *Papers in Jewish Demography* (1977): 83–102; S. Goldstein, *Tefutzot Yisrael*; L. Hirschowitz, "The Soviet Census 1970: New Data on the Jewish Minority," *Tefutzot Yisrael* 4 (1980): 95–126 (Hebrew).
79. S. Yosef, "The Family and Professional Composition of the Jewish Emigrants to the United States and Their Educational Level," in B. Dinur, A. Tartakower and J. Lestchinsky (eds), *Kollel Yisrael: Topics on the Sociology of the Jewish People*, in (Jerusalem, 1954), 179–80 (Hebrew).

Chapter 2: Emancipation

1. Compare S. Ettinger, *History of the Jewish People in Modern Times* (Tel Aviv, 1969), 17 (Hebrew).
2. Compare J. Katz, *Tradition and Crisis* (Jerusalem, 1958), 19–27

(Hebrew); J. Parkes, *The Jews in the Medieval Community* (London, 1938), 101–207.

3. J. Locke, *Of Civil Government*, vol. 2, part 4 (London, 1695); J. Toland, *Reason for Naturalizing the Jews of Great Britain and Ireland* (London, 1714); S. Ettinger, "The Beginning of the Change in Attitude of European Society Toward the Jews," *Scripta Hierosolymitana*, 7 (Jerusalem, 1961): 193–219.

4. G. E. Lessing, *Die Juden* (Berlin, 1749).

5. G. R. Mirabeau, *Sur Moses Mendelssohn, Sur La Réforme Politique des Juif* (Paris, 1787); R. R. Palmer, *The Age of Democratic Revolution: The Challenge* (Princeton, 1959), 178–79.

6. C. Roth, *A History of the Jews in England* (Oxford, 1978), 197–223.

7. W. O. McCagg Jr., *A History of Habsburg Jews, 1670–1918* (Bloomington, 1989), 140–80.

8. S. Stern, *The Court Jew* (Philadelphia, 1950).

9. P. Gay, *Voltaire's Politics: The Pact of Realist* (Princeton, 1959), 77.

10. M. Graetz, *The French Revolution and the Jews* (Jerusalem, 1990), 64.

11. J. Arieli, *Political Philosophy in the United States* (Jerusalem, 1968), 79 (Hebrew).

12. A. Hertzberg, *The French Enlightenment and the Jews* (New York), 210.

13. M. Graetz, *The French Revolution and the Jews*, 3–11.

14. M. Graetz, *The Periphery Became the Center* (Jerusalem, 1982), 34–35 (Hebrew); P. C. Albert, *The Modernization of French Jewry: Consistory and Community in the Nineteenth Century* (New Hampshire, 1977), 56–71.

15. S. Almog, *Nationalism and Antisemitism in Modern Europe, 1815–1945* (Jerusalem, 1985), 31 (Hebrew).

16. A. Altmann, *Moses Mendelssohn: A Biographical Study* (Philadelphia, 1973), 421–552; M. Meyer, *Response to Modernity – A History of the Reform Movement in Judaism* (Oxford, 1988), 121–24; A. Shochat, *In Time of Transition – Beginning of the Haskalah with German Jewry* (Jerusalem, 1960) (Hebrew); H. M. Graupe, *The Rise of Modern Judaism* (New York, 1978), 137–66.

17. Moses Mendelssohn, *Gesammelte Schriften,* in G. B. Mendelssohn (ed.), (Leipzig, 1843–1845), 669.

18. M. Meyer, *Response to Modernity – A History of the Reform Movement in Judaism*, 30ff.

19. A. Shochat, "The Integration of German Jewry with its Envi-

ronment at the Onset of the *Haskalah*," *Zion*, 21 (1955): 207–35 (Hebrew).

20. J. Katz, *Out of the Ghetto – The Social Background of Jewish Emancipation, 1770–1870* (New York, 1978).

21. P. G. Pulzer, *The Rise of Political Anti-Semitism in Germany and Austria* (New York, 1969); P. W. Massing, *Rehearsal for Destruction* (New York, 1967).

22. M. Meyer, *The Growth of the Modern Jew – Jewish Identity and European Culture in Germany, 1749–1824* (Jerusalem, 1990), 63–163 (Hebrew).

23. M. Graetz, *The Periphery Became the Center*, 75–164.

24. L. Greenberg, *The Jews in Russia*, vol. 1 (New York, 1976); S. Baron, *The Russian Jews Under Tsars and Soviets* (New York, 1976); S. M. Dubnow, *History of the Jews in Russia and Poland*, vols 1, 2 (Philadelphia, 1975); B. Pinkus, *The Jews of Russia and the Soviet Union – The History of a National Minority* (Jerusalem, 1986) (Hebrew).

25. S. Ettinger, "The Fundaments and Objectives Which Formed the Russian Regime's Policy Toward the Jews After the Partition of Poland," *He-avar*, 19 (1972): 20–35 (Hebrew); R. Pipes, "Catherine II and the Jews," *Soviet Jewish Affairs*, 2 (1975): 3–20; J. Klier, "The Ambiguous Legal Status of Russian Jewry in the Reign of Catherine II," *Slavic Review*, 3 (1976): 504–17.

26. S. Ettinger, "The Statute of 1804," *He-avar*, 22 (1977): 87–110 (Hebrew).

27. M. Stanislawski, *Tsar Nicholas I and the Jews: The Transformation of Jewish Society in Russia, 1825–1855* (Philadelphia, 1983).

28. S. Baron, *The Russian Jews Under Tsars and Soviets*, 37.

29. S. M. Berk, *Year of Crisis, Year of Hope – Russian Jews and the Pogroms of 1881–1882* (London, 1985).

30. S. Dubnow, *Evrei v tsarstvovanie Nikoloya II* (Petrograd, 1922), 33–111.

31. L. Wolf, *Legal Sufferings of the Jews in Russia* (London, 1912).

32. B. Dinur, "Ignatyev's Program for the Solution of the Jewish Problem and the Conference of the Community Representatives in Petersburg," *He-avar* (1962): 57–60 (Hebrew).

33. Compare, *Lopukhin's Memorandum, A Secret Police Report on the Zionist Movement, 1899–1902*, Introduction and notes by J. Goldstein (Jerusalem, 1988), 9–31 (Hebrew).

34. J. Lestschinsky estimated the number of Jews who lived off the income from leasing and tavern keeping at about 70 to

90 percent of overall Jewish wage earners. J. Lestchinsky, "The Situation of Ukrainian Jewry at the End of the 18th and Beginning of the 19th Centuries," *He-avar*, 7 (1960): 6–14 (Hebrew); J. Lestschinsky, *The Economic Situation of the Jews* (Tel Aviv, 1935) (Hebrew). On the other hand Gessen considerably reduces these estimates. Y. Gessen, *Istoriya evriskogo naroda v Rossii* (Leningrad, 1925), 1–130. Gessen's research is much more accurate, although I think he underestimates the number of Jews engaged in the leasing and distilling of alcoholic beverages.

35.   B. Brutskus, *Professionaliji sostov evreiskovo naselanie Rossii* (St Petersburg, 1908); E. Mendelsohn, *Class Struggle in the Pale: The Formative Years of the Jewish Worker's Movement in Tsarist Russia* (Cambridge, 1970).

36.   B. Dinur, "The Historical Image of Russian Jewry and the Problems in its Research," *Zion*, 22 (1957): 93–118 (Hebrew).

37.   B. Kedari, *The Role of Jews in the Industrial Development of Warsaw – 1816/20–1914* (Tel Aviv, 1985) (Hebrew).

38.   S. Ettinger, "The Image of the Jews in Russian Public Opinion up to the 1880's," in *Antisemitism in the Modern Period* (Tel Aviv, 1978), 145–68 (Hebrew).

39.   Ibid., 157.

40.   S. Witte, *Vespominaniie*, 3 (1922), 12–13, 19–20; A. Feldman, "The Manifest of October 17 1905, Count Witte and the Jewish Question," in *Raphael Mahler Festschrift* (Tel Aviv, 1974), 115 (Hebrew).

41.   H. Rogger, "Tsarist Policy on Jewish Emigration," *Soviet Jewish Affairs*, 1 (1973): 27.

42.   B. Pinkus, *The Jews of Russia and the Soviet Union – The History of a National Minority*, 192–95.

43.   L. Schapiro, "The Role of the Jews in the Russian Revolutionary Movement," *Slavonic and East European Review*, 40 (1961): 148–67; T. M. Riglu, *Communist Party Membership in the U.S.S.R. 1917–1967* (Princeton, 1968), 366–88.

44.   M. Altshuler, *The Yevsektsiya in the Soviet Union 1918–1938: Between Nationalism and Communism* (Tel Aviv, 1980) (Hebrew); Z. Gitelman, *Jewish Nationality and Soviet Politics: The Jewish Sections of the CPSU, 1917–1930* (Princeton, 1972).

45.   J. Lvavi, *Jewish Settlement in Birobidzhan* (Jerusalem, 1965) (Hebrew).

46.   R. Conquest, *The Great Terror* (London, 1968).

47. L. Stein, *The Balfour Declaration* (London, 1961); M. Verete, "The Balfour Declaration and its Makers," *Middle East Studies*, 6 (1970): 48–76.

48. O. I. Janowsky, *The Jews and Minority Rights, 1918–1919* (New York, 1933); M. Landau, *A Fighting Ethnic Minority, The Struggle of Polish Jewry 1918–1928* (Jerusalem, 1986) (Hebrew).

49. S. Goldman, *Jewish National Autonomy in the Ukraine* (New York, 1961) (Yiddish).

50. E. Mendelsohn, *The Jews of East Central Europe Between the World Wars* (Bloomington, 1983), 11–84, 171–212.

51. Ibid.; J. Marcus, *Social and Political History of the Jews in Poland, 1919–1939* (Berlin/New York, 1983).

52 E. Mendelsohn, "Jewish Reactions to Antisemitism in Interwar East Central Europe," in J. Reinharz (ed.) *Living with Antisemitism – Modern Jewish Responses* (Hanover, 1987), 296–312; C. Shmeruk, "Responses to Antisemitism in Poland, 1912–1936," in ibid., 275–312.

53. B. Kedari, *The Role of Jews in the Industrial Development of Warsaw – 1816/20–1914*, 245; R. Mahler, *Jews of Poland between the Two World Wars* (Tel Aviv, 1968), 61 (Hebrew).

54. R. Mahler, *Jews of Poland*, 164–66.

55. Ibid., 189–95.

56. H. I. Bach, *The German Jew: A Synthesis of Judaism and Western Civilization, 1730–1930* (New York, 1989), 136–250.

57. U. Tal, *Christians and Jews in Germany – Religion, Politics and Ideology in the Second Reich 1870–1914* (Ithaca and London, 1975).

58. L. Yahil, *The Holocaust: The Fate of European Jewry, 1932–1945* (New York, 1992); Lucy S. Dawidowicz, *The War Against the Jews, 1933–1945* (New York, 1975), 65–123.

59. L. Yahil, *The Holocaust*; Lucy Dawidowicz, *The War Against the Jews*; G. Fleming, *Hitler and the Final Solution* (Los Angeles, 1984).

60. S. Ettinger (ed.), *History of the Jews in Islamic Countries*, vol. 3 (Jerusalem 1986), 74–92, 333–43, 352–468 (Hebrew).

Chapter 3: Cultural Revolution

1. Compare S. Dubnow, *History of Hasidism* (Tel Aviv, 1944) (Hebrew); B. Dinur, "The Beginnings of Hasidism and its

Socialist and Messianic Roots," *Zion*, 9 (1943): 108–9, 186–87; (1944): 67–77, 144–74 (Hebrew); G. Scholem, *Explications and Implications* (Tel Aviv, 1976), 285–381; J. Weiss, *Studies in Eastern European Jewish Mysticism* (Oxford, 1985).

2. H. Graetz, *History of the Jews*, vol. 5 (1893), 175–301; A. Altman, *Moses Mendelssohn: A Biographical Study* (Philadelphia, 1973), 421–552, 638–759.

3. B. Dinur, "The Modern Era in Jewish History,"; B. D. Weinryb, *The Jews of Poland – A Social and Economic History of the Jewish Community in Poland from 1100 to 1800* (Philadelphia, 1972), 179–303.

4. B. D. Weinryb, *The Jews of Poland*; G. D. Hundert, *Security and Dependence: Perspectives on 17th Century Polish-Jewish Society Gained Through a Study of Jewish Merchants in Little Poland* (Ph.D. diss., Columbia University, 1978).

5. Scholars disagree regarding the severity of the economic crisis. B. Dinur claims it was severe – see "The Modern Era in Jewish History." Rosman calls the community "solid and prosperous' – see M. J. Rosman, "The Image of Poland as a Center of Torah Learning after the Massacres of 1648," *Zion*, 51 (1986): 435–48 (Hebrew); M. J. Rosman, *The Lands, Jews and Magnates in Old Poland* (Cambridge, 1987).

6. There is further disagreement amongst scholars regarding the factors which influenced the rise of Hasidism and its intensity. Some say it was caused by the crisis within the Polish-Lithuanian Commonwealth while others say it was the result of Kabbalah influence and the Shabbatean movement. My own sense is that there is truth in both claims.

   Compare S. Dubnow, *History of the Jewish People*, 8–24; B. Dinur, "The Modern Era in Jewish History,"; G. Scholem, *Major Trends in Jewish Mysticism* (New York, 1954); S. Werses, *Haskalah and Shabbateanism: The History of a Struggle* (Jerusalem, 1987), 94–124 (Hebrew); A. Rubenstein, "Between Hasidism and Shabbateanism," *Bar-Ilan University Year Book* (1966), 324–39 (Hebrew); J. Katz, *Tradition and Crisis; Jewish Society at the End of the Middle Ages* (New York, 1961), 36–95; I. Halpern, *Jews and Judaism in Eastern Europe* (Jerusalem, 1969), 30–83 (Hebrew).

7. Some scholars of Hasidism maintain that the *Besht* was not the one and only leader but rather one "of a group of charismatic and phenomenal personalities." See A. Rappoport-

Albert, "The Hasidic Movement after 1772: Structural Continuity and Permutation," *Zion* 55 (1989): 196 (Hebrew). This argument does not detract from the power of his leadership or the perception that he was the leader of Hasidism in his time.

8. For the *Besht*, his circle and the development of the "first stage" of Hasidism see S. Dubnow, *History of the Jewish People*, vol. 10, 41–75; B. Dinur, "The Modern Era in Jewish History"; G. Scholem, "The First Two Testimonies about the Circle of Hasidim and the *Besht*," *Tarbiz* 20 (1948): 228–40 (Hebrew); G. Scholem, "The Historical Image of Israel Ba'al Shem Tov," *Molad* 18 (1959): 339–47 (Hebrew); M. Rosman, "Medzibezh and Rabbi Israel Ba'al Shem Tov," *Zion*, 52 (1986): 177–90 (Hebrew); S. Ettinger, "The Hasidic Leadership in its Formation," in *Religion and Society in the History of the Jewish People and the Nations of the World* (Jerusalem, 1964), 122–23 (Hebrew); M. Peikaz, *The Period of Development of Hasidism* (Jerusalem, 1977) (Hebrew).

9. A. Rappoport-Albert, "The Hasidic Movement after 1772: Structural Continuity and Permutation," 201–8.

10. G. Scholem, *Major Trends in Jewish Mysticism* (New York, 1954).

11. G. Scholem, "The First Two Testimonies about the Circle of Hasidim and the *Besht*."

12. M. Wilensky, "The Singing of the Tyrants and the Knives of Flint," in *Hasidim and Mitngaggedim: The History of the Polemic between them from 1774 to 1815* (Jerusalem, 1970), 27–69 (Hebrew).

13. E. Etkes, "Ha-Gaon Rabbi Eliyahu and the Beginning of Opposition to the Hasidim," in *Changes in Contemporary Jewish History – A Tribute to Shmuel Ettinger* (Jerusalem, 1988), 439–58 (Hebrew).

14. I. Halpern, "Groups for Torah and *Mitzvot*: The Hasidic Movement in its Expansion," in *Jews and Judaism in Eastern Europe* (Jerusalem, 1969), 313–32. (Hebrew). D. Assaf, "The Expansion of Hasidism – The Case of R. Nehemiah Yehiel of Bychawa," in *Studies in Jewish Culture in Honour of Chone Shmeruk* (Jerusalem, 1993), 269–98 (Hebrew).

15. Scholars agree that the Enlightenment movement in Eastern Europe began to spread amongst a small circle of Jews in the Pale of Settlement in the 1820s and 1830s, and as a social movement only in the 1850s and 1860s. However, they dis-

agree as to whether it is possible to perceive the blossoming of the Enlightenment parallel to its emergence in Central Europe. The Vilna Gaon has been perceived as the harbinger of the Enlightenment by scholars such as: Raphael Mahler, *The History of the Jewish People in Modern Times*, vol. 4 (Tel Aviv, 1962), 53–57 (Hebrew); Joseph Klausner, *History of Modern Hebrew Literature* (Jerusalem, 1952), 17–18 (Hebrew); Benzion Katz, *Rabbinism, Hasidism, Haskalah* (Tel Aviv, 1956), 38–43 (Hebrew), and others. An opposing view is that of Emanuel Etkes, "Ha-Gaon Rabbi Eliyahu and the *Haskalah* – Appearance and Reality," in E. Etkes and J. Salmon (eds), *Chapters in the History of Jewish Society in the Middle Ages and Modern Times* (Jerusalem, 1980), 192–217 (Hebrew).

16. M. Eliav, *Jewish Education in Germany During the Enlightenment and Emancipation* (Jerusalem, 1961), 15–24 (Hebrew).

17. M. Bodian, "The Jewish Entrepreneurs in Berlin and the Civil Improvement of the Jews in the 1780s and 1790s," *Zion*, 49 (1984): 176 (Hebrew); J. Katz, *Out of the Ghetto* (New York, 1978), 19–50; A. Shochat, "Integration of German Jewry with their Surroundings at the Onset of the Enlightenment," *Zion*, 21 (1956): 207–35 (Hebrew).

18. M. Mendelssohn, *Jerusalem: Treatise on Ecclesiastical Authority and Judaism*, English trans. M. Samuels (Berlin, 1778), 312–18; A. Altman, *Moses Mendelssohn: A Biographical Study*, 214–23; J. Katz, *Jews and Gentiles* (Jerusalem, 1961), 170–79 (Hebrew).

19. N. H. Wessely, *Words of Peace and Truth* (Berlin 1782) (Hebrew); M. Eliav, *Jewish Education in Germany During the Enlightenment and Emancipation*, 39–51.

20. H. H. Ben-Sasson (ed.), *A History of the Jewish People*, vol. 3 (Cambridge, Mass., 1976), 3, 79.

21. M. Meyer, *The Growth of the Modern Jew – Jewish Identity and European Culture in Germany, 1749–1824* (Jerusalem, 1990), 64–96 (Hebrew); J. Katz, *Out of the Ghetto*, 123. Y. Meisel, "A Letter from David Friedländer," *YIVO Historical Journal*, 2 (1937): 390–412 (Yiddish).

22. S. Feiner, "Isaac Euchel – The Initiator of the Enlightenment Movement in Germany," *Zion*, 52 (1987): 427–70 (Hebrew).

23. H. D. Schmidt, "The Terms of Emancipation, 1781–1812," *Leo Baeck Year Book*, 1 (1956): 28–50.

24. M. Meyer, *The Growth of the Modern Jew – Jewish Identity and European Culture in Germany, 1749–1824*, 96–130.

25. H. Kohn, *Heinrich Heine: The Man and the Myth* (New York), 45–70.
26. M. Meyer, *The Growth of the Modern Jew – Jewish Identity and European Culture in Germany, 1749–1824*, 164–210.
27. N. N. Glatzer, "Principles of Zunz's Historical Perception," *Zion*, 26 (1960): 208–14 (Hebrew).
28. M. Meyer, *Between Tradition and Progress: History of the Reform Movement in Judaism* (Jerusalem, 1989), 58–59 (Hebrew).
29. Ibid., 17–79.
30. M. Meyer, "The Building of the Reform Temple in Hamburg," *Chapters in the History of Jewish Society in the Middle Ages and Modern Times*, 218–24.
31. M. Meyer, *Between Tradition and Progress: History of the Reform Movement in Judaism*, 58.
32. Ibid., 122–67.
33. R. Horowitz, *Zacharias Frankel and the Beginnings of Positivist Historical Judaism* (Jerusalem, 1984), 9–41 (Hebrew).
34. Rabbi Moses Sofer, *Sermons*, vol. 2 (1829), folio 311, recto (Hebrew).
35. J. Katz, "Contribution Towards a Biography of R. Moses Sofer," *Studies in Mysticism and Religion Presented to Gershom G. Scholem* (1967): 133–44. (Hebrew); J. Katz, *Out of the Ghetto*, 166–70; S. Spitzer, "Der Einfluss des Chatam Sofer und seiner Pressburger Schule auf die Jüdischen Gemeinden Mitteleuropas im 19 jahrhundert," *Studia Judaica Austriaca*, 8 (1986): 111–21.
36. J. Katz, *Out of the Ghetto*, 152–70; J. Katz, "Contributions Towards a Biography . . . ".
37. B. Katz, *Rabbinism, Hasidism, Haskalah*, 122; R. Mahler, *The History of the Jewish People in Modern Times*, vol. 4, 90.
38. For the beginnings of the Enlightenment in Eastern Europe, see R. Mahler, *The History of the Jewish People in Modern Times*; L. Greenberg, *The Jews in Russia, The Struggle for Emancipation*, vol. 1 (New York, 1976), 56–72.
39. Some scholars maintain that he was the harbinger of the Enlightenment in Eastern Europe, though there is no evidence to support this. See S. M. Dubnow, *History of the Jews in Russia and Poland*, vol. 1 (Philadelphia, 1975), 384–89.
40. S. Ettinger, "The Statute of 1804," *He-avar*, 22 (1977): 87–110 (Hebrew); Iulli Gessen [Julius Hessen], *Yvrei v Rossii* ["The Jews in Russia"] (St. Petersburg, 1906), 326–35.

41. M. Stanislawski, *Tsar Nicholas I and the Jews: The Transformation of Jewish Society in Russia, 1825–1855* (Philadelphia, 1983).
42. S. J. Zipperstein, *The Jews of Odessa, A Cultural History, 1794–1861* (Stanford, 1985), 44–55.
43. M. Levin, *Social and Economic Values in the Ideology of the Age of the Haskalah* (Jerusalem, 1975), 74–186 (Hebrew).
44. R. Mahler, *The History of the Jewish People in Modern Times*, vol. 6, 110–31; S. Verses, "Hasidism as Perceived by *Haskalah* Literature," *Molad* 18 (1960): 379–91 (Hebrew).
45. I. B. Levinsohn, *Beit Yehudah* ["House of Judah"] (Vilna, 1838), 134 (Hebrew); For additional material on Levinsohn see E. Etkes' Introduction to the book by I. B. Levinsohn, *Te'udah be-Yisrael* ["Testimony in Israel"] (Jerusalem, 1977), 8ff. (Hebrew).
46. Memorandum from Benjamin Mandelstamm to Max Lilienthal, 1842, *Hazon la-Moed* ["The Prophecy to be Fulfilled"], vol. 2 (Vienna, 1877), 14–15 (Hebrew).
47. M. Stanislawski, *Tsar Nicholas I and the Jews, The Transformation of Jewish Society in Russia, 1825–1855.*
48. Iulli Gessen [Julius Hessen] *Istoriia evreiskogo naroda v Rossii* ["History of the Jewish People in Russia"], vol. 1 (Leningrad, 1925), 74–143.
49. M. Levin, *Social and Economic Values in the Ideology of the Age of the Haskalah*; J. Raisin, *The Haskalah Movement in Russia* (Philadelphia, 1913).
50. L. Greenberg, *The Jews in Russia: The Struggle for Emancipation*, vol. 1, 76; Regarding the easing of laws by Alexander II see: Vitali Levanda, "Complete Chronological Collections of Laws and Regulations Concerning Jews from the Time of the Tsar Alexei Mikhailovich to the Present, 1649–1873" (St. Petersburg, 1874), 891–94.
51. B. Pinkus, *Jews of Russia and the Soviet Union – History of a National Minority* (Beer-Sheba, 1986), 88–90 (Hebrew); on *Haskalah* education, see S. Levin, "Elementary Schools for Children of the Mosaic Faith in Warsaw, 1830–1860", *Gal'ed* 3 (1976): 82–63 (Hebrew); S. Levin, "The First Elementary Schools for Children of the Mosaic Faith in Warsaw, 1828–1830," *Gal'ed* 1 (1973): 63–100 (Hebrew); S. Levin, "History of Secular Schools in Poland in the Last Forty Years of the 19th Century," *Gal'ed* 9 (1986): 77–90 (Hebrew).

52. Y. Slutsky, *The Russian-Jewish Press in the 19th Century* (Jerusalem, 1970), 27 (Hebrew).
53. This is evidenced by the large circulation of Russian-language Jewish newspapers. Compare Y. Slutsky, *The Russian-Jewish Press in the 19th Century*; and by the ever-growing number of Jewish pupils who studied in Russian high schools and universities. E. Schulman, *A History of Jewish Education in the Soviet Union* (New York, 1972), 22–25.
54. Data regarding the Jewish educational system in Russia from 1881 are taken from: S. Levin, *Social and Economic Values in the Ideology of the Age of the Haskalah*; B. Pinkus, *Jews of Russia and the Soviet Union – History of a National Minority*, 133–36; Z. Halevy, *Jewish University Students and Professionals in Tsarist and Soviet Russia* (Tel Aviv, 1976).
55. Compare M. Levin, *Social and Economic Values in the Ideology of the Age of the Haskalah*; an outstanding example of this change can be seen in the development of Ahad Ha'am. Compare J. Goldstein, *Ahad Ha'am: A Biography* (Jerusalem, 1992) (Hebrew); S. J. Zipperstein, *Elusive Prophet: Ahad Ha'am and the Origins of Zionism* (Los Angeles, 1993).
56. Compare for example: A. Coale, S. W. Watkins, *The Decline of Fertility in Europe* (Princeton, 1986); O. Chadwick, *The Secularization of the European Mind in the 19th century* (Cambridge, 1975).
57. Compare for example: P. Wengeroff, *Memoiren einer grossmutter* (Berlin, 1913–1919); A. Frank, *The Urbanites and the Jews in Poland* (Warsaw, 1921) (Hebrew); A. Frank, "The Struggle Against 'Wantonness' in Old-Time Warsaw", in *Almanac for the Tenth Anniversary of Der Moment* (Warsaw, 1921), 95–114 (Yiddish).
58. J. Teitel, *Aus meiner Lebensarbeit: Erinnenurngen eines judischen Richters in alter Russland* (Frankfurt, 1929); J. Shatzky, *History of the Jews in Warsaw*, vol. 3 (New York, 1953), 406–23 (Yiddish). Compare the sociological explanations regarding New York City, which no doubt apply to cities such as Warsaw, Łódź or Odessa. A. A. Goren, *New York Jews and the Quest for Community* (Philadelphia, 1970), 1–42.
59. Compare for example: B. Katz, *Memoirs* (Tel Aviv, 1963) (Hebrew).
60. Compare for example: J. Shatzky, "Alexander Kraushar and His Road to Total Assimilation," *YIVO Annual* 7 (1953): 146–74;

J. Shatzky, "Institutional Aspects of Jewish Life in Warsaw in the Second Half of the Nineteenth Century," *YIVO Annual*, 10 (1955): 9–44.

61. J. Frankel, *Prophecy and Politics: Socialism, Nationalism, and the Russian Jews, 1862–1917* (Cambridge, 1981), 52.
62. Ibid., 51.
63. Ibid., 40–61.
64. Ibid., 91–107; M. Mishkinsky, "The Initial Sources of the Jewish Labor Movement" *Zion*, 31 (1966): 87–115 (Hebrew); M. Mishkinsky, "The Jewish Socialist Movement Until the Founding of the Bund," *YIVO Historishe Shriftn*, vol. 3 (Vilna/Paris, 1939); E. Mendelsohn, *Class Struggle in the Pale: The Formative Years of the Jewish Workers Movement in Tsarist Russia* (Cambridge, 1970).
65. Regarding the Bund see: J. Frankel, *Prophecy and Politics*, 171–257; G. Aronson, J. S. Hertz (eds), *History of the Bund*, 4 vols (New York, 1956–1968) (Yiddish); H. J. Tobias, *The Jewish Bund in Russia: From its Origins to 1905* (Stanford, 1972); A. L. Patkin, *The Origins of the Russian-Jewish Labour Movement* (Melbourne, 1947).
66. *Yiddisher Arbeiter*, 2 December 1898.
67. Ibid., no. 12 (1901), 99.
68. Ibid.
69. Regarding *Hibbat Zion* and the Zionist Organization see: David Vital, *The Origins of Zionism* (Oxford, 1975); *Zionism: The Formative Years* (Oxford, 1982); *Zionism: The Crucial Phase* (Oxford, 1987); J. Klausner, *The Movement to Zion in Russia*, 3 vols (1962–1965) (Hebrew); A. Böhm, *Die Zionistische Bewegung*, 2 vols (1933–1935).
70. M. L. Lilienblum, *Derekh La'avor Golim – The Revival of the Jewish People in the Land of their Fathers*, in *An Autobiography* (Jerusalem, 1970), 9–18 (Hebrew).
71. E. Luz, *Parallels Meet* (Tel Aviv, 1985), 163–83 (Hebrew); J. Salmon, *Religion and Zionism – the First Confrontations* (Jerusalem, 1990), 312–13 (Hebrew).
72. Regarding Mohilever see J. Salmon, "Rabbi Samuel Mohilever – The Rabbi of *Hovevei Zion*," *Zion*, 56 (1990): 47–78 (Hebrew); regarding Rabbi Kook see: Z. Yaron, *Rabbi Kook's Philosophy* (Jerusalem, 1973) (Hebrew); S. Avineri, *The Zionist Idea in all its Nuances* (Tel Aviv, 1978), 216–26 (Hebrew); regarding Gush Emunim see Z. Ra'anan, *Gush Emunim* (Tel Aviv, 1980)

(Hebrew); J. Aviad, "The Messianism of Gush Emunim," *Studies in Contemporary Jewry*, vol. 7, ed. Jonathan Frankel (1991): 197–216.

73. Compare: E. Luz, *Parallels Meet*, 185–214; J. Salmon, *Religion and Zionism – the First Confrontations*, 314–34; S. Z. Landau, *Sefer Or la-Yesharim* (Warsaw, 1900) (Hebrew).

74. Ahad Ha'am, "The Wrong Way," *Ha-Melitz* 53 (1899) (Hebrew); Ahad Ha'am, "Following the Bier of a Wise Man," *Kaveret* (Odessa, 1890): 105 (Hebrew); Ahad Ha'am, "Torah of the Heart," *Writings of Ahad Ha'am* (Tel Aviv, 1964), 51, 54 (Hebrew); J. Goldstein "Ahad Ha'am's Attitude to Religion from a Historical Perspective," *Changes in Contemporary Jewish History – A Tribute to Shmuel Ettinger* (Jerusalem, 1988), 159–68 (Hebrew).

75. Herzl's opening address at the First Zionist Congress, *Die Welt*, 3 September 1897.

76. *Ha-Melitz* 61, 26 March 1899 (Hebrew).

77. On Benei Moshe, see J. Goldstein, "Benei Moshe: The Story of a Secret Order," *Zion*, 57 (1992): 175–206 (Hebrew); On the Democratic Faction, see: J. Reinharz, *Chaim Weizmann: The Making of a Zionist Leader* (Oxford, 1985), 65–91; Israel Klausner, *Opposition to Herzl* (Jerusalem, 1968) (Hebrew).

78. S. Baron, *The Test of Freedom* (Jerusalem, 1976), 234–46 (Hebrew); L. P. Gartner, *The Jewish Community in the United States, from its Inception Until the Present Day* (Tel Aviv, 1980), 78–82 (Hebrew); M. Davis, *The Development of American Jewry* (New York, 1951) (Hebrew); H. Feingold, "A New Religious Synthesis: Conservatism," in H. Feingold, *Zion in America* (New York, 1974): 179–93; N. Glazer, "Reformers and Conservatives, 1880–1900," *American Judaism* (Chicago, 1972): 43–59; J. S. Gurock, "Resisters and Accommodators: Varieties of Orthodox Rabbis in America, 1886–1983," *The American Rabbinate – A Century of Continuity and Change, 1883–1983* (New Jersey, 1983), 10–97.

79. M. Rischin, *The Promised City – New York Jews, 1870–1914* (Cambridge, Mass., 1962).

80. Compare, for example, the thousands of letters to the *Bintel Brief* ("Bundle of Letters"), a column in the Yiddish newspaper *Forward*. For a selection of these letters see: I. Metzker (ed.), *A Bintel Brief: Sixty Years of Letters from the East Side to the Jewish Daily Forward* (New York, 1971); I. Howe, *World of Our Fathers*

(New York, 1976), 533–37.

81. Regarding Jewish education compare: I. Howe, *World of Our Fathers*; M. Rischin, *The Promised City – New York Jews, 1870–1914*.

82. I. Howe, *World of Our Fathers*, 460–517; M. Rischin, *The Promised City – New York Jews, 1870–1914*, 133–38.

83. I. Friedlaender, "The Problem of Judaism in America," *Past and Present – Selected Essays* (New York, 1961), 159–83.

84. H. Hapgood, *The Spirit of the Ghetto* (New York, 1966), 67–70.

85. S. Schechter, "The Work of Heaven," *American Hebrew*, February 1913.

86. J. Rothenberg, "The Legal Status of Religion in the Soviet Union," in R. Marshall Jr. (ed.), *Aspects of Religion in the Soviet Union, 1917–1967* (Chicago, 1967), 61–100.

87. M. Altshuler, *The Yevsektsiya in the Soviet Union, 1918–1930 – Between Nationalism and Communism* (Tel Aviv, 1980) (Hebrew); Z. Gitelman, *Jewish Nationality and Soviet Politics: The Jewish Section of the CPSU, 1917–1930* (Princeton 1972).

88. J. Rothenberg, *The Jewish Religion in the Soviet Union* (New York).

89. A. Yodfat, "Jewish Religious Communities in the USSR," *Soviet Jewish Affairs* 2 (1971): 63.

90. E. Mendelsohn, *The Jews of East Central Europe Between the World Wars* (Bloomington, 1983), 17–32.

91. The details are from: J. Marcus, *Social and Political History of the Jews in Poland, 1919–1939* (Berlin/New York, 1983), 249–90; E. Mendelsohn, *The Jews of East Central Europe Between the World Wars* (Bloomington, 1983).

92. J. Marcus, *Social and Political History of the Jews in Poland, 1919–1939* (Berlin/New York, 1983), 149.

93. J. Salmon, "The Askenazi Urban Settlement in Erez Israel, 1880–1903," in *The History of the Jewish Community in Erez Israel* (Jerusalem, 1990), 539–620 (Hebrew).

94. J. Salmon, "The Confrontation between Haredim and Maskilim in the Hibbat Zion Movement," *Ha-Ziyyonut*, 5 (1978): 43–77 (Hebrew).

95. M. Friedman, "The Social Significance of the Shemitah [Sabbatical Year] Controversy," *Shalem*, 1 (1979): 455–80 (Hebrew).

96. J. Goldstein, *Ahad Ha'am: A Biography*, 122–72.

97. D. Kenaani, *The Workers of the Second Aliyah and their Attitude Towards Religion and Tradition* (Tel Aviv, 1976) (Hebrew).

98. Y. Haver, "In the Press and in Literature," *Ha-Po'el ha-za'ir*: 3, 26 (1911) (Hebrew).
99. R. Kark, *Jaffa – Its Development as a City, 1799–1917* (Jerusalem, 1984) (Hebrew); A. Shahori, *A Dream that Became a City: Tel Aviv, – Its Birth and Development: The City that Gave Birth to a State* (Tel Aviv, 1990) (Hebrew).
100. M. Friedman, *Society and Religion* (Jerusalem, 1978), 114–15 (Hebrew).
101. A. Shapira, "The Religious Motifs of the Labor Movement," in *Volume in Memory of Professor Shimon Reshf*, ed. A. Shapira and A. Kasher (Tel Aviv, 1991), 155–78 (Hebrew).
102. M. Friedman, *Society and Religion*, 130–31.
103. The definition "Haredim" is difficult and controversial. The reference in this article to *Haredim* or to the Jewish-Orthodox community is meant to relate to all the groups who, from the founding of Agudat Israel (1912), remained faithful to the Jewish religion, did not see themselves as nationalists (Zionists) and were stricter in observance of the *mitzvot*.
104. M. Attias, *The Jewish Community in Erez Israel* (Jerusalem, 1944), 29–35 (Hebrew); B. Eliav, *The Yishuv During the Period of the National Home* (Jerusalem, 1970), 151–205 (Hebrew).
105. Regarding the character of Mizrachi education in the 1920s, see for example M. Rinot, "The Controversy About Creating the Hebrew Educational System in Erez Israel, 1918–1920," *Ha-Ziyyonut*, 5 (1978): 78–114 (Hebrew).
106. M. Friedman, *Society and Religion*, 253–85.
107. Compare, for example, A. Shapira, "The Religious Motifs of the Labor Movement."
108. Regarding the various trends of education in Israel, compare H. Adler, "A Sociological View of Education in Israel," *Yahadut Zemanenu*, 4 (1988): 171–98 (Hebrew).
109. S. N. Eisenstadt, *The Transformation of Israeli Society* (London, 1985); U. O. Schmelz, S. Della Pergola and U. Avner, *Ethnic Differences Among Jews: A New Look* (Jerusalem, 1991).
110. Compare for example: M. Abitbol, "The Jews in North Africa and Egypt," in S. Ettinger (ed.) *The History of the Jews in Islamic Countries* (Jerusalem 1986), 316–406 (Hebrew).
111. U. O. Schmelz *et al.*, *Ethnic Differences Among Jews: A New Look*.
112. D. Caspi, A. Diskin and E. Gutman (eds), *The Roots of Begin's Success* (London, 1984).

113. M. Friedman, *Society and Religion*, 214.
114. A. Ravitzky, "Exile in the Holy Land: The Dilemma of Haredi Jewry," *Studies in Contemporary Jewry*, 5 (1989): 89–125.
115. For additional information about the reasons for the ideological cooperation between Agudat Israel and the Government of Israel in the 1980s, see A. Ravitzky, "Exile in the Holy Land," 108–9.
116. The information is from the Israel Government *Budget Book* for 1974/5, 1977/8, 1982/3, 1985/6 (Hebrew).
117. Ibid.
118. The figures for Yeshiva Students receiving exemption from army service are estimates based on press coverage. Compare, for example, *Ha'aretz*, 7 March 1991 (Hebrew).
119. U. O. Schmelz, S. Della Pergola and U. Avner, *Ethnic Differences Among Jews: A New Look* (Jerusalem, 1991).
120. Compare A. Ravitzky, "Exile in the Holy Land."
121. S. M. Cohen, *American Assimilation or Jewish Revival* (Bloomington, 1981); C. Goldscheider, *Toward the Fifth Generation: The Challenges to Assimilate in the American Jewish Community* (Chicago, 1982).
122. There is disagreement amongst the scholars regarding the percentage of mixed marriages and particularly about their significance. Compare: S. Della Pergola, U. O. Schmelz, "Demographic Transformations of American Jewry: Marriage and Mixed Marriages in the 1980s," *Studies in Contemporary Jewry*, 5 (1989): 169–200; C. Goldscheider, "American Jewish Marriages: Erosion or Transformation?," ibid., 201–8; E. Mayer, "Patterns of Mixed Marriages Amongst American Jews: Differences, Similarities, Dilemmas and Prospects," *Tefutzot Yisrael*, 4 (1979): 88–95 (Hebrew).
123. B. Pinkus, *Jews of Russia and the Soviet Union – History of a National Minority*, 452–54; *American Jewish Year Book* (1990): 385–87.
124. See for example: U. O. Schmelz, S. Della Pergola, "The Demography of Latin American Jewry," *Yahadut Zemanenu*, 4 (1988): 291–293 (Hebrew); *American Jewish Year Book* (1990): 314–18, 330–31, 397–400.
125. The figure is disputed. According to U. O. Schmelz and others (see note 109) there is a difference between Orthodox and traditionalists who together constitute about 35 percent of the population. The Orthodox who in the Knesset elections

vote for the Orthodox and *Haredi* parties are about 20 percent on average, together with another approximately 6 percent Orthodox and *Haredim* who vote for non-religious parties.

Chapter 4: Anti-Semitism

1. Cf. M. Stern, *Greek and Latin Authors on Jews and Judaism*, vols 1–2 (Jerusalem, 1976, 1980); A. Kasher, "The Propaganda Goal of the Mannon Libel Regarding the Base Origin of the Jews," in *Studies in the History of the People of Israel and the Land of Israel*, vol. 3, part 1 (1975), 69–84 (Hebrew); D. Flusser, "Blood Libel Against the Jews in the Light of the Views of the Hellenistic Period," *The Book of Yohanan Levi* (Jerusalem, 1949), 104–24 (Hebrew); M. Stern, "Jew-Hatred in Rome," in S. Almog (ed.), *Generations of Jew-Hatred* (Jerusalem, 1980), 27–40 (Hebrew); S. Ettinger, *Antisemitism in the Modern Era* (Tel Aviv, 1978), vol. 1 (Hebrew); L. Rott-Garson, "Jew-Hatred in Ancient Times," in *Jew-Hatred and Antisemitism*, vol. 2 (The Open University Tel Aviv, 1985), 89–149 (Hebrew).

2. Cf., for example, S. Ettinger, "Jew-Hatred in Historical Continuity," in in S. Almog (ed.), *Generations of Jew-Hatred*, 11–26; H. Shatzker, "The Dispute of the German Historians – or the Germans' Dispute with their History," *Pages on the Study of the Holocaust*, 6 (1988): 185–214 (Hebrew); H. Hoffman (ed.), *Gegen den Versuch Vergangenheit Zu Verbiegen* (Frankfurt am Main, 1987).

3. See for example J. Parkes, *The Conflict of the Church and the Synagogue* (New York, 1981); J. G. Gager, *The Origins of Anti-Semitism* (Oxford, 1985); E. L. Alel, *The Roots of Anti-Semitism* (London, 1975); J. Katz, *Jew-Hatred: From Blood Loathing to Denial of the Race* (Tel Aviv, 1979) (Hebrew).

4. See, for example S. W. Baron, "European Jewry before and after Hitler," in *American Jewish Year Book*, 63 (1962): 3–53.

5. See, for example E. Reichman, *Hostages of Civilization* (Boston, 1951).

6. See, for example S. Freud, *Moses and Monotheism* (London, 1939); T. W. Adorno *et al.*, *The Authoritarian Personality* (New York, 1964).

7. See, for example M. Rodinson, "Preface," in *La Conception Materialiste de la Question Juive* (Paris, 1968).

8. Most prominently, H. Arendt, *The Origins of Totalitarianism* (New York, 1951) and *Eichmann in Jerusalem* (New York, 1963).
9. Cf. L. Poliakov, *The History of Anti-Semitism*, vols 1–4 (New York 1968–1985); S. Ettinger, *Antisemitism in the Modern Era*, 1–28.
10. Cf., for example, S. W. Baron, "Changing Patterns of Anti-Semitism," in *In the Diaspora* 79/80 (1977): 125–52 (Hebrew); S. W. Baron, "European Jewry before and after Hitler," 3–53.
11. Cf., for example, S. Volkov, "Antisemitism as a Cultural Code," in *Leo Baeck Institute Year Book*, 22 (1978): 25–46.
12. T. Mason, "Intention and Explanation," in G. Hirschfeld, L. Kettennacker (eds), *Der Führerstaat: Mythos und Realitat* (Stuttgart, 1981), 23–41; C. Browning, "Attitudes toward the 'Final Solution' in German Historiography of the Last Two Decades," in Y. Gutman and G. Grace (eds), *The Holocaust in Historiography* (Jerusalem, 1987), 23–42 (Hebrew).
13. Nolte's essay appeared in the *Frankfurter Allgemeine Zeitung*, 6 June 1986, and afterward in *Das Vergehen der Verganenheit: Antwort an meine Kritiker im sogennantes Historikerstreit* (Frankfurt am Main, 1987).
14. *Die Zeit*, 11 July 1986.
15. Cf. H. Shatzker's summary, "The Dispute of the German Historians – or the Germans' Dispute with their History," *Pages on the Study of the Holocaust* 6 (1988), 185–214 (Hebrew).
16. J. Fest, *Frankfurter Allgemeine Zeitung*, 29 August 1986.
17. See the sources cited in note 13 above.
18. Cf., for example, S. Friedlander's response, *Ha'aretz*, 3 October 1986.
19. Cf. P. W. Massing, *Rehearsal for Destruction* (New York 1967).
20. R. S. Levy, The *Downfall of the Anti-Semitic Political Parties in Imperial Germany* (New Haven, 1975).
21. E. O. Sterling, "Anti-Jewish Riots in Germany in 1819: A Displacement of Social Protest," *Historia Judaica* 12 (1950): 105–92; J. Katz, "The 1819 'Hep Hep' Riots in Germany and their Historical Background," *Zion*, 38 (1973): 62–115 (Hebrew); J. Tori, "Self Defense in the 'Hep Hep' Riots," in *Yalkut Moreshet* (1972): 107–16 (Hebrew).
22. R. Rürap, "The European Revolutions of 1848 and Jewish Emancipation," in W. E. Mosse, A. Paucker, R. Rürap (eds), *Revolution and Evolution: 1848 in German-Jewish History*

(Tübingen, 1981), 1–53; S. Baron, "The Impact of the Revolution of 1848 on Jewish Emancipation," *Jewish Social Studies* 11 (1949): 195–248; J. Toury, *Tumult and Confusion in the 1848 Revolution* (Tel Aviv, 1968) (Hebrew).

23. M. Maoz, "The Background of the Damascus Libel," in *Pe'amim* (1984): 29–36 (Hebrew); J. Frankel, "Crisis as a Factor in Modern Jewish Politics, 1840 and 1881–1882," in J. Reinharz (ed.), *Living with Antisemitism* (Hanover, 1987), 42–43.
24. J. Katz, *Jew-Hatred: From Blood Loathing to Denial of the Race* (Tel Aviv, 1979), 292–97 (Hebrew).
25. J. Isaac, *Has Anti-Semitism Roots in Christianity?* (New York, 1961), 65; M. H., *Thy Brother's Blood* (Jerusalem, 1980) (Hebrew).
26. W. Marr, *Der Sieg Des Judentums über das Germanentum* (Bern, 1879), 75.
27. N. Cohn, *Warrant for Genocide* (Harmondsworth, 1970), 68, 70.
28. E. Drumont, *La France Juive*, vol. 1 (Paris, 1885), 37.
29. K. Marx, *A World Without Jews*, ed. D. D. Runes (New York, 1959).
30. A. Régnard, "Aryens et Sémites," *Revue Socialiste*, 6 (1887): 400.
31. M. Bakunin, *Oeuvres de Bakounine* 3 (Paris, 1899), 113.
32. *Arbeiter Zeitung*, 9 May 1890.
33. S. Ettinger, *Antisemitism in the Modern Era* (Tel Aviv, 1978), 15.
34. R. Wagner, "Das Judentum in der Musik," *Neue Zeitung fuer Musik*.
35. H. Treitschke, *Ein wort über unser Judentum* (Berlin, 1879), 12–13.
36. Ibid., 13.
37. A. Stoecker, *Unsere Forderungen an das Moderne Judentum* (1879), 23.
38. Ibid., 25.
39. A. de Gobineau, *Essai sur l'Inégalité des Races Humaines* (Paris, 121.
40. G. L. Mosse, *Toward the Final Solution: A History of European Racism* (Wisconsin, 1978), 72.
41. H. S. Chamberlain, *Die Grundlagen des XIX Jahrhunderts* 41 (1899): 207.
42. Ibid., 323.

43. Ibid., 324.
44. A. Hitler, *Hitler's Secret Book* (New York, 1961), 213.
45. P. W. Massing, *Rehearsal for Destruction* (New York 1967), 51–59.
46. R. S. Wistrich, *The Jews of Vienna in the Age of Franz Joseph* (Oxford 1990), 205–37.
47. N. Katzburg, *Antisemitism in Hungary, 1897–1914* (Tel Aviv, 1969), 106–54 (Hebrew).
48. On the Affair, see S. Wilson, "Catholic Populism in France at the Time of the Dreyfus Affair: The Union National," *Journal of Contemporary History*, 10 (1975); M. R. Marrus, *The Politics of Assimilation* (Oxford 1971); I. Cohen, "The Dreyfus Affair and the Jews," in S. Almog (ed.), *Generations of Jew-Hatred* (Jerusalem, 1980), 291–308 (Hebrew).
49. S. Dubnow, *History of the Eternal People*, vol. 10 (Tel Aviv, 1962), 3–59 (Hebrew).
50. S. Ettinger, *History of the Jewish People in the Modern Era* (Tel Aviv, 1969), 45 (Hebrew).
51. S. Ettinger, "The State of Muscovy and its Attitude Toward the Jews," *Zion*, 18 (1953): 136–68 (Hebrew); Ettinger, "Russia and the Jews – An Attempt at an Historical Summary," in his *Antisemitism in the Modern Era* (Tel Aviv, 1978), 169 (Hebrew).
52. S. Dubnow, *History of the Jews in Russia and in Poland*, vols 2–3, (Philadelphia, 1975); L. Greenberg, *The Jews in Russia*, vols 1–2 (New York, 1991); B. Pinkus, *The Jews in Russia and in the Soviet Union* (Beer-Sheva, 1986) (Hebrew).
53. R. Byrnes, *Pobedonostsev: His Life and Thought* (Bloomington, 1968).
54. S. Ettinger, "Ideological Background of the Antisemitic Literature in Russia," in his *Antisemitism in the Modern Era* (Tel Aviv, 1978), 100 (Hebrew).
55. S. Ettinger, ibid., 142–44.
56. I. Aksakov, "Will the Jews Cease Being Harmful Once they Become a Cultural Stratum?", *Rus* 1 (October 1883).
57. Cf. S. Breiman, "The Image of the Jew in 19th-Century Russian Literature," *He-avar*, 20 (1973): 38 (Hebrew).
58. J. Frankel, *Prophecy and Politics* (Cambridge, 1981), 49–133; S. M. Berk, *Year of Crisis, Year of Hope* (London, 1985).
59. Y. Gimpelson, L. Bamson, *Zakony O Ivreakh* 1, 2 (St. Petersburg 1914–15), 1991.

186   *Notes to pp. 88–97*

60. S. M. Berk, *Year of Crisis, Year of Hope.*
61. R. Byrnes, *Pobedonostsev: His Life and Thought.*
62. S. Dubnow, *History of the Jews in Russia and in Poland,* vol. 2, 391–410; S. Vermel, "The Expulsion from Moscow," *He-avar,* 18 (1971): 24–25 (Hebrew); Y. Maor, "Background of the Expulsion of the Jews from Moscow," ibid.: 25–34; A. Feldman, "The Expulsion from Moscow in the Reports of the British Ambassador in Russia," ibid., 55–62.
63. Y. Goren (ed.), *Testimony of Victims of the 1903, Kishinev Pogrom* (Tel Aviv, 1991) (Hebrew).
64. S. Dubnow, *Evarei V tsarstvovanie Nikolaya II* (St. Petersburg).
65. H. Rogger, "The Bailiss Case: Antisemitisim and Politics in the Reign of Nicholas II," *Slavic Review,* 25 (1966): 615–29.
66. U. Lohalm, *Völkischer Radikalismus* (Hamburg, 1970); H. Mommsen, "German Nationalism between the Two World Wars," in M. Zimmerman (ed.), *German Nationalism* (Jerusalem, 1983), 104.
67. K. D. Bracher, *The German Dictatorship* (New York, 1970), 168–227.
68. S. Neuman, *Die Parteien der Weimarer Republik* (Stuttgart, 1963).
69. W. Hofer, *Die Diktatur Hitler bis zum Beginn des Zweiten Weltkrieges* (Konstanz, 1959).
70. L. Yahil, *The Holocaust: The Fate of European Jewry, 1932–1945* (New York, 1992).
71. L. Dawidowicz, *The War Against the Jews 1933–1945* (New York, 1976).
72. A. Hitler, *Hitler's Secret Book,* 208–9.
73. The various details are from L. Yahil, *The Holocaust,* L. Dawidowicz, *The War Against the Jews 1933–1945,* K. D. Bracher, *The German Dictatorship.*
74. L. Dawidowicz, *The War Against the Jews 1933–1945,* 138–39.
75. A. D. Morse, *While Six Million Died* (New York, 1968), 270–88.
76. K. D. Bracher, *The German Dictatorship,* 425.
77. Ibid., 424.
78. Ibid.
79. Ibid., 428.
80. Ibid., 430.
81. Cf. J. Frankel, "The Paradoxical Politics of Marginality: Thoughts on the Jewish Situation During the Years 1914–1921," *Studies in Contemporary Jewry,* vol. 4 (1988): 3–21.
82. Y. Laschinski, *Jewry in Soviet Russia* (Tel Aviv, 1940), 53

(Hebrew); B. Pinkus, *Jews of Russia and the Soviet Union – History of a National Minority*, 190.

83. D. Weinryb, "Antisemitism in Soviet Russia," in L. Kochan (ed.), *The Jews in Soviet Russia since 1917* (Oxford, 1978), 310.

84. R. Conquest, *The Great Terror* (London, 1968).

85. B. Pinkus, *Jews of Russia and the Soviet Union – History of a National Minority*. Cf. also B. Pinkus, "The Extra-Territorial National Minorities in the Soviet Union, 1917–1939: Jews, Germans and Poles," *Studies in Contemporary Jewry* vol. 3 (1987), 72–97.

86. B. Pinchuk, *Soviet Jews in the Face of the Holocaust* (Tel Aviv, 1979), 24–28 (Hebrew).

87. B. Pinchuk, *Shtetl Jews under Soviet Rule* (London, 1990).

88. Y. A. Gilboa, *The Black Years of Soviet Jewry* (Tel Aviv, 1972), 14–15.

89. R. V. Daniels, *The Conscience of the Revolution* (Cambridge, 1960), 104–7; L. Schapiro, *The Origins of the Communist Autocracy* (London, 1956), 245–52.

90. S. Ettinger, "Russia and the Jews – an Attempt at an Historical Summation," in his *Antisemitism in the Modern Era* (Tel Aviv, 1978), 183–84 (Hebrew).

91. On the Jews being accused of sympathizing with Zionism, see, for example, Y. Ro'i, *Soviet Decision Making in Practice, on the USSR and Israel, 1947–1954* (New Brunswick, 1980).

92. B. Pinkus, *Jews of Russia and the Soviet Union – History of a National Minority*, 254–340.

93. The scholarly dispute as to whether the campaign against the "cosmopolitans" was directed specifically against Jews is irrelevant. The fact is that thousands of Jews, along with members of other nationalities, were imprisoned on that charge. Those emphasizing that the campaign was anti-Jewish include: H. Swayze, *Political Control of Literature in the USSR, 1946–1959* (Harvard, 1962); A. Yarmolinsky, *Literature under Communism* (Bloomington, 1960); and B. Pinkus, *Jews of Russia and the Soviet Union – History of a National Minority*. One of those who claimed that the campaign was not distinctively anti-Jewish was G. Struve, *Soviet Russian Literature, 1917–1950* (Oklahoma, 1951).

94. Cf. also Y. Ro'i, *The Struggle for Soviet Jewish Emigration, 1948–1967* (Cambridge, 1991), 39–54; B. D. Weinryb, "Antisemitism in Soviet Russia," 300–33.

95. N. J. Mandel, *The Arabs and Zionism before World War I* (Berkeley, 1976); Y. Ro'i, "The Zionist Attitude to the Arabs 1908–1914," in E. Kedourie and S. G. Haim (eds), *Palestine and Israel in the 19th and 20th Centuries* (London, 1982), 15–59; A. Be'eri, *The Genesis of the Israeli-Arab Conflict* (Haifa, 1986) (Hebrew).

96. N. A. Stillman, "Antisemitism in the Contemporary Arab World," in M. Curtis (ed.), *Antisemitism in the Contemporary World* (Boulder, 1986), 70–86.

97. Cf. S. D. Goitein, *Jews and Arabs: Their Contacts Through the Ages* (New York, 1974); B. Lewis, *The Jews of Islam* (Princeton, 1984).

98. M. Abitbol, "The Jews in North Africa and Egypt," in S. Ettinger (ed.), *The History of the Jews in the Islamic Countries* (Jerusalem, 1986), 412–20 (Hebrew).

99. On Soviet anti-Semitism that was camouflaged with anti-Zionist motifs, see *Extracts from the Soviet Press* (*Materialii iz Sovetskoi Pachati*) issued from 1962 by the Center for Research and Documentation of Eastern European Jewry, Hebrew University, Jerusalem; S. Ettinger (ed.) *Anti-Semitism in the Soviet Union*, vols 1–2 (Jerusalem, 1979–83).

100. N. A. Stillman, "The Response of the Jews of the Arab World to Antisemitism in the Modern Era," in J. Reinharz (ed.), *Living with Antisemitism*, 357–58.

101. Y. Harkabi, "On the New Arab Antisemitism," in S. Almog (ed.), *Antisemitism through the Ages* (Jerusalem, 1980), 247–59 (Hebrew).

102. Cf., for example, A. Rubinstein, "The Protocols of the Elders of Zion in the Arab-Israeli Conflict in Palestine in the Twenties," *The New East* 26, 1–2 (1976): 38 (Hebrew). Cf. also Y. Harkabi, *The Arabs' Lesson from their Defeat* (Tel Aviv, 1969) (Hebrew).

103. Characteristic, for example, is the book by Abdallah Al-Tall, *The Danger of the Jewish World to Islam and Christianity*; published in Arabic in Cairo in 1964, it was translated into many languages and generated a good deal of interest in the international community. Al-Tall's intellectual contortions, and his desire to show that he harbors no anti-Jewish prejudice, are poles apart from the crass, determined anti-Semitism of European intellectuals, who understood that there was no need for apologetics since virtually all levels of society supported their ideas.

104. Y. Harkabi, "On the New Arab Antisemitism," in *Antisemitism through the Ages* (Jerusalem, 1980), 247–59.

Chapter 5: Zionism and the State of Israel

1. N. Sokolow, *History of Zionism* (London, 1919); N. M. Gelber, *Zur Vorgeschichte des Zionismus* (Vienna, 1927); S. Almog (ed.), *Before Zionism* (Jerusalem, 1981) (Hebrew); Y. Klausner, *In the Paths of Zion* (Jerusalem, 1978) (Hebrew).
2. On Napoleon Bonaparte's attitude toward the creation of a Jewish state, see N. M. Gelber, "Napoleon I and the Land of Israel," in *Book of Dinaburg* (Jerusalem, 1949), 263–88 (Hebrew); on Lawrence Oliphant, see N. Sokolow, *History of Zionism*, 207ff.; on Yosef Salvador, see M. Graetz, "The Place of Yosef Salvador in the Emergence of a Distinctive Jewish Consciousness," *Zion* 37 (1972): 41–65 (Hebrew); on Emma Lazarus, see Sokolow, *History of Zionism*, 241ff.; on Emanuel Noah, see B. D. Weinryb, "Noah's Ararat Jewish State in its Historical Setting," *American Jewish Historical Society*, 40, part 3 (1954).
3. Cf. Y. Klausner, *In the Paths of Zion*, 81–114.
4. Cf. M. Verta, "The Idea of the Return to Zion in Protestant Thought in England from 1790–1840," *Zion* 33 (1968): 145–79 (Hebrew).
5. G. Krasel, "The First Society to Settle the Land of Israel," *Zion* 7 (1942): 197–205 (Hebrew).
6. *Israelit* 28 (1861): 340–41.
7. M. Hess, *Rome and Jerusalem* (Jerusalem, 1983), 96 (Hebrew).
8. Y. Alkalai, "Causes of the Crisis," in Y. Werfel (ed.), *Complete Writings of Rabbi Alkalai* (Jerusalem, 1944), 73 (Hebrew).
9. Z. H. Kalischer, *Quest for Zion*, (Thoren, 1870), 73.
10. On Moses Hess, see also M. Graetz, "The Return of Moses Hess to the Jewish People," in M. Hess, *Rome and Jerusalem*, 255–76; S. Avineri, *Moses Hess: Between Socialism and Zionism* (Tel Aviv, 1986) (Hebrew). On Rabbi Alkalai, see Y. Katz, "Messianism and Nationalism in the Doctrine of Rabbi Alkalai," in *Shivat Zion*, 4 (1955–56), 41–49 (Hebrew). On Rabbi Zvi Hirsch Kalischer, see *Shivat Zion*, 2–3 (1951–52): 26–41 (Hebrew). On their activity as "forerunners of Zionism," see Y. Katz, "The Jewish National Movement: A Sociological Analysis," in *Jewish Nationalism* (Jerusalem, 1979), 15–35 (Hebrew).

11. On their nationalist activity and its significance, see Y. Salmon, "The Emergence of a Jewish Nationalist Consciousness in Europe During the 1860s and 1870s," *Association for Jewish Studies Review* (1991): 107–32.

12. The details about Hovevei Zion are from D. Vital, *The Zionist Revolution*, vol. 1 (Tel Aviv, 1978), 65–179 (Hebrew); S. L. Zitron, *History of Hibat Zion* (Odessa, 1914); Y. Klausner, *The Movement for Zion in Russia*, vols 1–3 (Jerusalem, 1962–65).

13. See also Y. Goldstein, *Between Zion and Zionism*, vol. 1 (Tel Aviv, 1995) (Hebrew).

14. A copious literature exists on the national awakening in Europe in the late nineteenth century. Cf., for example, E. Gellner, *Nations and Nationalism* (Oxford, 1983).

15. On "Am Olam," see H. Turtel, "The Am Olam Movement," *He-avar*, 10 (1963): 124–43 (Hebrew).

16. *Razsveet* 41, 2 November 1892. On Lilienblum, see *Autobiographical Writings of M. L. Lilienblum*, vols 1–3 (edited, with introduction and notes, S. Breiman) (Jerusalem, 1970) (Hebrew).

17. Y. L. Pinsker, *Autoemancipation* (Jerusalem, 1952), 26.

18. On Mohilever, see Y. Salmon, "Rabbi Moshe Mohilever – Rabbi of Hovevei Zion," *Zion*, 56 (1991): 47–78 (Hebrew).

19. Y. L. Fishman (ed.), *The Book of Samuel* (Jerusalem, 1923), 144.

20. Ibid., 55.

21. Pinsker, *Autoemancipation*, 26.

22. "Minutes of the Kattowitz Conference," in *Writings on the History of Hibat Zion and the Settlement of the Land of Israel* (first compiled and ed., A. Druyanov, new edition by S. Laskov) (Tel Aviv, 1985), 573 (Hebrew).

23. On Ahad Ha'am, see Y. Goldstein, *Ahad Ha'am: A Biography* (Jerusalem, 1992) (Hebrew). S. J. Zipperstein, *Elusive Prophet: Ahad Ha'am and the Origins of Zionism* (Los Angeles, 1993).

24. On "Benei Moshe," see Y. Goldstein, "Benei Moshe: The Story of a Secret Order," *Zion*, 57 (1992): 175–205 (Hebrew).

25. To this day the real reasons for the failure of the 1890–1891 immigration are not clear. Research on the subject is scarce. A few details may be gleaned from R. Kark, "Land Purchases and New Agricultural Settlement in the 'Tiomkin Period,' 1890–1892," *Zionism*, 9 (1984): 182ff. (Hebrew); Y. Goldstein, "On the History of the First Voyage of Ahad Ha'am: Truth from the Land of Israel," *Katedra*, 46 (1987): 91–108 (Hebrew).

26. Y. Goldstein, "The Status of Ahad Ha'am Until the Advent of Herzl as Reflected in the 'Libel Trial' Against Margalit," *Zion*, 52, (1987): 471–88 (Hebrew).
27. The details on Herzl are from A. Bein, *Theodor Herzl: A Biography of the Founder of Modern Zionism* (New York, 1970); E. Pawel, *The Labyrinth of Exile* (London, 1990); J. Kornberg, *Theodor Herzl: From Assimilation to Zionism* (Bloomington, 1993).
28. T. Herzl, *The Jewish State* (Tel Aviv, 1978), 22 (Hebrew).
29. Ibid., 28.
30. Ibid.
31. Cf., for example, L. Yoffe (ed.), *Book of the Congress* (Jerusalem, 1940) (Hebrew).
32. *Zionisten – Congress in Basle, 29/30 und 31 August. Officielle protocol* (Vienna, 1898), 119.
33. On the "Uganda affair," see M. Heymann, *The Uganda Controversy* vols 1 and 2 (Jerusalem, 1970, 1977) (Hebrew).
34. Cf. Y. Goldstein, *Between Political Zionism and Practical Zionism: The Early Zionist Movement in Russia* (Jerusalem, 1991), 186–220 (Hebrew).
35. On Wolffsohn's policy, see M. Eliav, *David Wolffsohn: The Man and his Time* (Jerusalem, 1967), 139–254 (Hebrew).
36. B. Lewis, *The Emergence of Modern Turkey* (Oxford, 1961).
37. On the "Old Yishuv" and the "New Yishuv," see Y. Bartal, "'Old Yishuv' and 'New Yishuv' – Image and Reality," *Katedra*, 2 (1977): 3–19 (Hebrew); Y. Kaniel, "The Terms Old Yishuv and New Yishuv in the Eyes of Contemporaries and in Historiography," *Katedra*, 6 (1978): 3–19 (Hebrew).
38. R. Aharonson, "Stages in the Establishment and Development of the First Aliyah Moshavot," in M. Eliav (ed.), *Book of the First Aliyah* (Jerusalem, 1982), 83 (Hebrew).
39. The various data on the First *Aliyah* are from *The Book of the First Aliyah* vols 1 and 2; R. Aharonson, *The Baron and the Moshavot* (Jersualem 1990) (Hebrew); Y. Kaniel, *Continuity and Change* (Jerusalem, 1982) (Hebrew); Y. Ben-Artzi, *The Hebrew Moshava in the Land of Israel Landscape, 1882–1914* (Jerusalem, 1988) (Hebrew).
40. On Baron Rothschild, see R. Aharonson, *The Baron and the Moshavot*; S. Shama, *The House of Rothschild and the Land of Israel* (London, 1982); D. Giladi, M. Naor, *Rothschild* (Jerusalem, 1982) (Hebrew); Y. Margalit, Y. Goldstein, "The Enterprise of

Baron Edmond de Rothschild, 1882–1929," in Moshe Lissak, Gavriel Cohen (editors-in-chief), *The History of the Jewish Community in Erez Israel, The Ottoman Period*, ed. Y. Kolatt (Jerusalem, 1990), 419–502 (Hebrew).

41. Cf. M. Shilo, "From a *Moshav* Orientation to a General Yishuv Orientation," *Zion*, 57 (1992): 85 (Hebrew).

42. For details on the expansion of the Jewish community in Jerusalem, see Y. Ben-Arieh, *Jerusalem in the 19th Century – The Old City* (New York, 1984).

43. The data on Jaffa is from R. Kark, *Jaffa: Growth of a City, 1799–1917* (Jerusalem, 1982) (Hebrew).

44. The details on the Second Aliyah are from Y. Kolat, *Ideology and Reality in the Labor Movement in the Land of Israel, 1905–1919* (Ph.D. diss., Hebrew University of Jerusalem, 1964) (Hebrew); M. Shilo, *The Settlement Policy of the Palestine Office, 1908–1914* (Ph.D. diss., Hebrew University of Jerusalem, 1985) (Hebrew).

45. Z. Zahor, "The Encounter between the Farmers and the Workers of the Second Aliyah in Petah Tikva, *Katedra*, 10 (1979): 142–50 (Hebrew).

46. M. Shilo, "Degania – First Model of Cooperative Settlement on State-Domain Land," *Katedra*, 39 (1986): 78–98 (Hebrew).

47. H. Near, *The Kibbutz Movement: A History* (Oxford, 1992), 7–57.

48. The information on the Arab-Jewish conflict before World War I is from N. Mandel, *Arabs & Zionism Before World War I* (Berkeley, 1976); Y. Gorni, *The Arab Question and the Jewish Problem* (Tel Aviv, 1985), 108–19 (Hebrew).

49. Najib Azouri's remarks of 1905 are quoted in A. Hourani, *Arabic Thought in the Liberal Age* (London, 1962), 279.

50. *Filistin* (Haifa), 16 September 1911 (Arabic).

51. A. Almaliah, *The Land of Israel and Syria During the World War*, vol. 1 (Jerusalem, 1928), 175 (Hebrew).

52. Y. Hermoni, "The Arab Movement and The Progress of Asia," *Ha-shiloah*, 16 (1905): 463–64 (Hebrew).

53. *Ha-poel Ha-tza'ir*, 7 (1910) (Hebrew).

54. Y. Katz, "The Ahuzat Bayit Society, 1906–1909 – Laying the Foundations for the Building of Tel Aviv," *Katedra*, 33 (1984): 161–91 (Hebrew).

55. N. Druyan, *Pioneers of the Yemenite Immigration* (Jerusalem, 1982) (Hebrew); Y. Nini, "Yemen Immigrants in the Land of Israel 1802–1914," *Katedra*, 5 (1978): 30–82 (Hebrew).

56. Y. Salmon, "The Ashkenazi Urban Community in the Land of Israel, 1880–1903," in *The History of the Jewish Community in Erez Israel*, 605–20.

57. The details on World War I are from M. Eliav (ed.), *In Distress and in Despair – The Land of Israel in World War I* (Jerusalem, 1991) (Hebrew); N. Efrati, *From Crisis to Hope: The Jewish Yishuv in the Land of Israel in World War I* (Jerusalem, 1991) (Hebrew).

58. On Nili, see E. Livneh, Y. Nedava, Y. Efrati (eds), *History of Political Audacity* (Jerusalem, 1961) (Hebrew).

59. L. Stein, *Foundation of the State of Israel: The History of the Balfour Declaration* (Tel Aviv, 1962) (Hebrew); M. Verete, "The Balfour Declaration and its Makers," *Middle East Studies*, 6 (1970): 48–76.

60. There is some doubt as to whether Palestine was in fact included in the territories promised the Arabs. Cf. G. Antonius, *The Arab Awakening* (London, 1961), 176–83; Y. Porath, *The Emergence of the Palestinian-Arab National Movement, 1918–1929* (Tel Aviv, 1976), 34–38 (Hebrew).

61. N. Caplan, "The Yishuv, Sir Herbert Samuel, and the Arab Question in Palestine, 1921–1925," in E. Kedourie and S. G. Haim (eds), *Zionism and Arabism in Palestine & Israel* (London, 1982), 1–51; B. Wasserstein, *Herbert Samuel: A Political Life* (Oxford, 1992), 230–70.

62. Data from R. Bachi, *The Population of Israel* (Jerusalem, 1974), 396, 399.

63. On the artisans and the capitalists, cf. Y. Drori, "The Beginnings of Economic Organizations in the Land of Israel in the Twenties," *Katedra*, 25 (1983): 99–112 (Hebrew); Drori, "The Beginnings of the Organization of Artisans in the Land of Israel," *Katedra*, 34 (1985): 145–74 (Hebrew).

64. Some estimates put the number of members of the pioneering movements among the Third *Aliya* at only about 8,000. See Y. Erez (ed.), *Book of the Third Aliyah*, vol. 1 (Tel Aviv, 1964), 78ff. (Hebrew); Z. Zahor, *The Roots of Israeli Politics* (Tel Aviv, 1987), 59 (Hebrew).

65. Cf., for example, Y. Erez, *Book of the Third Aliyah*, 1–2; Y. Slutzky, "From Defense to Struggle," in B. Dinur (ed.), *History of the Haganah*, vols 1 and 2 (Tel Aviv, 1959), 9–22 (Hebrew); Y. Slutzky, "From the Balfour Declaration to the 1936 Disturbances," in B. Eliav (ed.), *The Yishuv During the Period of the*

National Home (Jerusalem, 1976), 22–23 (Hebrew); M. Naor and D. Giladi, *The Land of Israel in the Twentieth Century: From Yishuv to State, 1900–1950* (Tel Aviv, 1992), 126–42 (Hebrew).

66. A. Shapira, "On the Shattering of One Dream: The Yosef Trumpeldor Labor Battalion," in *Visions in Conflict* (Tel Aviv, 1990), 157 (Hebrew); A. Margalit, "The Labor Battalion – From the Sphere of Imagination of a General Commune to Practical Experience," *Katedra*, 7 (1977): 49–98 (Hebrew); Z. Zahor, "Sad Victory: Ben-Gurion and the Labor Battalion," *Katedra*, 43 (1987): 33–51 (Hebrew).

67. Z. Al-Peleg, *The Grand Mufti* (Tel Aviv, 1989), 13–20 (Hebrew).

68. On the development of the Arab national movement in the 1920s, see Y. Porath, *The Growth of the Palestinian Arab Movement, 1918–1929* (Tel Aviv, 1976) (Hebrew).

69. On the early history of the Histadrut, see Z. Zahor, *On the Road to Leadership of the Yishuv: The Beginnings of the Histadrut* (Tel Aviv, 1982) (Hebrew).

70. On the Fourth *Aliyah* and its outcome, see D. Giladi, *The Yishuv During the Fourth Aliyah* (Tel Aviv, 1973) (Hebrew).

71. Z. Zahor, *Roots of Israeli Politics*, 61.

72. On the events of 1929, see ibid., vol. 2, 301–415.

73. On the events of 1936–1939, see *History of the Haganah*, vol. 2, 622ff.

74. Y. Metzer and E. Kaplan, *Jewish Economic Sector and Arab Economic Sector in the Land of Israel* (Jerusalem, 1990), 54–74 (Hebrew).

75. Y. Porath, *From Riots to Rebellion* (Tel Aviv, 1971), 137–71 (Hebrew); Y. Arnon-Ohana, "The Beginnings of Palestinian Radicalism, 1930–1937," *Katedra*, 12 (1979): 91–109 (Hebrew).

76. S. Lachman, "Arab Rebellion and Terrorism in Palestine 1929–39: The Case of Sheik Al-Din Al Qassam and his Movement" in E. Kedourie and S. G. Haim (eds), *Zionism and Arabism in Palestine and Israel* (London, 1982); and N. Caplan, "The Yishuv, Sir Herbert Samuel, and the Arab Question in Palestine, 1921–1925," in E. Kedourie and S. G. Haim (eds), *Zionism and Arabism in Palestine and Israel* (London, 1982), 52–99.

77. A. Ilan, "The Political and National Struggle for the Land of Israel, 1917–1947," in Y. Porath and Y. Shavit (eds), *History of the Land of Israel* (Jerusalem, 1982), 37–43 (Hebrew).

78. Cf. Y. Porath, *In the Crucible of Political Action* (Jerusalem, 1985), 216–68.

79. Cf. the analysis by G. Shefer, "Principles of British Pragmatism: A Reassessment of British Policy Toward Palestine in the Thirties," *Katedra*, 29 (1983): 113–44 (Hebrew).

80. Y. Porath, *From Riots to Rebellion*, 259–328; N. Katzburg, *From Partition to White Paper* (Jerusalem, 1974). On the controversy among the Jews, Ben-Gurion's assent to partition and the ensuing dispute, see S. Dotan, *The Partition Controversy During the Mandate Period* (Jerusalem, 1980), 37ff.

81. M. J. Cohen, *Palestine: Retreat from the Mandate* (London, 1978).

82. Cf. Y. Porath, *From Riots to Rebellion*, 325–78; L. Hirszowicz, *The Third Reich and the Arab World* (London, 1966).

83. N. Katzburg, *From Partition to White Paper*, 74ff.

84. A. Friesel, *Zionist Policy in the Aftermath of the Balfour Declaration, 1917–1922* (Tel Aviv, 1977) (Hebrew); B. Halpern, *A Clash of Heroes* (Oxford, 1987).

85. Y. Eilam, *The Jewish Agency: The Initial Period* (Jerusalem, 1990).

86. On the immigration from Germany, cf. M. Getter, "Immigration from Germany from 1933–1939," *Katedra*, 12 (1979): 125–47 (Hebrew); Y. Gelber, *New Homeland* (Jerusalem, 1990) (Hebrew).

87. Cf. the data of Y. Metzer and E. Kaplan, *Jewish Economic Sector and Arab Economic Sector in the Land of Israel*.

88. On the size of the Yishuv in the 1930s, see S. Reichman, *From Foothold to Stronghold* (Jerusalem, 1979), 161–276 (Hebrew).

89. On economic development in Palestine in the 1930s, see D. Giladi and S. Avidor, "The Growth and Development of the Jewish Economic Sector," in *History of the Land of Israel*, 138–46, 193–201; N. Gross, "The Economic Policy of the Mandate Government," *Katedra*, 24 (1982): 106–37; F. L. Fingold, *British Economic Policy in Palestine, 1920–1948* (Ph.D. diss., London, 1978). On British investments in development, see N. Gross, "The Economic Policy of the British Mandatory Administration in Palestine," *Katedra*, 24 (1982): 153–80; and 25 (1982): 135–68 (Hebrew).

90. Y. Goldstein, *The Land of Israel Workers' Party – Causes of its Creation* (Tel Aviv, 1975) (Hebrew); A. Shapira, *Berl*, vol. 1 (Tel Aviv, 1983), 291–97 (Hebrew); Y. Gorny, *Achdut Ha'avoda 1914–1930* (Tel Aviv, 1973) (Hebrew); Y. Shapiro, *The Historic Achdut Ha'avoda: The Strength of a Political Organization* (Tel Aviv, 1975) (Hebrew).

91. Cf. Y. Shavit, *From Majority to State* (Tel Aviv, 1978), 23–68 (Hebrew); Y. Heller, *Lehi 1940–1949*, vol. 1 (Jerusalem, 1989), 19–30 (Hebrew); D. Niv, *The National Military Organization*, vol. 1 (Tel Aviv, 1983), 302–33 (Hebrew); Y. Goldstein, "The Creation of the Land of Israel Workers' Party and the Emergence of a Leadership Pattern in the Yishuv," *Katedra*, 23 (1982): 156–65 (Hebrew).
92. Y. Goren, *The Determining Confrontation* (Tel Aviv, 1986) (Hebrew).
93. Y. Goldstein, *The Road to Hegemony: Mapai – The Emergence of its Policy 1930–1936* (Tel Aviv, 1980) (Hebrew).
94. On the policy of restraint, see *History of the Haganah*, vol. 2, 833–50.
95. Y. Porath, *A Trapped Leadership* (Tel Aviv, 1985), 42ff. (Hebrew).
96. G. Cohen, *Churchill and the Palestine Question* (Jerusalem, 1976).
97. R. Zweig, "Britain, the Haganah and the Fate of the White Paper," in Y. Shavit (ed.), *Struggle, Revolt, Resistance* (Jerusalem, 1987), 168 (Hebrew).
98. On the debate between Weizmann and Ben-Gurion on the same issue, cf. Y. Gorny, *Partnership and Struggle* (Tel Aviv, 1976), 130ff. (Hebrew); N. Rose, *Chaim Weizmann: A Biography* (Jerusalem, 1990), p. 238ff. (Hebrew).
99. N. Rose, *Chaim Weizmann*, 237–240.
100. Y. Bauer, *From Diplomacy to Resistance* (Tel Aviv, 1963), 189–211.
101. A. Ilan, *America, Britain and Palestine* (Jerusalem, 1979), 92ff.
102. Y. Metzer and E. Kaplan, *Jewish Economic Sector and Arab Economic Sector in the Land of Israel*, 146.
103. D. Ofer, "Illegal Immigration to Palestine, 1939–1942" (Ph.D. diss., Hebrew University of Jerusalem, 1981) (Hebrew); Ofer, *Road on the Sea* (Jerusalem, 1987) (Hebrew).
104. Cf. R. Zweig, "Britain, the Haganah and the Fate of the White Paper"; A. Ilan, "Containing the Constitutional Aspects of the White Paper and Freezing Them from 1940–1942," *Zionism*, 6 (1981): 275–322 (Hebrew).
105. On volunteering for the British Army, see Y. Gelber, *The History of Volunteering*, vols 1–2 (Jerusalem, 1979, 1981) (Hebrew).
106. On the Haganah in World War II, see *Book of the Haganah*, vol. 3.
107. Y. Bauer, *From Diplomacy to Resistance*, 202.

108. On Lehi's actions, see Y. Heller, *Lehi 1940–1949*.

109. On Etzel actions following the declaration of the "revolt," see D. Niv, *The National Military Organization*, vol. 4.

110. On the policy of informing, see D. Niv, *The National Military Organization*, vol. 1, 96–124; *Book of the Haganah*, vol. 3, 531–43 (Hebrew); Y. Gelber, "British and Zionists Politics in Palestine and the Possibility of a Jewish Revolt, 1942–1944," *Zionism*, 7 (1982): 352ff. (Hebrew).

111. Y. Bauer, "From Biltmore to Paris – The Impact of the Holocaust on Zionist Policy 1942–1946," *Sixth World Zionist Conference on Jewish Studies*, vol. 2 (Jerusalem, 1976), 475 (Hebrew); Y. Bauer, *Flight and Rescue – Brichah* (New York, 1970), 257–58; unlike Bauer, Y. Heller does not think that the DP problem furnished the motivation that led the Zionists to revise their policy: Y. Heller, "From 'Black Sabbath' to Partition – Summer 1946 as a Turning Point in the History of Zionist Policy," *Zion*, 43 (1978): 314–15 (Hebrew).

112. Cf. *Book of the Haganah*, vol. 3, 836–940.

113. Y. Bauer, *Flight and Rescue – Brichah*.

114. A. Ilan, *America, Britain and Palestine*, 178–203.

115. Y. Heller, "Zionist Policy in the International Arena after World War II – The Affair of the Anglo-American Commission, 1945–1946," *Shalem* 3 (1981): 213–93 (Hebrew).

116. *History of the Haganah*, vol. 3, 889ff.

117. Ibid., 1091–90.

118. A. Ilan, *America, Britain and Palestine*, 78ff.; Z. Ganin, *Truman, American Jewry and Israel, 1945–1948* (New York, 1979); Ganin, "The Partition Plan and Nahum Goldmann's Mission to Washington, Summer 1946, and the American Cabinet," *Ha-Tziyyonut*, 5 (1978): 256 (Hebrew).

119. A. Ilan, "Withdrawal without Recommendation: Britain's Decision to Relinquish the Palestine Mandate, 1947"; M. Y. Cohen, "The British Decision to Leave Palestine," *Katedra*, 15 (1980): 143–56 (Hebrew); A. Ilan, "When Did the British Decide to Leave?", 156–75.

120. Cf. *History of the Haganah*, vol. 2, 898ff.; D. Niv, *The National Military Organization*, vol. 1, 281ff.

121. Cf. Y. Heller, "From 'Black Sabbath' to Partition," 360–61.

122. M. V. Hadari, *Refugees Defeat an Empire: The Aliya B Episodes 1945–1948* (Tel Aviv, 1985) (Hebrew).

123. Details on the War of Independence are from *History of the*

Haganah, vol. 3; U. Milstein, N. Lorch, *History of the War of Independence* (Ramat Gan, 1958); Y. Ben-Arieh (ed.), *History of the Land of Israel* (Jerusalem, 1983).

124. B. Morris, *The Birth of the Palestinian Refugee Problem, 1947–1949*, (Cambridge, 1987).

125. Z. Ganin, *Truman, American Jewry and Israel, 1945–1948*; M. Kaufmann, "The American Trusteeship Plan for Resolving the Palestine Question," *Yahadut Zemanenu*, 1 (1984): 249–73 (Hebrew).

Conclusion

1.   F. Furet, *Penser la Révolution française* (Paris, 1978), 3.

2.   See the Introduction.

3.   *Cambridge Modern History* (Cambridge, 1960) vol. I, 2.

Index

Aaron the Great, Rabbi of Karlin, 48
Acre, 23, 142
Adler, Cyrus, 67
Agudat Israel, 68, 70, 72–73
Agudat ha-Sotzyalistim ha-Ivrim, 62
Ahad Ha'am (Asher Zvi Ginsberg), 64–65, 69, 109–10, 111, 115, 118, 121, 144
Aharonson, Aharon, 121
Ahdut Ha'avoda, 133
Ahuzat Bayit, 120
Aksakov, Ivan, 86–87
Albania, 96
Alexander I, 15, 35, 37, 50, 55–56
Alexander II, 36, 58, 86, 88
Alexander III, 15, 36, 37, 87, 88
Algeria, 20, 21, 25, 102
Aliyah, 25
  First (1881–1903), 12–13, 69, 115, 120
  Second (1904–14), 12–13, 69, 117, 120
  Third (1919–23), 18, 69, 123, 124
  Fourth (1924–28), 18–19, 69, 123, 127
  Fifth (1929–39), 19, 69, 123, 132
  from Islamic countries, 21–22
  in period 1969–74, 24
Alkalai, Yehuda, 105
Allenby, Edmund, 122
Alsace, 8
Am Olam movement, 12, 107
Amsterdam, 11
Anglo-American Commission (1946), 140
Anti-Semitism, 2, 26, 76–103, 149
  Arab, 2, 46, 100–2, 103

Austria, 45, 90
Austro-Hungarian Empire, 9, 83, 84
Europe, 9, 78, 80, 84–85, 100, 106–7, 111
France, 9, 83, 84
Germany, 2, 9, 18, 44–46, 78, 80–82, 83, 90–97, 130
Hungary, 103
Poland, 98
Russia, 36–37, 85–90, 103
Soviet Union, 2, 39, 40–41, 97–100, 103
Ukraine, 97, 98
Arab-Jewish conflict, 100–2
  during Fifth *Aliyah*, 128–30, 134, 137
  during First/Second *Aliyah*, 118–20
  during Second World War, 138
  during Third *Aliyah*, 124–26
  post Second World War, 21–22, 140, 142–44
Arabs
  anti-Semitism, 2, 46, 100–2, 103
  Balfour Declaration, 122
  during War of Independence, 23, 24
  in Erez Israel, 13, 21
  population ratio, 24–25, 123
Argentina, 9, 11, 13–14, 17, 75, 112
Arlosoroff, Chaim, 133–34
Aryan race, 44, 81–82, 92, 94, 102
Ascher, Saul, 33
Asefat ha-Nivharim, 70
Ashkenazi, 22, 63, 71, 121
Auschwitz-Birkenau, 45, 95
Australia, 9, 12

Austria
  anti-Semitism, 45, 90
  displaced persons camps, 21
  emancipation, 46
  emigration, 93
  Kristallnacht, 45
Austro-Hungarian Empire
  annexation of Galicia, 34
  anti-Semitism, 9, 83, 84
  emancipation, 2, 28, 32, 35, 36,
    43–44, 78, 147
  emigration, 8, 9, 10, 146
  internal migration, 8
  Jewish education, 59
  Jewish Reform Movement, 53, 54
  nationalist movements, 106
  Toleranzpatent, 30
Axelrod, Pavel Borisovich, 62

Ba'al Shem Tov (Besht), 47–48, 49,
    147
Ba'al Teshuvah movement, 73
Baden, 78
Baer, Yitzhak, 3–4
Bakunin, Mikhail, 80
Balfour, Arthur James, 122
Balfour Declaration (1917), 2, 18, 41,
    122, 124–25, 126, 129
Baltic states, 16, 20, 43, 98
Banet, Mordecai, 54
Bar Giora organization, 118
Baron, Salo, 4, 146
Bavaria, 78
Begin, Menachem, 73, 138–39
Beiliss, Mendel, 90
Beit David, 116
Belgium, 20
Belorussia
  emigration, 7, 8, 146
  Hasidism, 48
  Mitnaggedim, 49, 50
  nationalist movements, 106
  Russian annexation, 34
Belzec, 45, 95
Ben-Gurion, David, 117, 130, 134,
    135–36, 139, 141
  declaration of independence, 143,
    149
  head of provisional government
    (1948–49), 72
  and Histadrut, 126–27, 133

and U.S., 136
Ben-Zvi, Yitzhak, 117
Benei Moshe order, 64, 69, 110, 111
Berihah, 20
Berlin
  Haskalah movement, 50
  Jewish Reform movement, 52,
    53, 54
  migration to, 8
  Rothschild family, 33
  transit city, 11
  Zionist Organization, 121
  see also Wannsee Conference
Besht, The, 47–48, 49
  see also Ba'al Shem Tov
Bevin, Ernest, 139
Bibas, Judah, 105
Biltmore Plan, 135–36, 141
Bilu, 108
Binyamina, 121
Birobidzhan, 16, 40
Birth rate, 7, 25
Black Sabbath, 140
"black years" of Soviet Jewry, 99
Bochum, 83
Bolshevism, 15, 39, 41, 67–68
Bormann, Martin, 95
Börne, Ludwig, 80
Bracher, Karl Dietrich, 91
Braffmann, Jacob, 87
Brandeis, Louis, 131
Brazil, 9, 12, 17, 75
Bremen, 11
Brenner, Joseph Hayyim, 69
Breslau, 53
Brody, 11
Brunswick, 53
Buchenwald, 93
Budapest, 8
Bulgaria, 16, 17
Bund, The (General Jewish Workers'
    Union), 62–63, 72, 104

Cairo, 139
Canada, 9, 12, 17, 75
Catherine II, Empress of Russia,
    34–35
Chamberlain, Houston Stewart,
    81–82, 103
Chamberlain, Joseph, 113
Chelmno, 45

Chile, 17
Chlenov, Yehiel, 114, 121
Christian Socialist Workers' Party, 83
Churchill, Winston, 126, 134–35
Clermont-Tonnerre, Comte de, 30
Concentration camps, 45–46, 93, 95–96
Conservatism *see* Jewish Conservative movement
Cracow, 94
Crémieux, Adolphe, 105
Crimea, 8
Cuba, 93
Cultural processes *see* secularization
Cyprus, 21, 113
Czechoslovakia, 16, 20, 144

Dachau, 93
Damascus blood libel (1840), 78
Darwin, Charles, 81, 102
Dawidowicz, Lucy, 91
Degania, 118
Deir Yassin, 143
Deists, 29
Demographic growth *see* population
Derzhavin, Gabriel, 35, 37
Deutsch, Leo, 62
Diderot, Denis, 30
Dinur, Ben Zion, 3, 4, 5, 146
Dnepropetrovsk, 8
Dnieper, River, 38
"Doctors' plot", 99
Dostoevsky, Fyodor Mikhalovich, 87
Dresden, 83
Dreyfus, Alfred, 84, 103, 111
Drugoznik, 109
Drumont, Edouard, 79, 84, 111
Dubnow, Simon, 3, 4, 5, 28, 84, 146, 147

Egypt, 20, 21, 24, 46, 101, 143, 144
Eichmann, Adolf, 95
Eisenstadt-Barzilai, Yehoshua, 110
Einstein, Albert, 44
Ekron, 115
El-Arish, 113
Eliasberg, Mordecai, 63
Emancipation, 2, 28–46, 147
  Austria, 46
  Austro-Hungarian Empire, 2, 28, 32, 35, 36, 43–44, 78, 147

Europe, 28, 39, 46, 77, 102, 106, 107
  France, 2, 4, 28, 30, 31–32, 35, 36, 41, 46, 146, 147
  Germany, 2, 28, 32, 35, 36, 43–44, 46, 51, 78, 91–92, 147
  Great Britain, 30, 46, 146
  Lithuania, 42
  Netherlands, 146
  Poland, 42–43
  Romania, 42, 43, 77
  Russia, 2, 28, 34–39, 77, 85, 87, 97, 147
  Soviet Union, 39–40
  Ukraine, 42
  United States, 28, 30–31, 36, 41
Emigration *see* migration
Engels, Friedrich, 80
Enlightenment movement *see* Haskalah
Erez Israel *see* Israel
Ermland, 34
Estonia, 16
Ettinger, Shmuel, 4, 146, 149
Etzel, 137, 138–39, 140, 141, 142
Euchel, Isaac, 51
Europe
  absolutism, 4
  anti-Semitism, 9, 78, 80, 84–85, 100, 106–7, 111
  attitude to Jews, 28–30, 34
  enlightenment movement, 34
  emancipation, 28, 39, 46, 77, 102, 106, 107
  emigration, 1, 9–14, 17–19, 20–21, 24, 26, 147
  Haskalah movement, 50, 51, 55, 59
  impact of French Revolution, 4
  internal migration, 7–9, 14–17, 26
  Jewish economic involvement, 33–34, 78, 79
  Jewish Reform movement, 53, 54
  migration to, 23, 146
  national movements, 106
  Orthodox Judaism, 72
  secularization, 61, 65, 67–68
  see also Holocaust
Exodus, 142

Fein, Shmuel Yosef, 109
Fest, Joachim, 77
Feisal I, King of Iraq, 125

Fichte, Johann Gottlieb, 80
Final Solution *see* Holocaust
France
　anti-Semitism, 9, 83, 84
　attitude to Jews, 29, 31
　displaced Jews, 20
　emancipation, 2, 4, 28, 30, 31–32,
　　35, 36, 41, 46, 146, 147
　emigration, 8
　Jewish education, 59
　loss of influence, 22
　migration to, 25
　Orthodox Judaism, 75
　ports of embarkation, 11
　Revolution (1789), 4, 28, 30, 78, 146
　Syria, administration of, 125
　see also Dreyfus, Alfred
Frankel, Zacharias, 52, 54
Frankfurt, 33, 53, 79
Franz Joseph, Emperor, 83
Freud, Sigmund, 44
Friedlander, David, 51
Friedländer, Nathan, 105
Fries, Friedrich Jacob, 33
Friesal, Ivan, 35, 37
Furet, François, 146

Galicia, 8, 14, 34, 48, 49, 50
Gans, Eduard, 52
Gaza Strip, 24, 25, 100, 144
Gederah, 69, 115
Geiger, Abraham, 52, 53
German Popular Defense League, 90
Germany
　Agudat Israel, 72
　anti-Semitism, 2, 9, 18, 44–46, 78,
　　80–82, 83, 90–97, 130
　conflict with Soviet Union, 98
　displaced persons camps, 21
　emancipation, 2, 28, 32, 35, 36,
　　43–44, 46, 51, 78, 91–92, 147
　emigration, 8, 9, 19, 21, 65, 93,
　　146–47
　Haskalah, 51, 56
　Jewish education, 59
　Jewish Reform movement, 52–53
　ports of embarkation, 11
　secularization, 146
　see also Holocaust; Nazis
Ghettos, 45, 94, 95, 96
Ginsberg, Asher Zvi *see* Ahad Ha'am

glasnost, 24
Gobineau, Comte Arthur de, 81
Goering, Hermann, 93, 95
Golomb, Eliahu, 137
Gomperz family, 30
Gorbachev, Mikhail, 24
Gordon, Aharon David, 69, 117
Gordon, Yehuda Leib, 105
Graetz, Heinrich, 3–5, 28, 146, 148
Grabski, Ładisław, 127
Great Britain
　attitude to Jews, 29, 30
　emancipation, 30, 46, 146
　emigration, 9
　Erez Israel, 17, 18, 19
　internment of Jews, 21
　loss of influence, 22
　Orthodox Judaism, 75
　Palestine Mandate, 122–41
　ports of embarkation, 11
　and Zionism, 121–22
　see also Balfour Declaration
Greenberg, Avraham, 109
Grégoire, Abbé, 30, 31
Grodna District, 109
Gruenbaum, Yitzhak, 42
Guenzburg, Mordecai Aaron, 56
Guenzburg family, 39, 79
Gush Etzion, 142

Ha-meliz, 59
Ha-Zefirah, 59
Ha'Achdut, 120
Habad Hasidim, 64
Habermas, Jürgen, 77
Hadarim, 59, 65
Haganah, 136, 137–38, 139, 140, 141,
　142
Haifa
　Arab attacks (1929), 128
　Arab groups in, 118
　Arab-Jewish friction, 119
　expansion of port, 123, 124, 132
　immigrants settle in, 23, 117, 120,
　　123, 127
　Jewish capture of (1948), 142
Halakhah, 49, 52, 54
Halukah, 68
Ha-magid, 105
Hamburg, 11, 52, 53, 54
Ha-po'el Ha-tza'ir, 119, 120

Ha-po'el Ha-tza'ir (Young Worker
  Party), 120
Hapsburg Empire *see* Austro-
  Hungarian Empire
Haredim, 69, 70, 71, 73–75
Hashomer organization, 118
Hasidism, 2, 47–50, 55, 57, 58, 74,
  104, 147–48
Haskalah, 4, 47, 50–59, 74, 106, 109
Hebrew language, 120
Hebrew Socialist Union, 62
Hebron, 117, 128
Hechler, Henry, 111
He-halutz, 123
Heine, Heinrich, 52, 80
"Hep-Hep" riots, 78
Herder, Johann, 80
Hermoni, Aharon, 119
Herut, 72
Herzl, Theodor
  Arab-Jewish relations, 119
  and Argentina, 14, 112
  Zionism, 2, 64, 104, 111–14, 122,
    130, 144, 149
Herzlia Hebrew Gymnasium, 69
Hess, Moses, 105
Heydrich, Reinhard, 94–95
He-hasid, Judah, 4, 5
HIAS (United Hebrew Sheltering
  and Immigrant Aid Society), 11
Hibbat Zion, 63, 64
  see also Hovevei Zion
Himmler, Heinrich, 92, 94, 95, 96, 97
Hirsch, Baron Maurice de, 14, 111,
  115
Histadrut, 126–27, 128, 133, 137
Hitler, Adolf
  anti-semitic ideology, 19, 44, 79,
    82, 103, 149
  failed putsch (1923), 44
  Final Solution, 45, 76–77, 93–94, 95
  gains power, 44, 91, 130
  race theory, 2
Hofer, Walther, 91
Holocaust, 6, 19–20, 45–46, 76–78,
  93–97, 103, 147
Hovevei Zion, 12, 69, 104, 106, 107–11,
  113, 115, 130, 149
  see also Hibbat Zion
Hungary
  Agudat Israel movement, 72

anti-Semitism, 103
becomes independent state, 16
displaced Jews, 20
Hasidism, 48, 50
Holocaust victims, 20
  see also Austro-Hungarian Empire
Hurwitz, Phinehas Elijah, 55
Hussein, Sharif, 122
al-Husseini, Hajj Amin, 125–26, 130
al-Husseini, Mussa Kazim Pasha, 125

ICA (Jewish Colonization
  Association), 14
IDF *see* Israel Defense Forces
Ignatyev, Count Nikolai, 37, 88
India, 141
Iraq, 21, 46, 71, 101, 102, 143
Islamic countries, 20, 21–22, 26,
  71–72, 102, 147
Islamic fundamentalism, 101–2
Israel
  Arab Jewish population ratio,
    24–25
  creation of State, 5, 21, 104
  Declaration of Independence, 143,
    144, 149
  Elected Assembly, 70, 133
  emigration, 23–24, 25, 128
  migration to, 1, 4, 12–13, 17, 18–19,
    20–25, 26, 102, 127, 147
  secularization, 68–75
  see also Aliyah; Arab-Jewish
    conflict; Yishuv; Zionism
Israel Defense Forces (IDF), 143–44
Istoczy, Viktor, 83
Italy, 9, 21, 26

Jabotinsky, Ze'ev, 126, 131, 133,
  134
Jacobson, Israel, 52
Jaffa
  Arab attacks (1929), 128
  British capture of (1917), 122
  expansion of, 116–17, 119, 120
  immigrants settle in, 23
  "Palestine Office", 114
  secular centre, 69
Jerusalem
  anti-British demonstrations (1920),
    125
  Arab attacks (1929), 128

Arab-Jewish conflict (1948), 142, 143, 144
Arab-Jewish friction, 119
Arab population, 13
British capture of (1917), 122
immigrants settle in, 23, 116, 117, 120, 123, 127
internationalization of, 142
King David Hotel bombing (1946), 141
Yishuv, 115
"Jerusalem School", 4
Jewish Agency, 18, 22, 71, 132, 133, 135–36
Jewish Anti-Fascist Committee, 99
Jewish Brigade, 137
Jewish Colonial Bank, 112, 117
Jewish Colonization Organization (JCO), 115–16
Jewish Committee, 37, 58
Jewish Conservative movement, 2, 54, 67, 148
Jewish National Fund, 112, 114
Jewish nationalism *see* Zionism
Jewish Reform movement, 2, 10, 52–54, 65, 148
Jewish Statutes, 15, 35, 56
Jezreel Valley, 118, 127
Jordan, 24, 101, 143, 144
Joseph II, Holy Roman Emperor, 30
Judaism, 2, 50–54, 64, 148
see also Orthodox Judaism

Kabbalists, 47, 48, 49
Kahal, 36, 58
Kalischer, Zwi Hirsch, 105
Kaminev, Lev, 97
Kaplan, Eliezer, 134
Katznelson Berl, 117
Kehillah, 49, 50, 51
Keitel, Wilhelm, 95
Kenya, 113
Keren Hayesod, 131
Kerensky government, 28, 39, 41
Kharkov, 15, 16, 108
Kherson, 8
Kibbutz, 118
Kiev, 15, 16, 61, 90
Kirovgrad, 8
Kishinev, 89, 103
Knesset, 71, 72, 73, 74

Kook, Abraham Isaac, 63
Kossovsky, Vladimir, 63
Kostomarov, Nicholas, 86, 87
Kovno, 14
Kranz, Jacob Ben Wolf, 55
Kremer, Arkadi, 63
Kristallnacht, 45, 92, 93
Krushevan, Pavolaki, 89
Kurland, 14
Kvutza, 118

Labor Battalion, 124
Labor movement, 123, 126–27, 133–34
Labor party, 69–70, 71
Latin America, 9, 11–12, 17, 24
Latvia, 14, 16, 106
Law of Return (1950), 21
Lazarus, Emma, 105
League of Nations, 122
Lebanon, 101, 143
Lebensohn, Abraham Dov, 56
Lehi, 138, 139, 140
Lenin, Vladimir Ilyich, 39, 67
Leningrad *see* St. Petersburg
Lessing, Ephraim, 29
Levin, Judah Leib (Yehalel), 12
Levin, Yitzhak Meir, 72
Levinsohn Isaac Behr, 57
Levy, Richard S., 77
Libya, 21
Liebermann, Aaron Samuel, 62
Likud, 72
Lilienblum, Moses Leib, 12, 63, 107, 108, 109, 110
Lithuania
  Agudat Israel, 72
  becomes independent state, 16
  Bund, The, 62
  displaced Jews, 20
  emancipation, 42
  emigration, 7, 8, 146
  Hasidism, 48
  Jewish Statute, 35
  Mitnaggedim, 49, 50
  nationalist movements, 106
  Russian annexation, 34
  see also Poland–Lithuania
Lloyd George, David, 122
Locke, John, 29
Lod, 23

Łódź
  extermination camps, 45, 95
  ghettos, 94
  Jewish factory ownership, 38
  Jewish population increase, 8
  secularization process, 61
Łomza, 14
London
  Hebrew Socialist Union, 62
  migration to, 8
  Rothschild family, 33, 79
  Zionist Conference (1920), 131
Lopukhin, Alexei, 37
Lorje, Hayyim, 105
Lubarsky, Avraham Eliahu, 110
Lublin, 14, 94
Lueger, Karl, 44, 83, 84
Luxemburg, Rosa, 44
Lvov, 94

Ma'barot, 23
Macdonald, Ramsay, 129
Maggid of Mezhirech, 48
Mahaneh Yisrael, 116
Mahler, Raphael, 3, 4
Majdanek, 95
Mandelstamm, Benjamin, 57
Mandelstamm, Max, 64
Mapai, 133–34
Marr, Wilhelm, 78, 79
Marshall, Louis, 67
Marx, Karl, 79–80
Marxist party, 62
Maskilim, 2, 50, 51, 52, 55, 56–59, 148
Mauthausen, 93
"May laws", 37
Meah She'arim, 116
Mein Kampf, 44, 77, 94
Meisel, Elijah Hayyim, 64
Mendel, Menahem, 48
Mendelssohn, Felix, 80
Mendelssohn, Moses
  attitude to civil and religious
    obligations of Jews, 32
  Haskalah movement, 47, 50–51,
    54, 148
  impact on Jewish history, 3–5,
    28, 29
Merhavia, 118
Metternich, Klemens von, 34
Meyerbeer, Giacomo, 80

Migration, 1, 6–27, 146–47
  to Argentina, 13–14
  from Austria, 93
  from Austro-Hungarian Empire, 8,
    9, 10, 146
  within Austro-Hungarian Empire,
    8
  from Belorussia, , 7, 8, 146
  from Europe, 1, 9–14, 17–19, 20–21,
    24, 26, 147
  to Europe, 23, 146
  within Europe, 7–9, 14–17, 26
  from France, 8
  to France, 25
  from Germany, 8, 9, 19, 21, 65, 93,
    146–47
  from Great Britain, 9
  from Islamic countries, 21–22, 26,
    71–72, 102, 147
  from Israel, 23–24, 25, 128
  to Israel, 1, 4, 12–13, 17, 18–19,
    20–25, 26, 102, 127, 147
  from Italy, 9
  to Latin America, 9, 11–12, 17
  from Lithuania, 7, 8, 146
  from Poland, 1, 7, 8, 14, 17, 18, 21,
    123, 127, 146
  to Polish cities, 7, 8, 38, 146
  from Romania, 8, 10, 17
  from Russia, 1, 8–9, 10, 11, 18,
    123, 147
  in Russia, 8, 14–16, 26, 58, 67, 146
  from Soviet Union, 21, 24, 25, 124
  from Spain, 9
  from Ukraine, 7, 8, 14, 15
  to Ukraine, 146
  from U.S., 24
  to U.S., 1, 8, 9–11, 12, 13, 17, 18, 23,
    24, 25, 26, 65, 127, 146, 147
  see also Aliyah
Mill, Joseph Solomon, 63
Mirabeau, Honoré-Gabriel Riqueti,
  29
Mishkenot Sha'ananim, 116
Mitnaggedim, 49–50, 58, 74
mitzvot, 51, 52, 54, 55, 59–60, 64
Mohilever, Samuel, 12, 63, 108, 109
Molotov, Vyacheslav Mikhailovich,
  98
Montefiore, Moses, 105, 116
Morocco, 20, 21, 46, 102

Moscow
  expulsion from (1891), 15, 89
  Sacred Fraternity, 88
  settlement in after 1915, 14, 16,
    39, 67
  university restrictions, 59
Moser, Moses, 52
Moshavot, 13
Motzkin, Leo, 65, 121
Moyne, Lord, 139
Mueller, Heinrich, 95
Muslim Higher Council, 125

Nahalat Shiva, 116
Naharayim power plant, 128
Naples, 79
Napoleon Bonaparte, 31, 46, 105
al-Nashashibi, Ra'ab, 119
"National home", 41, 63, 122, 126,
    130
National Military Organization *see*
  Etzel
National Religious Party, 72
National Socialist Party *see* Nazis
Nationalism *see* Zionism
Natok, Joseph, 105
Nazis, 28, 41, 91–97, 99, 103
  ideological roots, 77–78, 79
  race theory, 82
  rise to power, 43, 76, 84–85, 91,
    130
  see also Holocaust
Netherlands, 11, 20, 146
Neumann, Sigmund, 91
New York, 10, 11, 20, 65, 147
Nicholas I, Tsar of Russia, 35–36, 37,
    56, 57–58, 86
Nicholas II, Tsar of Russia, 36, 87, 89
"Nili", 121
Noah, Emanuel, 105
Nolte, Ernst, 77
Nordau, Max, 111, 119
Nuremberg Laws, 2, 44, 92, 96, 147

October Manifesto (1905), 89
Odessa, 11
  Am Olam Society, 12
  Jewish population increase, 8, 16
  maskilim, 55, 56, 58
  secularization process, 61
Odessa Committee, 110–11

Oliphant, Lawrence, 105
Oppenheimer, Franz, 118
Oppenheimer, Joseph Suess, 30
Orthodox Judaism, 72, 73–75, 148
  in Israel, 68, 73–74, 75
  in Poland, 68
  in U.S., 66–67, 75
  and Zionism, 64, 65, 112
  see also Agudat Israel
Ottoman Empire *see* Turkey

Pale of Settlement, 34
  abolition (1915), 14, 39
  Bund, The, 62, 63
  Hasidism, 48, 49
  Haskalah movement, 50, 56, 59
  Jewish factory ownership, 38
  migration, 15–16
Palestine, 18, 100
  British Mandate, 122–41
  Jewish settlement, 110, 112–20
  UN responsibility, 141–42
  see also Aliyah; Arab-Jewish
    conflict; Yishuv
Palmach commando squads, 144
Panama Canal Affair, 111
Paris, 8, 33, 79
Paris Peace Conference (1919), 42
Passfield, Lord, 129
Patria, 136
Paul I, Emperor of Russia, 35
Paulsten, Friedrich, 81
Peel Commission, 130, 134
Perier family, 79
Perestroika, 24
Petah Tikva, 115
Petrograd *see* St. Petersburg
Pilsudski, Jozef, 42, 43
Pinsker, Judah Leib, 12, 107–8, 109,
    110, 111
Plehve, V.K, 89
Po'alei Agudat Israel, 72
Po'alei Zion, 120, 133
Pobedonostev, Konstantin, 37, 85, 88
Podolia, 34, 47
Podolinski, Sergey, 38–39
Pogroms, 78
  Arab states, 102
  Germany, 45, 95
  Russia, 36–37, 87–88, 89, 90, 103
  Soviet Union, 99

Ukraine, 97
see also anti-Semitism; Holocaust
Poland
  Agudat Israel, 72
  anti-Semitism, 98
  becomes independent state, 16
  Bund, The, 63
  displaced Jews, 20
  division of (1772–95), 85
  emancipation, 42–43
  ghettos, 94
  Hasidism, 48
  Holocaust victims, 19–20
  invasion (1939), 93
  Jewish community size, 147
  emigration, 1, 7, 8, 14, 17, 18, 21,
    123, 127, 146
  migration to cities, 7, 8, 38, 146
  nationalist uprisings, 106
  partitions, 15, 34, 48, 55
  secularization, 61, 67, 68
  Sejm, 42
Poland–Lithuania, 34, 47
Political movements, 61–63
Polyakov brothers, 39, 79
Pomerania, 34
Population
  Eastern Europe, 7, 8, 16, 107
  in Israel, 17–19, 21, 24–25, 116, 120,
    123, 127, 132
  world Jewish, 6–7
Poznan, 8
Poznanski brothers, 39
Preuss, Hugo, 44
Proudhon, Pierre Joseph, 80
Prussia, 34, 53

Race theory, 81–82, 102
  Nazism, 2, 44, 46, 92, 94, 96
  Zionism, 101
Radek, Karl, 97
Radom, 14, 94
Ramle, 23
Rathenau, Walter, 44
Rationalism, 29
Ravnitsky, Yehoshua Hana, 110
Raziel, David, 138
Razsvet, 59
Reform *see* Jewish Reform movement
Reines, Isaac Jacob, 63
Revisionist Party, 133–34, 142

Ribbentrop, Joachim von, 98
Rishon Lezion, 115
Romania
  becomes independent state, 16
  emancipation, 42, 43, 77
  emigration, 8, 10, 17
  Hasidism, 48, 50
  Holocaust victims, 20
  Jewish population growth, 7
  Palestine colonies, 115
  Zionist movement, 105
Rosenberg, Alfred, 95
Rosenthal, Leon, 39
Rosenzweig, Franz, 44
Rosh Pina, 115
Rothschild, Baron Edmond de, 13,
  111, 115
Rothschild family, 33, 79
Rotterdam, 11
Rousseau, Jean-Jacques, 29
Ruppin, Arthur, 114, 118
Russia
  annexation of Poland, 34
  anti-Semitism, 36–37, 85–90, 103
  emancipation, 2, 28, 34–39, 77, 85,
    87, 97, 147
  emigration, 1, 8–9, 10, 11, 18, 123,
    147
  Hasidism, 48, 50
  Haskalah movement, 55–59, 74
  Hovevei Zion, 104, 108, 109, 115
  internal migrations, 8, 14–16, 26,
    58, 67, 146
  Jewish community size, 147
  Jewish population growth, 7
  nationalist movements, 106
  Novorussia, 8, 16, 61
  October Manifesto (1905), 89
  Orthodox Judaism, 75
  political movements, 61–63
  secularization, 67
  urbanization, 60–61
  Zionist movement, 105, 113
  see also Pale of Settlement
Russian Orthodox Church, 85–86

Sabbatian movement, 4, 147
Sacred Fraternity, 88
Safed, 128
St. Louis, 93
St. Petersburg

Enlightenment movement, 74
settlement in after 1915, 14, 16,
    39, 67
Sacred Fraternity, 88
university restrictions, 59
Salvador, Joseph, 105
Samuel, Herbert, 122, 123, 125, 126,
    131
San Remo Conference (1920), 122
Saper, George, 62
Schechter, Solomon, 67
Schiff, Jacob Henry, 67
Schneorsohn, Isaac Dov Baer, 64
Schoenerer, Georg Ritter von, 83
Scholem, Gershom, 4, 147
Secularization, 2, 47–75, 147–48
    in Europe, 61, 65, 67–68
    in Germany, 146
    in Israel, 68–75
    in Poland, 61, 67, 68
    in Soviet Union, 67–68
    in U.S., 65–67
    and Zionism, 63–65, 72
    see also Hasidism; *Haskalah*; Jewish
        Conservative movement;
        Jewish Reform movement
Seesen, 52, 53
Sejm, 42
Sephardi-Haredi Shas party, 73
Sabbateanism, 47, 49
Shabbetai Zevi, 47
Shemitah, 69
Shertok, Moshe, 134
Shick, Baruch, 55
Silver, Abba Hillel, 135
Simferopol, 8
Simonyi, Ivan, 83
Smolenskin, Peretz, 105
Sneh, Moshe, 141
Sobibor, 45, 95
Social-cultural processes
    see secularization
Sofer, Moses, 54
Sokolonikov, Grigori, 97
Sokolow, Nahum, 114, 121
South Africa, 12, 75
South America *see* Latin America
"Southern Storms", 36, 87–88, 103
Soviet Union, 16, 98
    anti-Semitism, 2, 39, 40–41,
        97–100, 103

Bolshevik Jewish policy, 39
conflict with Germany, 98
displaced Jews, 20
emancipation, 39–40
emigration, 21, 24, 25, 124
Holocaust victims, 20, 97
Jewish state, 142
Orthodox Judaism, 75
secularization, 67–68
Spain, 9
Sprinzak, Yosef, 117
SS (Schutzstaffel), 92, 94, 96
Stalin, Joseph, 40–41, 68, 77, 97, 98,
    99–100, 103
Stern, Avraham, 138
Stoecker, Adolf, 81, 83
Streicher, Julius, 91
Struma, 136
Stürmer, Der, 91
Switzerland, 59
Syria, 46, 101, 102, 125, 143

Tel Aviv
    Arab attacks (1929), 128
    founded, 119–20
    immigrants settle in, 123
    population growth, 18–19, 127, 132
    secularism, 69
Tiberias, 117, 118, 142
Tiomkin, Vladimir, 110
Tisza-Eszlar, 83, 103
Toland, John, 29
Toleranzpatent, 30
Torah study, 49, 67, 148
Treblinka, 45, 95
Treitschke, Heinrich von, 33, 80
Trotsky, Lev, 97
Truman, Harry, 140, 141
Tsederbaum, Alexander, 110
Tunisia, 20, 21, 46
Turkey, 13, 17, 112, 113, 121
    Young Turks, 114, 118, 119

Uganda, 113, 114
Ukraine
    anti-Semitism, 97, 98
    emancipation, 42
    emigration, 7, 8, 14, 15
    Hasidism, 47–48
    Jewish Statute, 35
    migration to, 146

nationalism, 86, 106
Orthodox Judaism, 75
Russian annexation, 34
"Um Juni", 118
United Nations, 46, 100, 101, 141, 142
United Religious Front, 72
United Resistance Movement,
  139–40, 141
United States
  American Constitution, 46
  Anglo-American Commission
    (1946), 140
  Biltmore Plan, 135–36
  Declaration of Independence, 30
  emancipation, 28, 30–31, 36, 41
  emigration, 24
  First World War, 122
  Jewish Conservative movement,
    54, 67
  Jewish Reform movement, 53, 65
  Jewish state, 142, 143
  as leading Jewish community, 20
  migration to, 1, 8, 9–11, 12, 13,
    17, 18, 23, 24, 25, 26, 65, 127,
    146, 147
  Orthodox Judaism, 66–67, 75
  secularization, 65–67
  Zionist support, 140–41
Urbanization, 7, 8, 33, 60–61, 65, 67
Uruguay, 17
Ussishkin, Menachem, 114, 126, 131
U.S.S.R. *see* Soviet Union

Versailles Peace Treaty (1919), 42
Vienna, 8, 11, 33, 79
Vilna, 50, 55, 61, 109
Vilna Gaon, 49, 55
Volhynia, 34
Voltaire, Françoise Marie Arouet
  de, 30

Wagner, Richard, 80
Wannsee Conference, 20, 45, 95, 96
War of Independence, 22, 23, 24, 144
Warburg, Otto, 114, 119
Warsaw, 11
  ghettos, 94
  Jewish factory ownership, 38
  Jewish population increase, 8
  maskilim, 58
  secularization process, 61

Weizmann, Chaim, 65, 123, 130–32,
  133
  and Britain, 121, 126, 135, 136
Werfel, Franz, 44
Wertheimer, Samson, 30
Wesssely, Naphtali Herz, 51
West Bank, 24, 25, 100, 144
Westphalia, 52, 54
Williams, Roger, 29
Wilson, Woodrow, 42
Witte, Sergey, 37, 38, 39
Wolffsohn, David, 111, 114, 119
Würzburg, 78

Yalta Conference (1945), 139
Yehiam, 142
Yahil, Leni, 91
Yekaterinoslav, 8, 16, 61
Yelizavetgrad, 8, 16, 61
Yemen, 21, 71, 120
Yesud Hama'alah, 115
Yevsektsiya, 40, 68
Yiddish culture
  Bund, The, 62
  maskilim, 57
  Stalinism 97–98
  in U.S., 11, 66
Yishuv, 22
  anti-Turkish feelings, 121
  and Arab population, 19, 128, 134
  and Britain, 125, 126, 134, 136, 137,
    139–40
  domestic tensions, 120–21
  economic growth, 132, 133, 136
  and Haganah, 137, 138
  and Histadrut, 126, 127, 128
  Jewish state, 142
  language conflict, 120
  New, 114–16, 120, 121
  partition acceptance, 141
  political control of, 133
  secularization, 68–69
  terrorist activity, 139
Yosef, Ovadiah, 73
Young Turks, 114, 118, 119
Yugoslavia, 16

Zaddik, 48, 57
Zaddikim, 48
Zalman, Elijah ben Solomon, 49, 55
Zhitomir, 58

Index

Zichron Ya'akov, 115, 121
Zinoviev, Grigori, 97
Zionism, 2, 5, 104–45, 146, 149
  and Agudat Israel, 72–73
  Arabs, 46, 101–2, 103
  Jewish Reform movement, 52, 54
  "national home" demand, 41, 63,
    122, 126, 130
  and secularization, 63–65, 72
  UN definition (1974), 101
  in U.S., 135
  see also Hibbat Zion; Hovevei Zion
Zionist Conference (1920), 131
Zionist Congress, 104, 112, 113–14,
  134

Zionist Executive, 134, 135, 136
Zionist Organization, 112–14, 131–32
  and Britain, 126, 130
  during World War I, 121
  founding of (1897), 2, 112
  investment in Erez Israel, 18
  languages dispute, 120
  political control of, 133, 134, 135
  secularization, 63, 69, 71
  Tel Aviv founded, 120
Zola, Emile, 84
Zuker, Alois, 33
Zunz, Leopold, 52
Zweig, Stefan, 44